The Teacher Residency Model

The Teacher Residency Model

Core Components for High Impact on Student Achievement

Edited by
Cheryl A. Torrez and Marjori Krebs

LEXINGTON BOOKS
Lanham • Boulder • New York • London

Published by Lexington Books
An imprint of The Rowman & Littlefield Publishing Group, Inc.
4501 Forbes Boulevard, Suite 200, Lanham, Maryland 20706
www.rowman.com

6 Tinworth Street, London SE11 5AL, United Kingdom

Copyright © 2020 by The Rowman & Littlefield Publishing Group, Inc.

All rights reserved. No part of this book may be reproduced in any form or by any electronic or mechanical means, including information storage and retrieval systems, without written permission from the publisher, except by a reviewer who may quote passages in a review.

British Library Cataloguing in Publication Information Available

Library of Congress Control Number: 2019950453
ISBN 978-1-7936-0636-5 (cloth : alk. paper)
ISBN 978-1-7936-0638-9 (pbk : alk. paper)
ISBN 978-1-7936-0637-2 (electronic)

Contents

List of Figures and Tables	vii
Foreword *Cheryl A. Torrez and Marjori Krebs*	ix
Introduction: Teacher Residency Programs *National Center for Teacher Residencies*	xiii
1 The Importance of Partnerships: A Focus on the Albuquerque Teacher Residency Partnership *Viola Florez and Marjori Krebs*	1
2 Identifying and Recruiting Quality Residents *Ashley Clark, Sarah B. Glover, and Jessamyn Lockhart*	21
3 Identifying and Recruiting Quality Mentor Teachers *Tamara L. Sober*	31
4 Residency Year Curriculum *Marisa Bier*	61
5 High-Leverage Resident Practices *Sherryl Browne Graves and Susan Gonzowitz*	83
6 Alignment of Coursework to the Clinical Experience: Bridging Theory and Practice *Brandon Ware, Holly Gonzales, and Harry Ervin*	115
7 An Examination of the Teaching and Learning Structures at the Dudley Street Neighborhood Charter School *Lilly Siu, Marcie Osinsky, and Lynne Godfrey*	131

8	Evaluating and Continuously Improving Program Quality in the Teacher Residency *Marisa Harford and Rachelle Verdier*	153
9	Moving from Resident to Teacher-of-Record *Bill Kennedy and Rebecca Hendrickson*	187
10	Principal Involvement in Teacher Residencies *Danaya Lamker Franke, Shelley Neilsen Gatti, and Amy Steele*	205
11	Scale and Sustainability of Residency Programs *Carrianne Scheib, Christine Brennan Davis, and the National Center for Teacher Residencies*	223

Index	237
About the Editors and Contributors	241

List of Figures and Tables

FIGURES

Figure 3.1	CRC Informational Recruitment Flyer.	37
Figure 4.1	STR Formal Observation Guide.	73
Figure 5.1	EHTR Program Timeline.	87
Figure 5.2	TeachingWorks EHTR and HLP Comparison.	103
Figure 6.1	Organizational Chart for the KUTR Partnership.	117
Figure 6.2	KUTR Programmatic Shifts over Time.	119
Figure 7.1	Excerpt of DSNCS Student Data Tracker.	144
Figure 8.1	Sample Individual Resident Profile for One Assessment.	164
Figure 8.2	Sample of Score Analysis Comparing Average School Administrator Danielson Framework Assessment of Residents to Mentor Assessment by Rubric Component.	165
Figure 8.3	Learning Structures for All Stakeholders.	169
Figure 8.4	The UTR Teacher Inquiry Cycle.	171

TABLES

Table 3.1	CRC Observation Score Sheet	40
Table 4.1	Culturally and Linguistically Diverse Students STR Curricular Map 2018–2019	66
Table 4.2	STR Classroom Management Curricular Map 2018–2019	67

Table 5.1	EHTR Version of TeachingWorks Adult Learning Cycle	93
Table 5.2	EHTR Coaching Structure	105
Table 7.1	DSNCS Teaching Academy Structure	139
Table 8.1	Gathering and Using Data in UTR	167
Table 9.1	UChicago UTEP Praxis Cycle for Coaching	193
Table 10.1	SUTR Demographic Data	210

Foreword

Cheryl A. Torrez and Marjori Krebs

The Teacher Residency Model: Core Components for High Impact on Student Achievement is rooted in the work of outstanding teacher residency programs across the United States that are affiliated with the National Center for Teacher Residencies (NCTR). In the early stages of the residency program in which we are involved, the Albuquerque Teacher Residency Program, NCTR's guidance and support was invaluable. Early on as we navigated the teacher residency landscape we began to wonder, "What are other residency programs doing that we could learn from?" We contacted our colleagues at NCTR, Anne Matz and Carrie Scheib, who have both contributed to this book, and asked if there might be interest in an edited book about the teacher residency model. Matz and Scheib, along with their NCTR colleagues, provided the approval for the book and recommended the exemplary residency programs that have contributed chapters to this book.

Each chapter is focused on a specific area of teacher residency development, implementation, and sustainability. Authors have painted a picture of their unique residency programs and kindly shared their lessons learned and insights. The book begins and ends with chapters from the National Center for Teacher Residencies, and each chapter addresses a different key component of residency programs. Individual chapter authors explain the need for residencies as teacher preparation programs, along with their own definitions of residencies, and their operationalization of the NCTR framework.

We are grateful to each of the chapter authors for their commitment to making a positive difference in the lives of K-12 students and educators. In each chapter, we have found conceptual and operational suggestions that caused us to say, "That is a great idea, we're going to implement that!" We are confident that the readers of this book will take away a plethora of ideas whether at the inchoate stages of working with residencies, or as seasoned veterans of residency programs.

The Chicago-Based National Center for Teacher Residencies (NCTR) provides a detailed, clear overview of NCTR, along with its research-based philosophy and framework of residencies. This introductory chapter, "Teacher Residency Programs," is an important first-read. Taking the time to review this chapter before delving into each stage of teacher residencies is time well spent. The reader will benefit from looking first at the residency framework and vocabulary presented in this chapter before moving on to specific phases of residencies.

Chapter 1, "The Importance of Partnerships: A Focus on the Albuquerque Teacher Residency Partnership (ATRP)," is a good place to begin the exploration of residencies, as strategic partnerships between school districts and educator preparation providers is foundational for successful residency programs. Krebs (one of the editors of this book) and Florez, both from the University of New Mexico, explain the roles and responsibilities of each partner in ATRP, as shared by representatives from each of the partnering organizations.

Clark, Glover, and Lockhart, with the Denver-Based Public Education and Business Coalition (PEBC), introduce the key aspects of successful resident recruitment. In chapter 2, "Identifying and Recruiting Quality Residents," the authors explain that producing a diverse group of high-quality teachers after the residency year begins with identifying and recruiting a diverse, strong cohort of residents. Their recruitment and application process focuses not on how to identify a large *number* of residents to apply, but specifically on how to find the *right* residents for the areas in which they will serve. PEBC seeks to learn about the applicants in addition to taking the opportunity to educate them to understand the inequities in the education system and taking time to reflect on which communities they would like to serve.

Another part of a successful residency is placing the residents with high-quality classroom teachers who can mentor and model excellent teaching strategies and a strong commitment to knowing and understanding their students and families. Sober, with Virginia Commonwealth University, explains these strategies in chapter 3, "Identifying and Recruiting Quality Mentor Teachers." Sober shares experiences in working with veteran teachers and assisting them in learning coaching strategies for working with residents. A significant part of their continuous improvement in working with mentor teachers is their evaluative feedback they receive each year, which allows them to continually analyze and improve their practices.

In chapter 4, "Residency Year Curriculum," Bier, the program director, shares what the residents actually learn throughout the residency year. She describes how Seattle Teacher Residency combines instruction in teaching methods with residency field experience and mentor teacher expertise. Bier explains the specific professional development opportunities provided for mentor teachers in order to increase the residents' classroom skills and knowledge.

Graves and Gonzowitz in chapter 5, "High-Leverage Resident Practices," detail exactly *what* the residents learn. Graves works with the Hunter College School of Education in New York City and Gonzowitz is the founding managing director for the East Harlem Tutorial Program. The authors explain how they leverage the nineteen High-Leverage Teaching Practices of TeachingWorks with their residents to assist them in developing and honing effective teaching skills.

Obtaining an understanding of teaching practices and skills is a key component to teacher success, but this alone is not enough. High-quality teachers also need to understand the theory behind those practices. In chapter 6, "Alignment of Coursework to the Clinical Experience: Bridging Theory and Practice," Gonzalez, Ware, and Ervin of Bakersfield City School District in California describe how the Kern Urban Teacher Residency assists residents in making these connections.

The relationship between resident and mentor teacher is a key component to making such connections. Siu, Osinsky and Godfrey, of the Boston Teacher Residency (BRT), authored chapter 7: "An Examination of the Teaching and Learning Structures at the Dudley Street Neighborhood Charter School." In this chapter, the authors explain how they have designed structures and routines for the mentor teachers and residents to collaboratively engage in the work of teaching. Through providing routines and structures, both mentor teachers and residents focus on student learning through the use of data and "making their reasoning public," by explaining practices and decisions in real time, to improve student learning.

Even with all these frameworks and strategies in place, residencies understand the importance of continuous improvement. Authors Harford and Verdier with New Visions for Public Schools Urban Teacher Residency in New York City share their processes in chapter 8, "Evaluating and Continuously Improving Program Quality in the Teacher Residency." Readers will learn about the feedback loops and protocols that New Visions implements to effectively use data to inform their decision-making.

Following the residency year, the next step is matriculation of the residents to their own classrooms. In chapter 9, "Moving from Resident to Teacher-of-Record," Kennedy and Hendrickson, with the UChicago Urban Teacher Education Program, explain their three-year model of induction to the field of teaching, from the residency year, followed by two years of support and continued coaching, directly resulting in success and retention of teachers in the field.

Leadership is one of the most important aspects of successful teacher residencies. In chapter 10, "Principal Involvement in Teacher Residencies," Franke, Gatti, and Steele, with the Saint Paul Public Schools Urban Teacher Residency (SUTR), describe the role of the principal as critical to a successful residency. SUTR partners closely with its principals, relaying on their expertise through conversations, collaboration, and regular participation in design team planning sessions.

In chapter 11, "Scale and Sustainability of Residency Programs," Scheib and Davis from the National Center for Teacher Residencies, explain the importance of planning for scaling up and sustaining residencies in order for districts to realize their long-term success. Important to this success are the elements of financial strategies and engagement of leadership with all partner organizations, and especially implementing strategies to minimize cost and maximize revenue.

In closing, we express our gratitude to Anne Matz and Carrie Scheib, and all those with the National Center for Teacher Residencies, who embarked on this project with us, recommending outstanding residency practitioners from which we can all learn and grow. Anne and Carrie trusted us with this project and have supported us all along the way. In addition, we sincerely appreciate the tireless work of Allison Stansbury, our project editor, who worked days, nights, and weekends to meet our deadlines, assisting us with proofing and editing the chapters, with expertise and a cheerful attitude throughout.

As we introduce this book to you, we invite you to hear the voices of these on-the-ground practitioners, facing the challenges of preparing caring, intelligent, purposeful teachers for our children. This is challenging work as the need for teachers continues to grow. Yet, these practitioners are doing the work, learning from their experiences and the experiences of others, and making an impact on teacher recruitment, preparation, and retention of teachers. We invite you to read, hear, learn, and put into practice what our authors share with you in the following chapters.

Introduction
Teacher Residency Programs
National Center for Teacher Residencies

Imagine a typical teacher taking on her very own classroom for the first time. She is the teacher-of-record; the students' success rests on her shoulders. She sought a job where she knew she would be most needed: in an urban school, one where most of the children live in poverty, and many do not speak or hear English at home. Few perform on grade level.

How was this teacher prepared for this classroom? Like four out of five new teachers in this country, she earned her credentials through a university program.[1] Her foundations classes taught her theories of learning, and her methods classes taught her approaches to pedagogy. She left school with good grades, many ideas, and ten weeks of student teaching under her belt.

What, though, was she lacking? She took many of those classes a year or more before she started her teaching job, and they weren't connected in a meaningful way to the practice of teaching. Some of the elements we have come to understand are most crucial to effective teaching—managing student behaviors, planning lessons with the proper pacing and questions to engage and challenge students, designing assignments aligned to career and college-readiness standards, refining instruction based on assessment data—were touched on, but were not thoroughly coordinated with her time in the classroom. When she student taught, her cooperating teacher did not have any special skills in mentoring an apprentice, so there was little useful feedback. The classroom was so different from her own classroom experiences, both demographically and culturally, and she wasn't present at the beginning of the year, when a teacher does some of her most important work: setting the norms for the classroom and establishing expectations for students.

On her first day, like many—if not most—of her peers across America, she was not prepared.

Contrast that with the experience of a new teacher who entered the profession through a teacher residency in the National Center for Teacher Residencies' network. She spent the entire previous year—from the first bell to the last—in one or more classrooms in a high-needs school, receiving in-depth coaching by a teacher who has proven to successfully prepare students to meet challenging academic standards. With the continuous support of her mentor, she planned lessons; delivered instruction; participated in parent-teacher conferences, school-wide professional development and every team meeting; managed student behaviors; designed assessments; and developed instruction based on its results.

All of her graduate coursework took place during that year. Her assignments always required her to apply what she was learning to her actual students—and she spent one day a week in a seminar with other residents, learning instructional techniques that closed the normally wide gap between theory and practice. She sat down for a few hours of feedback each week from her mentor, who himself was receiving regular feedback and instruction on how to be a better coach. Over the course of the school year, there was a gradual release of the classroom from the mentor teacher to the resident so that she was leading the learning in the classroom with daily feedback from her mentor teacher.

Her day 1, then, was really day 181.

Given the extraordinary challenges of teaching, especially in underserved urban and rural schools, it is a decided advantage to students, schools, and districts to have teachers whose training is rigorous, practical, and completely relevant to the environment they will be hired into. It is an advantage that teacher residency graduates have committed to teach at least three to five years in high-needs schools. And because every day counts for every child, it is not just an advantage but an imperative to do all we can to develop a highly capable cadre of committed new teachers able to hit the ground running, to ensure that students are never solely the responsibility of teachers who still have on their training wheels.

Given that residency programs have these advantages, the national conversation around teacher preparation is turning its attention to teacher residencies. Teacher residency programs are at the heart of student-focused teacher preparation, and ensure that all new teachers enter the classroom prepared to teach from the start of their first year as teacher of record. Residencies are ideal for creating a dedicated pipeline of excellent teachers for our highest-need schools. The strategies employed by residency programs to select, train, and support new teachers emphasize the ideal for how every new teacher should be prepared.

Teacher residency programs are, by definition, district-serving teacher education programs that pair a rigorous full-year classroom apprenticeship with university-level education content. Most resident programs pair the apprenticeship with master's-level coursework, although some programs offer bachelor's level coursework and degrees paired with the clinical-oriented preparation. Building on the medical residency model, teacher preparation programs provide residents with both the underlying theory of effective teaching and a year-long, in-school "residency" in which they practice and hone their skills and knowledge alongside an effective teacher-mentor in a high-need classroom. Residents receive stipends as they learn to teach, and commit to teaching in their districts often for three or more years beyond the residency. Residents are prepared to help meet the districts hiring needs, whether that's in hard-to-staff schools or high-need certifications.

With a belief that access to a quality teacher is a right for all children, the National Center for Teacher Residencies (NCTR) works to advance a network of high-performing teacher residency programs across the country dedicated to preparing highly effective teachers that will transform educational practices nationwide. NCTR (formerly named Urban Teacher Residency United) was founded in Chicago in 2007 as a network of practice for three partner teacher residency programs in Boston, Denver, and Chicago. NCTR now partners with school districts, charter management organizations, institutions of higher education, nonprofit organizations, and states to develop teacher residency programs as quality pipelines of effective and diverse new teachers. It is the only organization in the nation dedicated to developing, launching, supporting, and accelerating the impact of teacher residency programs. As of 2019, NCTR has provided technical assistance to over fifty partner programs. NCTR-affiliated residency programs have graduated over 3,600 residents. NCTR is pleased to introduce this text, which highlights the work of our partner programs, as a resource for transforming teacher preparation.

ORIGINS OF THE TEACHER RESIDENCY MOVEMENT

NCTR partner teacher residency programs align to the shifts in the last four decades in teacher preparation. The origins of the residency movement date back to the 1980s. The Holmes Group, a consortium of deans and a number of chief academic officers from research institutions in each of the fifty states, was organized around the twin goals of the reform of teacher education and the teaching profession in 1986. Members of the group represented colleges of teacher education that were the leading research institutions in their respective states and regions. The Holmes Group and other practitioners such as the National Network for Education Renewal began to recommend grand shifts in the preparation of teachers, proposing the establishment of professional development schools, which would bring the main setting for teacher preparation into the PK-12 school, instead of the university.[2] In recognizing the popularity of alternative routes and the specific demands of districts for an increased supply of novice teachers, the Holmes deans advocated for additional preparation, induction, and ongoing development supports for teacher candidates. Years later, the implementation of the *No Child Left Behind Act* in 2001 strengthened support for new teacher preparation models that could focus on developing "highly qualified" teachers capable of meeting every student's needs.

The 2010s then found increased support for residency and other clinically oriented teacher preparation as a way to transform and improve teacher preparation.[3] The teacher residency model was created as a response to calls to reform traditional teacher preparation which typically consisted primarily of theory-heavy coursework detached from the PK-12 teaching experiences.[4] Recognizing the need for candidates to engage in more clinical experiences, more university-based teacher education programs and alternative teacher certification routes have also incorporated the tenets of the residency model to transform their methods.

CORE COMPONENTS OF A TEACHER RESIDENCY PROGRAM

High-quality teacher residencies are typically a partnership between a school district or charter management organization, an institution of higher education or other teacher-certifying agent, and sometimes a nonprofit organization. The residency is a teacher preparation program that builds on the medical residency model of intense clinical practice with expert instruction, supervision and coaching. Teacher residencies draw from the strengths of traditional as well as alternative approaches to teacher selection, preparation, and support.

Residencies incorporate:

- Partnership between a high-need school district(s), institution of higher education, and other stakeholders
- Data-based recruitment and selection of residents to serve a district need, with a living stipend or salary to attract high-potential candidates
- Selection process for mentor teachers based on multiple criteria that includes demonstrated effective classroom practice and the skills to coach adult learners
- Rigorous, full-year classroom apprenticeship alongside a well-trained mentor teacher that integrates coursework and theory in a school-based environment

- Ongoing learning, feedback, and evaluation cycles
- Placement and/or hiring assistance coupled with the resident's commitment to teach in the district for three to five years
- Intensive induction support for graduates of the residency program

There are certainly variations in the model that come as a result of decisions that must be made around program design and partnership. For example, some residencies, such as the East Harlem Teaching Residency, place residents in a classroom with a mentor teacher for one year while the resident concurrently serves as lead teacher of his or her own after-school time classroom. Other residencies, such as the Richmond Teacher Residency, are housed within a university but provide a separate track for residency candidates versus traditional program candidates. The Kansas City Teacher Residency enables program staff and university faculty to lead coursework, then residents are certified and can take additional courses to earn a master's degree through a partner university after their residency experience. Additionally, living stipends, tuition reduction and reimbursement, and housing support are all options some residencies employ to offset the financial burden of additional education.

The residency approach to teacher preparation incorporates a district-serving, data-driven, and capacity-building perspective not seen in most other teacher-preparation programs. A well-designed residency program has a number of positive effects on the ecosystem in which it was designed. The residency program raises recruitment and selection standards to attract high-potential candidates and select and prepare new teachers with the specific skill sets necessary to work in high-need schools and subject areas. Teacher educators in residency programs revamp the teacher preparation curriculum to put teacher practice and improvement at the center of preparation, wrapping coursework and theory around the classroom-focused learning experiences. A strong residency program capitalizes on existing assets in schools, leverages effective classroom teachers as mentors, and supports those experienced educators in their own classroom performance and professional development. The residency program creates a long-term, sustainable pipeline of highly effective new teachers who positively impact student learning and school success.

Despite the varied residency programs that exist among partners, all NCTR residency programs strongly believe that to select, train, and retain effective teachers for high-need schools, candidates must participate in a teacher preparation model that centers on a rigorous, school-based clinical experience, teaching and learning alongside an effective master teacher, and ongoing mentoring, including observations, feedback, and coaching based on teacher and student performance data. Programs must select high-priority teacher practices that are aligned to the vision of effective teaching of the districts they serve. Residents' engagement in the learning, rehearsal, enactment, and analysis of these teaching practices is central to the residency year experience.

A Rigorous, School-Based Clinical Experience

These two vignettes from NCTR's *Clinically Oriented Teacher Preparation* differentiate a rigorous, school-based clinical experience from one less connected to schools and districts. The vignettes are drawn from the experiences of individuals who completed teacher education programs as undergraduates. The first example typifies a non-clinically focused university-based teacher preparation program,[5] and the second features a university-based teacher preparation program that has made significant shifts toward clinically oriented preparation. While the names of the two teachers are fictitious, the details are drawn from observations, interviews, and document reviews.

Traditional Teacher Preparation: The Case of Ms. Reynolds

Elizabeth Reynolds completed her student teaching in a teacher preparation program in Ms. Meyer's ninth-grade classroom in the suburban town where she grew up, where students were mostly like her, and in a high school with a strong academic reputation. In her 120-credit undergraduate program for secondary Biology, Ms. Reynolds was required to take 36 credits of teacher education courses and 12 credits of student teaching in addition to the general education and biology courses required by her major. Student teaching was a capstone experience that took place during the final semester of her undergraduate training. Student teaching began at the end of January and spanned twelve weeks. She began the semester by observing her cooperating teacher and slowly took on increasing levels of responsibility for instruction. In the last two weeks of student teaching, she completed her "full-time teach" where she taught for the entire day. Ms. Reynolds was the first student teacher to whom Ms. Meyer had mentored, though Ms. Meyer had not received training in mentoring or coaching.

Ms. Reynolds's university supervisor came three times during the semester to observe and evaluate her teaching. Additionally, Ms. Reynolds attended an hour-long weekly teaching practicum class with other student teachers in her program to talk about their experiences and offer each other support. This was the only course she took with direct connections to her practicum experience during her time as a student teacher.

There were no open teaching positions in the district where Ms. Reynolds' student taught (and the district rarely hires first-year teachers). Students at Ms. Reynolds's university typically land their first teaching jobs at challenging and underperforming schools nearby, which is exactly where Ms.

Reynolds landed a seventh-grade science teacher position. She was excited for her first teaching job and felt she had the content and instructional knowledge needed to teach the required topics in the school's Next-Generation Science Standards aligned curriculum. Her first month, however, proved exceptionally difficult. Despite having received an honors distinction and consistently strong evaluations from her university supervisor during student teaching, Ms. Reynolds reports feeling inadequately prepared for the challenges she faces on a daily basis in her classroom. She has almost no support in her school to guide her as she navigates her first year of teaching science to students who do not have strong science backgrounds. Ms. Reynolds wants her students to be successful in science but does not know how to achieve this goal and does not know where to turn for support.

Clinically Oriented Teacher Preparation: The Case of Ms. Williams

Contrast Ms. Reynolds' student teaching experience with the experience of Keesha Williams, a new sixth-grade science teacher in Toppenish, Washington. Ms. Williams recently graduated from Heritage University's HU105 program, a residency-based approach to teacher preparation where she spent four semesters student teaching in a middle school in one of the program's partner districts. The students served by HU105's partner schools and districts live in an area of central Washington with the second highest poverty level in the state.

In lieu of traditional courses during her preparation, Ms. Williams was held accountable to a set of core competencies through rigorous performance assessments driven by HU105's Professional Competency Assessment Instrument (PCAI). Throughout her clinical experience, she was part of a four-member Teaching and Learning Team consisting of three candidates learning to teach at different stages of development and one core teacher who went through a rigorous selection process as well as continuous training on coaching and mentoring. Ms. Williams had regular opportunities to teach independently, co-teach, and receive feedback. She met daily with her team to discuss lessons, rehearse and role-play teaching scenarios, problem-solve particular instructional challenges, and receive support to progress on her individual PCAI goals.

In addition to the on-site support received from her team, Ms. William's site advocate (an HU105 faculty member who supports a cohort of teams in a school or group of schools) visited her classroom one to three times a week to provide additional guidance on assessments, classroom management, instructional design and implementation, and school operations and expectations as well as to co-teach or model particular practices when needed. Ms. William's teaching team and site advocate worked collaboratively to assess and evaluate her practice throughout her clinical experience.

Graduates of the HU105 program are often hired by the schools where they apprentice (if there are openings) and almost always by the district. The school where Ms. Williams now teaches is a few miles away from where she completed her residency. Having had hundreds of "at bats" in science teaching in a supportive environment with an abundance of feedback on her teaching practice, she began her school year confident to take on a position in another school. Her first month of school was not easy, but because she had seen two school years launch, she worked hard to establish solid management routines and relationships with her students, 100 percent of whom passed her first end-of-unit assessment. The learning and teaching opportunities afforded to Ms. Williams during her HU105 experience are consistent with the shifts toward clinically oriented teacher preparation being made by many programs across the country.

Belief in the centrality of the clinical experience is shared among leaders in the education sector. "Teacher education has too often been segmented with subject-matter preparation, theory, and pedagogy taught in isolated intervals and too far removed from clinical practice," concluded a panel of leaders in higher education and federal and state education policy tasked with evaluating the state of teacher preparation in 2010. "But teaching, like medicine, is a profession of practice, and prospective teachers must be prepared to become expert practitioners who know how to use the knowledge of their profession to advance student learning and how to build their professional knowledge through practice. In order to achieve this we must place practice at the center of teaching preparation." The panel, convened by the National Council for Accreditation of Teacher Education, pushed for programs "that are fully grounded in clinical practice and interwoven with academic content and professional courses."[6]

Teacher residency programs are exemplars in placing practice at the center of teacher preparation. National Council on Teacher Quality's 2018 Prep Review notes the rigor of the residency year experience, "Residencies stand out in our analysis, because more than a third earn 'A's for their clinical experience. They do this by providing candidates up to one year of experience in the classroom of a mentor who is a strong instructor and able to mentor adults, and by sending program staff to observe the teachers frequently."[7]

Impact of NCTR Teacher Residency Programs

Research clearly shows that teachers are the leverage point for improving student learning. Traditional teacher quality indicators such as post-graduate schooling and passing scores on licensing exams are becoming obsolete. Gauging quality now rests more than ever before on a teacher's ability to increase student achievement and learning,[89] and this paradigm shift holds teacher preparation programs accountable for selecting and training candidates who can show measurable improvement in the knowledge and skill sets of their students. Teacher residencies uniquely prepare teachers and ensure their effectiveness.

An evaluation on the effectiveness of the one of NCTR partner programs, Urban Teacher Residency (UTR) at New Visions for Public Schools in New York City, concluded that the residency is producing highly effective and diverse new teachers who are staying in their classrooms longer and are accelerating achievement among their students. UTR is a partnership between New Visions for Public Schools, Hunter College, and the New York City Department of Education. Between 2009 and 2014, the program developed and placed over 150 new English, mathematics, science, and special education teachers for some of the city's highest-need secondary schools. According to the researchers: "A selective admissions process, a skill- and confidence-building full year in the classroom, built-in accountability—all seemed to have paid off: UTR was increasing the numbers of teachers-effective teachers-in the pipeline."

On student achievement, researchers concluded that students of UTR-trained teachers outperformed those who had teachers developed through other pathways: "In 27 comparisons of (state test) scores where differences between students taught by UTR- and non-UTR-trained teachers were statistically significant, the UTR group's performance was higher 89 percent of the time." Evaluators also found that student achievement grew stronger as UTR-trained teachers gained more experience in the classroom. When the evaluators looked at special education teachers, they concluded that students who had UTR-trained teachers saw higher attendance rates and earned more credits than those in schools with no UTR-trained teachers. These benefits were especially notable among black and Hispanic students. Results were extremely positive when it came to teacher retention: "UTR graduates had a lower rate of attrition—by half—than other new (New York City) high school teachers. Retention rates decline slightly over time, but, after six years, close to three-fourths of UTR's first cohort are still teaching." "Overall, our findings portray a teacher preparation model that, thus far, stands the test of time," the report concluded.[10]

Additional research on the outcomes of teacher residency graduates shows promising trends: graduates are more likely to come from diverse backgrounds, to teach in shortage subject areas, to remain in the classroom, and to earn high principal satisfaction ratings.[11]

Principals who hire and work with these residency graduates report that they are exceptionally well prepared for today's classrooms and that they outperform typical new teachers in their districts' evaluation systems:

- Of thirty-nine teacher preparation programs in Tennessee in 2015, the Memphis Teacher Residency has the highest percentage of graduates meeting and exceeding student growth averages on the state's value-added assessment system, according to state data. Memphis Teacher Residency finished 2018 as one of the state's top performers on Tennessee's Educator Preparation Report Card, earning nearly 95 percent of the evaluation's possible points.[12]

- In 2014–2015, Denver Teacher Residency graduates teaching in Denver Public Schools outperformed all other new teachers in every aspect of the district's evaluation system, and 97 percent of its principals said they would be more likely to hire a residency graduate than one from any other teacher preparation program.[13]
- In 2015, 70 percent of residents in the San Francisco Unified School District received "Highly Effective" or "Outstanding" ratings on the district's teacher evaluation framework—the top two ratings on a five-tiered scale.[14]

Attracting and retaining great teachers is a significant challenge, particularly for high-need schools. The annual data that NCTR collects from its partner programs shows that residency programs are meeting this retention challenges and other challenges. Residency programs provide schools with much-needed stability: 86 percent of residency graduates from NCTR residency partner programs are still teaching in their high-need schools after three years; in a typical urban district half of new teachers will leave during that same time span. With districts spending, on average, $20,000 to recruit, train, and support every teacher they hire,[15] the lower attrition rates of residency graduates mean substantial savings for their districts. Their longevity also strengthens a school's collective expertise and professional capacity.

Finally, residencies attract a larger percentage of people of color to the profession. More than half of residency graduates from NCTR partner programs are people of color; nationally fewer than 20 percent of teachers are people of color.

NCTR also administers perception surveys to stakeholders in its partner programs in the middle and end of the academic year. The NCTR end-year survey asks residents, graduates, mentors and principals from NCTR Network residency programs to assess resident and graduate preparedness in four areas of practice: planning and instruction, learning environment, engagement, and professionalism. An overwhelming majority of principals who hire residency program graduates say graduates are well prepared to enter the classroom as teachers of record and are ready for the rigors of teaching in high-need schools. Survey data from 2016 to 2017 also show:

- 91 percent of principals agree that graduates outperformed teachers prepared through non-residency pathways
- 91 percent of principals agree that the residency program improved achievement and student learning at the school

- 95 percent of graduates agree that residents entered the classroom with more effective skills than the average teacher
- 92 percent of principals agreed that the residency program positively impacted the school culture
- 94 percent of principals agreed that the mentors grew into more effective practitioners through participation in the residency program
- 96 percent of mentors agreed that participation in the residency program made them more effective teachers
- 98 percent of mentors agreed that participation in the residency program improved their abilities as a teacher leader

A slice of the qualitative data from NCTR perception surveys reasons candidates from diverse backgrounds are attracted to teacher residency programs. As one residency program candidate noted of the recruitment experience:

She [the recruitment manager] was just really reassuring [...] I would have had second thoughts about school, with grad school especially. It sounded really scary. I wasn't even supposed to really go to college, so the fact that I was going to get a Master's was not really even in my lane of focus at all. So, the fact that [the recruiter] was kind of like, you're already proving these things in your job as a para, so why don't you do the extra steps to get yourself to a different financial standpoint and just a happier lifestyle. She saw the bigger picture for me before I even saw it for myself.

A different residency program candidate shared this of the recruitment experience:

I think that right away it wasn't just like, hey, you're just another case in another interest meeting. But like, hey, I want you. And we need you, and you could grow. I felt like this program truly did take the time [and] wanted to get to know me right away and to be invested in me right away.

One graduate of an NCTR partner program noted:

I didn't do the best in undergrad with my grades [...] and just keeping up with the workload, but in the recruiting process with [the director], I did feel like I was going to be supported. In the cohort model everybody takes the same classes. It really was nice. The fact that I didn't have to worry about signing up for classes or anything like that because that was kind of a pain in undergrad.

Others mentioned the impact of the resident stipend on recruitment:

I don't think I would have gone to college after undergrad, if I didn't find a program that would at least subsidize some of the cost because that was the number one factor for me. And then I heard about [the residency program] that would subsidize the cost somehow, if you worked for them for about five years. [...] With [another program], you would have paid around $17,000 to have gone [...] but through the program I ended up paying a little over $7,000. That discount definitely sold the deal for me.

What really pulled me to this program was the time and that they offered a stipend. I wanted my degree, and I knew I wanted to teach, and this was a perfect add on to—and I had a public relations degree. So, this is a nice add on to that degree, which then got me the Master's. I think what really pulled me to it was how fast the program was. It was only 15 months, and we were able to get a teaching license and a Master's in that time.

Others noted the coursework and the cohort model as important parts of the value proposition of a residency program.

What really sold the program for me was during the interview process we get to sit in on a class and it was—I remember it was one of the foundation classes, and they were talking about how trauma in a child's life can impact their performance in school and how that affects their relationship with their teachers. And I think it's the fact that they were having those discussions that really sold the program for me. Whereas I was actually interviewing for Teach for America at the same time, and I think just when compared to—comparing those two programs it just felt like [the residency program] was much more aware of these issues and was actually taking the steps to prepare us to be successful in the same classrooms that Teach for America is sending its candidates into.

I think we were all held to the same standard and I just made it. The cohort of residents that I came in with was amazing. They were really supportive. I felt like anything that I lacked intellectually that they would definitely help me pick up on and vice versa [. . .] The program was still able to hold us to the same standards, and none of us felt like we were not able to meet their expectations.

The body of research on the impact of the residency model will grow in decades to come as the number of teachers prepared through this model increases. Individually, NCTR Network programs have tremendous impact in their community; collectively, they demonstrate the power of the residency model as the gold standard for clinical-based teacher preparation nationwide.

PARTNERING WITH NCTR

In just the past years, numerous prominent stakeholders in education have emphasized these strengths of the teacher residency program as a high-quality pathway grounded in rigorous clinical preparation. Done in partnership with local school districts, residencies ensure that new teachers are prepared with a mastery of content, depth of practice, and deep understanding of the students and communities where they work. This level of attention shows that residencies as a teacher preparation route are building momentum as a movement. In the individual programs of the NCTR Network, and as the only national network of teacher residency programs, NCTR partner programs are the leading examples that local, state, and national policymakers are referencing as they deeply examine the current state of teacher preparation.

National Center for Teacher Residencies

All of the residency programs who have authored chapters of this text are members of NCTR's robust network of innovate residency programs. NCTR's network is a dynamic, engaged professional learning community whose members are transforming how teachers are prepared for America's classrooms. Our invitation-only network includes high-quality residencies who meet *NCTR Standards for Effective Teacher Residencies*. Through the network participants collaborate, innovate, and learn from each other with the shared goal of developing skilled, effective teachers for the students and schools that most need them. NCTR's network partners are the country's most innovative and effective teacher residency programs.

NCTR is the only national nonprofit organization devoted to developing and expanding high-quality teacher residencies. NCTR's staff of experts and practitioners delivers programming and targeted consulting that helps network members strengthen, improve, and grow their residencies. NCTR provides members opportunities to engage with national leaders in teacher preparation and to have a voice in the national conversation about teacher quality and student equity. NCTR also engages network partners in its advocacy and communications efforts so that they can drive sustainability and ensure residencies are included in key federal and state policy decisions.

NCTR provides members of its network with a robust selection of in-person and virtual programs and technical assistance, including:

- Instructional Rounds: NCTR conducts on-site visits to network residencies where members systematically collaborate on a problem of practice by observing how partner programs implement the residency model and improve instruction for students.
- Symposium: Held in Chicago each spring, NCTR Symposium invites partners from all over the country to build their knowledge and skills on a critical theme or topic area. Experts present and share their latest research and promising teacher preparation practices.
- Consulting: Guided by *NCTR Standards for Effective Teacher Residencies*, network partners engage with NCTR on continuous, data-driven improvement efforts.

- Policy: NCTR provides network partners with expert analysis and help navigating state and federal policy, as well as local advocacy strategies to improve access to funding and resources.
- Research and Data: NCTR collaborates with partners to collect and use data in order to assess their residencies, continually improve, and compile a national look at the collective impact of the network and residency movement.
- Teacher Preparation Portal: A one-of-a-kind members-only website enables network members to share information, learn from others, analyze data, and collaborate online.
- Tools: NCTR offers partners access to innovative resources, like *Design for Impact*, the financial modeling tool for a residency program that enables programs to identify, plan for, and overcome financial barriers.

All NCTR programming is designed and facilitated to support our partners' improvement in strengthening partnerships to improve schools and communities, using data for continuous improvement, building teacher competency through practice, improving teacher educator effectiveness, and retaining and improving effective graduates. NCTR also assists members of the network with grant applications and collaborates on solving problems specific to their program.

NCTR also offers programming for those exploring the launch of a teacher residency program. NCTR's Residency Foundations Program is designed to support early-stage programs as they assess viability and sustainability of a residency. Through an innovative curriculum series, Residency Foundations explores residency program alignment with the human capital ecosystem of the district, identifying potential high-quality teacher preparation partners, and ensuring that all parties clearly understand their roles and responsibilities. NCTR guides potential programs in building and strengthening local institutional partnerships, while simultaneously drafting a sustainable program management infrastructure, which includes financial and human capital (staffing) planning and allocation.

From this planning work, partnerships are invited to participate in NCTR's Residency Development Program, a two-year strategic consulting engagement with school districts, nonprofit organizations, and universities that are creating residency-based teacher preparation programs built from and mapped to *NCTR's Standards for Effective Residency Programs*. The Residency Development Program consists of both in-person institutes and remote consultation. The institutes provide a structured series of multiday sessions that engage participants to analyze, design, and execute on the core components of a high-quality residency. NCTR provides data-based consultation linked to the institutes by addressing the specific design needs of each program as they execute on the core components of the residency model.

NCTR also designs programming and other support products for districts and university schools of education that wish to broadly adopt—at the systems level—the teacher residency model or other clinically oriented teacher preparation. NCTR created tools for programs to use to evaluate and examine the adoption of the elements of the residency model across a system in order to improve the preparation and effectiveness of teachers. Finally, NCTR conducts research, advocates for residency-friendly policies at the state and federal levels, and disseminates best practices throughout the field of teacher preparation.

By preparing a new kind of teacher inside the classroom—providing the practical learning, the hands-on experience and the support network they need to be effective right away—NCTR and its teacher residency program partners are building a real movement for education reform from the ground up. NCTR and teacher residency programs are raising the bar for teacher preparation, specifically for teachers preparing to serve in high-need areas and in high-need schools across the nation. For too long, teacher preparation programs have relied on course grades to demonstrate a preservice candidate's ability to teach—this measure is too narrow and indicates the teacher preparation candidate's knowledge of theory, not readiness for a classroom. Teacher residencies are leading as a twenty-first-century teacher preparation pathway that measures and monitors a resident's knowledge and skills prior to entering the classroom as teacher of record. The ability to positively impact students must be observed, demonstrated, and honed in real-school environments with intensive immersion experiences that use master educators as the translator of theory to practice.

Learn more about NCTR at https://nctresidencies.org/[16]

NOTES

1. "Digest of Education Statistics 2017." U.S. Department of Education, 2018, https://nces.ed.gov/pubs2018/2018070.pdf.

2. "Nine Essentials." National Association for Professional Development Schools, 2008. napds.org/nine-essentials/.

3. Staub, Shari Dickstein, and Roberta Trachtman. nctresidencies.org/wp-content/uploads/2016/10/NCTR-Landscape-Analysis-The-Four-Drivers-Project.pdf.

4. LiBetti, Ashley, and Justin Trinidad. "Trading Coursework for Classroom: Realizing the Potential of Teacher Residencies." Bellwether Education Partners, bellwethereducation.org/sites/default/files/TeacherResidencies_Bellwether.pdf.

5. Zeichner, Ken. "Re-thinking the Connections between Campus Courses and Field Experiences in College and University-based Teacher Education." *Journal of Teacher Education*, vol. 61, no. 1, pp. 89–99.

6. *National Council for Accreditation of Teacher Education*, www.highered.nysed.gov/pdf/NCATECR.pdf.

7. Drake, Graham, et al. "Teacher Prep Review 2018: A Review of the Nation's Teacher Preparation Programs." *National Council for Accreditation of Teacher Education*, www.nctq.org/publications/2018-Teacher-Prep-Review.

8. Hanushek, Eric A., and Steven G. Rivkin. "Generalizations About Using Value-Added Measures of Teaching Quality." *American Economic Review Papers and Proceedings*, vol. 100, no. 2, 2010, pp. 267–271.

9. Kane, Thomas J., et al. "Identifying Effective Classroom Practices Using Student Achievement Data." *The Journal of Human Resources*, vol. 46, no. 3, 2011, pp. 587–613.

10. Rockman, Saul, et al. "New Visions for Public Schools-Hunter College Urban Teacher Residency Project: A Different, More Durable Model." rockman.com/docs/downloads/TQPXCombinedReport_10.23.18-1.pdf.

11. LiBetti, Ashley, and Justin Trinidad. "Trading Coursework for Classroom: Realizing the Potential of Teacher Residencies." Bellwether Education Partners, bellwethereducation.org/sites/default/files/TeacherResidencies_Bellwether.pdf.

12. "2018 Educator Preparation Report Card." Tennessee State Board of Education, 2019, teacherprepreportcard.tn.gov/profiles/9906.

13. "2015 Network Impact Overview." National Center for Teacher Residencies, 2016, nctresidencies.org/wp-content/uploads/2016/04/NCTR-2015-Network-Impact-Overview.pdf.

14. "2015 Network Impact Overview." National Center for Teacher Residencies, 2016, nctresidencies.org/wp-content/uploads/2016/04/NCTR-2015-Network-Impact-Overview.pdf.

15. "What's the Cost of Teacher Turnover?" Learning Policy Institute, 2017, learningpolicyinstitute.org/product/the-cost-of-teacher-turnover.

16. *National Center for Teacher Residencies*, https://nctresidencies.org.

BIBLIOGRAPHY

"2018 Educator Preparation Report Card." Tennessee State Board of Education (2019). https://teacherprepreportcard.tn.gov/profiles/9906 (retrieved April 23, 2019).

"2015 Network Impact Overview." National Center for Teacher Residencies (2016). https://nctresidencies.org/wp-content/uploads/2016/04/NCTR-2015-Network-Impact-Overview.pdf (retrieved April 23, 2019).

"Building Effective Teacher Residencies." National Center for Teacher Residencies (2014). https://nctresidencies.org/wp-content/uploads/2014/11/NCTR-BETR-v2-Final.pdf (retrieved April 23, 2019).

"Clinically Oriented Teacher Preparation." National Center for Teacher Residencies (2015). https://nctresidencies.org/wp-content/uploads/2015/07/NCTR-COTP-Final-Single-Pgs.pdf (retrieved April 23, 2019).

Drake, Graham, Laura Pomerance, Robert Rickenbrode, and Kate Walsh. "Teacher Prep Review 2018: A Review of the Nation's Teacher Preparation Programs." National Council on Teacher Quality. https://www.nctq.org/publications/2018-Teacher-Prep-Review (retrieved April 23, 2019).

Hanushek, Eric A., and Steven G. Rivkin. "Generalizations about Using Value-Added Measures of Teaching Quality." *American Economic Review Papers and Proceeding*, 100(2) (2010), 267–71.

Kane, Thomas J., Eric S. Taylor, John H. Tyler, and Amy L. Wooten. "Identifying Effective Classroom Practices Using Student Achievement Data." *The Journal of Human Resources*, 46(3) (2011), 587–613.

"Leap Year: Assessing and Supporting Effective First-Year Teachers." TNTP (2013). https://tntp.org/assets/documents/TNTP_Leap_Year_2013.pdf (retrieved April 23, 2019).

LiBetti, Ashley, and Justin Trinidad. "Trading Coursework for Classroom: Realizing the Potential of Teacher Residencies." https://bellwethereducation.org/sites/default/files/TeacherResidencies_Bellwether.pdf (retrieved April 23, 2019).

"Nine Essentials." National Association for Professional Development Schools (2008). https://napds.org/nine-essentials/ (retrieved April 23, 2019).

Rockman, Saul, Kay Sloan, Alison Allen, Julie Blazevski, and Fatima Carson. "New Visions for Public Schools-Hunter College Urban Teacher Residency Project: A Different, More Durable Model." http://rockman.com/docs/downloads/TQPXCombinedReport_10.23.18-1.pdf (retrieved April 23, 2019).

Snyder, Thomas, Christobal De Brey, and Sally A. Dillow. "Digest of Education Statistics 2017." U.S. Department of Education. https://nces.ed.gov/pubs2018/2018070.pdf (retrieved April 23, 2019).

Staub, Shari Dickstein, and Roberta Trachtman. "Drivers of Teacher Preparation." https://nctresidencies.org/wp-content/uploads/2016/10/NCTR-Landscape-Analysis-The-Four-Drivers-Project.pdf (retrieved April 22, 2019).

"Transforming Teacher Education Through Clinical Practice: A National Strategy to Prepare Effective Teachers." National Council for Accreditation of Teacher Education (2010). http://www.highered.nysed.gov/pdf/NCATECR.pdf (retrieved April 23, 2019).

What's the Cost of Teacher Turnover? Learning Policy Institute (2017). https://learningpolicyinstitute.org/product/the-cost-of-teacher-turnover (retrieved April 23, 2019).

Zeichner, Ken. "Re-thinking the Connections between Campus Courses and Field Experiences in College and University-based Teacher Education." *Journal of Teacher Education*, 61(1) (2010), 89–99.

Chapter 1

The Importance of Partnerships

A Focus on the Albuquerque Teacher Residency Partnership

Viola Florez and Marjori Krebs

HISTORY AND CONTEXT OF ATRP

The College of Education (COE) at the University of New Mexico (UNM), the Albuquerque School District (APS), and the Albuquerque Teachers Federation (ATF) have a long history of collaboration focusing on improving education for P-20 students. The ongoing goal of all three organizations has been to ensure all students have equal access to high-quality teachers. Due to the teacher shortage in New Mexico and the need for more high-quality teachers, UNM, APS, and ATF submitted a grant to the National Center for Teacher Residencies (NCTR). NCTR provides high-level support to institutions of higher education and school districts wishing to develop and implement teacher residency programs to meet teacher shortages by recruiting quality professionals prepared in partnership. In 2017, NCTR funded these three partners to begin conceptualizing and implementing a teacher residency specifically for APS. Through this grant, the Albuquerque Teacher Residency Partnership (ATRP) was created. With grant funding from NCTR, we developed and implemented a residency pathway to improve the preparation and retention of effective, diverse teachers for high-need schools.

The Partners

Albuquerque Public Schools, the Albuquerque Teachers Federation, and the University of New Mexico College of Education are the key partners in this work. The Design Team, composed of representatives from each of these organizations, plans, directs, supervises, and evaluates the work.

Albuquerque Public Schools

APS is the largest school district by enrollment in New Mexico, with almost 85,000 students scattered over 1,200 square miles. With 12,000 employees, including 6,000 teachers, APS is also the largest employer in the city of Albuquerque. Of the 143 schools in APS, 68 percent are Title I schools. Sixty-four percent of students are eligible for free and reduced lunch, 17 percent are English language learners, and 17 percent are students with disabilities. In terms of ethnicity, 66 percent of students identify as Hispanic (many of whom are Spanish-speaking), 23 percent Caucasian, 6 percent American Indian (representing a variety of Indigenous languages from within and outside of New Mexico), 3 percent African American, and 2 percent Asian (Albuquerque Public Schools, 2019).

Albuquerque Teachers Federation

ATF is a "professional, progressive union" serving APS teachers and other support professionals. The ATF mission is to be "committed to improving the conditions of teaching and learning in our public schools, while advancing the causes of social justice and democracy for our members, students, and the ABQ community" (Albuquerque Teachers Federation, 2019, para. 1). ATF is dedicated to teacher quality and is engaged at all levels addressing the unique needs of schools within the Albuquerque Public School District and the partners who help prepare educators. Having the teachers' union representatives at the table as partners in preparing high-quality teachers is a unique opportunity because the voice of the teachers is consistently represented. In addition, the ATF representative is familiar with the induction year for the residents in their first year of teaching, and helps with the smooth transition from *resident* to *teacher-of-record*.

University of New Mexico

Founded in 1889, the University of New Mexico currently occupies 600 acres along old Route 66 in the heart of Albuquerque, a city and metro area of more than 900,000 people. In the fall of 2017, the campuses of the University of New Mexico served 26,278 students. UNM qualifies as an institution "with high Hispanic enrollment" (University of New Mexico, 2019, para. 6).

UNM College of Education

The mission of the UNM College of Education is the study and practice of education through teaching, research, and service, emphasizing excellence and diversity through people, ideas, and innovation. The COE has 5 departments with an undergraduate and graduate enrollment of 2,635 students as of fall 2017. The college offers multiple teacher preparation programs for undergraduate and graduate students interested in the teaching profession (University of New Mexico, 2019).

DEMOGRAPHIC CHALLENGES IN NEW MEXICO: THE OPPORTUNITY GAP

In New Mexico, poverty is a predominant condition and a major challenge. Thirty-one percent of children live in poverty, with poverty being defined as an annual income below $23,850 for a family of four. Also, 42 percent of children live in single-parent families and 18 percent of children grow up in families where the head of the household lacks a high school diploma (*New Mexico Voices for Children*, 2017). In APS, district-wide academic proficiency in math is 21 percent and English/Language Arts is 30 percent. APS third grade reading proficiency is 31 percent (New Mexico Public Education Department, 2018b).

Our three ATRP residency schools, Emerson Elementary School, Van Buren Middle School, and Highland High School, are facing high dropout challenges due to the lack of proficiency in reading and mathematics. In these three schools, 100 percent of students are eligible for free and reduced lunch. Additionally, proficiency levels for math and reading are extremely low. The proficiency rates in reading and math at our three residency partner schools range from 7 percent to 15 percent (New Mexico Public Education Department, 2018a).

Creating strong partnerships with elementary, middle, and secondary schools to address early literacy skills in reading and core academic subjects by grade level is important to impact student learning.

HOW DOES ATRP WORK?

ATRP is preparing teachers specifically ready for the challenges listed above. Our ATRP residents have already earned undergraduate degrees. Through ATRP, residents complete graduate coursework in either elementary or secondary education and yearlong clinical experiences in these high-need schools. After successful completion of ATRP, each resident will have earned a master's degree, is eligible to apply for licensure in New Mexico, and is guaranteed a teaching job in APS. In return, the residents agree to teach in APS for a minimum of two years. Elementary and secondary education program faculty teach courses and supervise residents. For their clinical experience, ATRP residents teach alongside master teachers who mentor them throughout the year. Each school site has an embedded faculty member who serves as the link between the university and the school site. This embedded faculty member conducts informal classroom observations and weekly seminars designed to make certain that residents acquire the skills necessary to be successful in the classroom. Embedded faculty members, along with university supervisors, also mentor the residents and provide support as deemed essential. In addition, the embedded faculty members and other faculty members conduct monthly professional development sessions for the master teachers.

Each resident receives a scholarship stipend of $20,000 to assist with tuition and also to supplement living costs. The funding for these stipends was, in part, from our grant from NCTR and additional funds from APS. APS also allowed all current APS employees, secretaries, and educational assistants, to maintain their health insurance through APS while completing ATRP. Master teachers in ATRP receive stipends of $2000 to mentor, coach, supervise, and participate in monthly professional development sessions led by university faculty. In the first year of ATRP, APS secured external funding to provide stipends for the master teachers to serve as resident mentors. In the future, APS plans to utilize state funds received for the purposes of mentoring and recruiting new teachers to pay master teacher stipends.

THE ATRP DESIGN TEAM—WHERE THE PARTNERS COME TOGETHER

The Power of Partnership

Residency programs across the country align with the concept of the partnership model between school districts and institutions of higher education. This alignment of efforts allows for the preparation of teachers to fit with the needs of the local community. "A hallmark of residency programs is the focus on recruiting and preparing candidates to fit the specific needs of the partner district or charter management organization" (Guha, Hyler, & Darling-Hammond, 2017, p. 35). Residents become part of their school communities while also being supported in their preparation as educators by the university and district.

The ATRP Design Team is at the center of the work of ATRP and was established to assist with the planning and implementation of the residency initiative. Each Design Team member contributes to the vision of ATRP and works collaboratively to implement and problem-solve issues around teaching courses, planning, recruiting, marketing, and other tasks as needed. Design Team members serve as advisors to key administrators in the organizations for whom they represent.

Design Team members include the executive director of Labor Relations and Staffing representing Albuquerque Public Schools; the president of the Albuquerque Teachers Federation representing the APS teachers' union; and several faculty members and instructors in the Department of Teacher Education, Educational Leadership, and Policy representing the University of New Mexico College of Education. The research assistant for grant work in the department prepares the agendas, follows up on the work between meetings, and maintains the ATRP website. These members commit to ninety-minute meetings each week, held at various locations, depending on the purposes of the meetings.

The representatives of each of the three organizations play key roles. For example, the APS representative secures the funding from the district to provide stipends for the residents and master teachers and recommends schools that would be strong partners for resident field experiences. The AFT representative knows the excellent school leaders and teachers in the district and assists us in matching residents with master teachers. AFT sponsors the first-year teacher-mentoring program, which assists us in creating a seamless transition for our residents into their first year of teaching. The UNM faculty teach the courses and conduct seminars and supervision of residents. In addition, they review the applicants for full admission into graduate programs in elementary and secondary education, and assist residents with graduate advising issues. UNM faculty also connect residents with programs on campus such as financial aid and student health care.

One of our first Design Team assignments as an NCTR-funding recipient was to create a mission statement and a vision. This detailed, in-depth process required representatives from each organization to come together to articulate exactly what we hoped to accomplish together. Our Mission Statement is as follows: "The mission of the Albuquerque Teacher Residency Partnership is to recruit, prepare, and retain what every student deserves: A competent, caring, and qualified teacher" (Albuquerque Teacher Residency Partnership, 2019, para. 1). The ATRP Vision states:

> Our program integrates rigorous academic coursework and theory with ongoing clinical experiences so that aspiring teachers are well prepared to inspire students, empower learning, and work within diverse communities. The ATRP will guide transformative experiences, shape teacher practice, affirm the cultural identities of both teachers and students, and work to build a more just society. (Para. 2)

Communication Is Key

All Design Team members are responsible for communicating with others in their organizations, and for soliciting feedback on various aspects of ATRP.

Topics for discussion include but are not limited to: admission of teacher residents to graduate programs, payment of master teachers and residents, feedback from APS School Board members, professional development for participants, feedback on coursework and field experiences, mentoring and professional development for master teachers, and many other topics. One major reason for the success of ATRP has been the effective communication among partners, emanating from Design Team members.

Even though this feedback loop is an important aspect of ATRP, there are still challenges with communication and making sure members of each partnership organization understand the work of ATRP and see their connection with ATRP. For example, when potential residents apply to ATRP and are reviewed by the Design Team, the faculty of the elementary and secondary Education programs in the College of Education are part of that discussion because in order for participants to be in ATRP, they must be admitted to the Masters' Degree Programs in elementary and secondary Education. Just because an applicant is qualified to be a teacher candidate in ATRP does not mean he is qualified for admission into a graduate program at UNM.

The Design Team addresses implementation and coordination issues and plans for sustainability of the teacher residency partnership. Because the grant with NCTR was for one year, the team is working to sustain funding from other sources, such as the district, college, or state legislation. We are currently working with APS to find sustainable resources to support ATRP, including considering reallocating resources, redesigning staffing structures, and working in close partnership with APS to ensure the program meets persistent district needs.

The Design Team also communicates with key community leaders to sustain this effort. For example, the New Mexico Workforce Connection Department provides stipends to apprentices in high-need career areas for the state. The residents meet the criteria for consideration since they are not working full time for a year and are working toward licensure to become teachers. The ATRP Design Team has secured an agreement Workforce Connection leadership to fund the graduate course work tuition costs for the residents.

Our Partnership at Work: A Meeting Agenda Review

To serve as an operational example of the Design Team partnership in action, the following example is a Design Team Agenda. Following this example are specific notations in *italics* explaining how the tasks connect to the partner roles.

    ATRP Design Team Meeting Agenda
    March 28, 2019, 9:30 a.m.–11:00 a.m.
    Location: Albuquerque Teachers Federation Building

1. Cohort 2 Updates
   a. Educational Assistant Recruitment Efforts
   b. Review Elementary and Secondary Admissions
2. NES Content Test Requirements
3. Course Schedule and Instructors
4. Graduate Induction Plan—Due to NCTR March 30
5. Alumni Engagement Plan—Due to NCTR March 30
6. NCTR Symposium in Chicago May 14
   a. Choose one of these three (Graduate Marketing and Hiring Plan, Graduate Induction Plan OR Alumni Engagement Plan) to bring and share with the NCTR Cohort
   b. Determine deliverable or slice of work showing how we used midyear NCTR Survey Data Analysis to make program improvements. What did we improve? How? What data showed that this needed to be improved? Etc.
   c. RSVP for Symposium May 14–16 in Chicago. We can bring five people from ATRP.
7. Master Teacher Issues
8. Resident Issues
9. Review Master Teachers to invite to mentor next year
10. Next Meeting: April 4. Location?

Meeting Agenda as a Sample of Our Partnership in Action

The agenda above is an agenda from our Design Team Meeting and serves as one example of how we work together as a team in decision-making. Below in *italics* are explanations of the different parts of the agenda and the roles of those involved in moving our work forward, highlighting our partnership.

1. Cohort 2 Updates
   (We are currently recruiting, screening, and interviewing our second group of residents. This update allows for university, school district, and union representatives to share their recruitment efforts for our next cohort, and to learn who have accepted our offers as a result of interviews held the week before.)
   a. Educational Assistant (EA) Recruitment Efforts
      (EAs are one potential pool of applicants. Design Team Members from APS and AFT reported on the emails sent out and the meeting scheduled specifically to target current EAs in classrooms to discuss opportunities with ATRP.)
   b. Review Elementary and Secondary Admissions

(ATRP residents are not only teaching in classrooms, but also are graduate students at UNM. The university faculty on the Design Team shared the admissions requirements, admissions process, and the timeline to be followed for UNM graduate admission.)
2. NES Content Test Requirements

    (The State of New Mexico requires all students admitted to licensure programs to pass three "essential skills" examinations in Reading, Writing, and Mathematics prior to admission. In addition, Secondary Education students must pass the Content Exams for their teaching field. UNM faculty shared these requirements and discussed possibilities of support for applicants who would need test preparation in order to pass these tests.)
3. Course Schedule and Instructors

    (As graduate students, residents take their required licensure methods courses as part of their graduate coursework. UNM faculty updated the Design Team on who would be teaching these courses for Cohort 2. The Program Faculty in Elementary and Secondary Education have agreed that the ATRP Design Team can select the instructors for the ATRP courses.)
4. Graduate Induction Plan—Due to NCTR March 30
5. Alumni Engagement Plan—Due to NCTR March 30

    (Both of these items above are requirements of the National Center for Teacher Residencies [NCTR]. Our Design Team began our work with a $500,000 grant from NCTR. As a result of that status, we have "deliverables" throughout the grant cycle to show NCTR we are making progress on our work and that we are following their "Best Practices" to deliver a quality residency program. As indicated by the two agenda items above, we are working on a plan for how our residents will be inducted into APS as full-time classroom teachers, and what support will continue for them in this new role. AFT directs the district's mentoring program, and as such, AFT discussed how the residents will be paired with mentors during their induction year who would be familiar with their work as residents and can pick up where their residency preparation left off. In addition, all parties discussed our roles in the Alumni Engagement Plan, to continue to bring Cohort 1 residents together on a regular basis to learn from their experiences as classroom teachers and to provide support for them in subsequent years of teaching. By continuing to engage with our previous residents, we hope that they will become our Master Teachers for future residents once they have three to five years of teaching experiences.)
6. NCTR Symposium in Chicago May 14

(Representatives of the Design Team attend regular meetings in Chicago with NCTR and other teacher residency programs to learn from each other and gain support.)
   a. Choose one of these three (Graduate Marketing and Hiring Plan, Graduate Induction Plan OR Alumni Engagement Plan) to bring and share with the NCTR Cohort
      (The Design Team discussed which focus area about which we would present at this next meeting with NCTR.)
   b. Determine deliverable or slice of work showing how we used midyear NCTR Survey Data Analysis to make program improvements. What did we improve? How? What data showed that this needed to be improved? Etc.
      (In addition, we determined what part of the data we would share at this meeting. As part of our grant with NCTR, they conducted surveys with our residents and master teachers, then provided us with the data collected. We spent one Design Team meeting evaluating this data, and then shared some of our findings as well as actions taken as a result of the data. We decided to share the midyear data from our residents and Master Teachers about their coursework, and their desire to have that be more connected with their classroom experiences. As a result of this information, we are working to schedule regular meetings with university course instructors and master teaches to help co-design the syllabi to better meet the needs of students in their specific residency classrooms.)
   c. RSVP for Symposium May 14–16 in Chicago. We can bring five people from ATRP.
      (The Design Team determined who would represent our team, making sure all three partners were represented. We decided that one UNM faculty member, one APS school board member, and the Human Resources representative of our Design Team would attend the meeting. One catch is that each participant has to find funding to finance their own travel costs. The APS representative said she would scour the budgets to see what was available to help pay for travel for the entire group. Faculty can also use their university travel allocations if necessary.)
7. Master Teacher Issues
   (Each meeting we spend time discussing any issues that have come up with master teachers. These issues range from questions regarding solo-teaching expectations to requirements from methods courses to professionalism of residents. Depending on the issue, either a UNM faculty member, the embedded faculty member, or the APS representative meets with the master teacher to resolve the issue.)

8. Resident Issues

    (We also spend time at each meeting discussing any issues that have arisen with our residents. These issues can range from concerns with methods coursework to personality conflicts with master teachers to illness or family obligations that must be negotiated. Typically, a UNM faculty member will meet with the resident to resolve these issues. On rare occasions, the Design Team will determine that a resident needs to be paired with a different master teacher. In these instances, the entire Design Team discusses the best options for this decision.)

9. Review Master Teachers to invite to mentor next year.

    (As part of our recruitment efforts for Cohort 2, we also must retain and/or retain master teachers for this new group to begin next year. The Design Team listens to feedback from university supervisors who observe the residents and their master teachers in their classrooms, along with information from UNM faculty who have conducted professional development sessions with master teachers. Not all master teachers will be invited to participate next year. During this discussion we also determined that we need to bring an additional elementary school on board as a residency school with our growing number of elementary resident applicants in Cohort 2. The Design Team will consider future school sites at subsequent meetings, then meet with the principal, and then with the teachers to determine their levels of interest. The school will then go through the residency school application process to secure their designation as a residency school.)

10. Next Meeting: April 4. Location?

    (This may not seem to be a major item on the agenda, but it is a symbol of our true partnership. We do rotate our meeting sites between the AFT Union Offices, APS Administrative Offices, and the UNM Campus. This simple decision is an indicator of the equal partnership of all organizations and their commitment to this residency partnership.)

As evidenced by the above agenda with notations, the weekly Design Team meetings, with representatives from all partnership organizations present, is the key to the success of ATRP. All issues are brought forth for all partners to consider and to give input. In this way, all partners are vested in the work, and work in true partnership.

THE VOICES OF OUR PARTNERS

In order to gain further insight, we interviewed one representative from each of our partner organizations regarding their thoughts on the ATRP partnership. The partners specifically addressed why each organization decided to be a part of ATRP, what has worked well, what challenges they see, what changes they would like to see moving forward, and their hopes for the future. These are our interviewees:

- Karen Rudys is the executive director of Labor Relations and Staffing for Albuquerque Public Schools. Ms. Rudys has served in this position for twelve years, and in Human Resources for a total of eighteen years. Prior to this work, she was a classroom teacher for five years.
- Dr. Ellen Bernstein serves as president of the Albuquerque Teachers Federation. Prior to this position, in which she has served for nineteen years, Dr. Bernstein was a classroom teacher for seventeen years, with an expertise in multiage-level teaching and inclusion.
- Dr. Viola Florez, co-author of this chapter, is a professor in the Department of Teacher Education, Educational Leadership, and Policy at the University of New Mexico. Dr. Florez spearheaded the writing of the NCTR grant that resulted in ATRP. She has held executive administrative positions such as, dean of the College of Education at UNM, interim provost, and cabinet secretary of Higher Education for the state of New Mexico. Dr. Florez has also served as a classroom teacher in New Mexico, Arizona, Colorado, and Texas.

Why Join ATRP?

All three representatives stated varying reasons why their organizations joined ATRP, but all agreed that ATRP matched the goals of their organizations and assisted them in their own roles in meeting those goals. Specifically, all partners stated that as part of their work within their own organizations, they were responsible for attracting, preparing, and retaining high-quality teachers, and that this partnership assisted them in meeting that overarching goal.

Ms. Rudys addressed her challenge in Human Resources with trying to minimize teacher *churn*, and to consistently recruit and retain the most highly qualified teachers. She stated,

> As far as the goals of HR and the District, it's really important to have those prepared quality teachers in the classroom for vacancies. We had 170 classroom teacher vacancies at the beginning of the school year. We are hoping that these twenty-five ATRP residents can fill those vacancies and stay with us because they are adequately prepared for the classroom.

Dr. Bernstein noted that she had been aware of teacher residencies for a long time, but recently credited Dr. Karen DeMoss of Bank Street College and the

MACP Prepared to Teach Grant with revitalizing the idea in Albuquerque. In addition, Dr. Bernstein took a more global approach to teacher preparation to explain why this work is important to her personally as well as to the teacher's union:

> It is in the national interest to have teachers well-prepared to work with the students of that country. Unlike what we have been doing in the recent past in America, where we believe that states should compete for the money they need to educate our nation's children. Other countries are actually saying, "It is our job to prepare teachers to prepare students to be citizens." What a novel idea!

Dr. Bernstein continued,

> I remember thinking even before I talked to Karen DeMoss, "What would it look like if we valued the profession so much and valued the role of the profession in the greater good of our country, that in order to get into teacher prep, not only did you have to excel and be accepted, but then we totally supported you to focus on college work and research, and actually learning how to teach?"

Dr. Florez took a more personal approach to the importance of teacher preparation through ATRP and the importance of "giving students a rich experience in the classroom, high-quality course work so they could become really effective teachers . . . being in the classroom for a full year, more mentoring, more supervision, and the planning that went with it." In summary, all partners agreed that the residency model of ATRP helped each of them individually meet their own goals within their organization, but more importantly, everyone collectively could meet the goal of placing high-quality teachers in every classroom.

What Has Worked Well with ATRP?

In addition to having a vested interest in common outcomes, all partners agreed that one key to ATRP's success was the establishment of the Design Team, its organizational structure, and weekly Design Team meetings which allow for regular, consistent communication among all partners. A strength of ATRP is the importance of working together in partnership to solve problems instead of working individually within our own organizations. In Ms. Rudys's words, "The partnership has worked really well." Dr. Florez spoke about the power in the group's "collective will" to succeed:

> One of the things that has worked well with ATRP is the fact that we really wanted to do this. This may sound kind of silly, but we went after the grant together as partners, as a school-university partnership. And we really wanted

to address some of the needs, such as the teacher shortage, which was one thing, but also the effectiveness of how we prepared our students to meet the "ready to teach" concept.... So I think what has worked well was the fact that we wanted to do it, we thought it through, we problem-solved together, we met the challenges. Yes, we've had some frustrating moments, but we are learning together, so we have a lot of lessons learned from this year now that we are planning for the second cohort.... So we have basically been able to work together in a problem-solving kind of a situation which I think has really worked well.

Dr. Bernstein spoke specifically to the collaboration of the group, when she stated, "I think UNM for the most part, in their role in preparing teachers, are used to dealing with the problems in the schools by themselves, and [through the Design Team structure] they can bring those to the table sooner." Ms. Rudys confirmed that collaboration was key, especially in connection with the bigger picture of preparing high-quality teachers,

The communication between the union, the district, and the UNM College of Ed has been extremely well done . . . because [the Design Team] meets every week. . . . The other thing is because we all have a vested interest in this, and regardless if people come and go in this partnership, we all really want to sustain it because we know it's the best practice and it's how teacher ed prep programs should be across the nation.

All partners agree that organizational qualities of regular open communication, group problem-solving, and belief in a common goal have been significant factors in the success of ATRP thus far.

What Are the Challenges of ATRP?

Even though all partners concur the partnership, as operationalized through the Design Team, has been successful in its first year, they also agree that ATRP does face challenges. All partners cited funding sustainability and institutionalization as important areas needing continued attention. Faculty buy-in at the university and continued meaningful faculty involvement are challenges to institutionalization with the elementary and secondary programs. In addition, partners stated that funding sustainability is complicated by the desire to expand teacher residencies to undergraduate students also.

Dr. Florez posed the following questions that need to be answered for ATRP to continue on a successful path: "How do we make it so that there is ownership within the College for it?" She further queried, "How do we make it so that there is ownership with the elementary and secondary faculty so that we want to sustain it, and that we all want to contribute to it in different ways?"

Ms. Rudys also cited the issue of faculty ownership from her perspective as a district partner, along with greater connections between classroom curriculum and university methods coursework:

> Challenges are getting the faculty buy in on designing the curriculum [to match with resident needs], and this is something that is probably going to take a couple of years, because we know that from learning from other programs across the nation, that it is a different way to teach, and we all have to change our thought processes on how to provide curriculum in the classroom hands-on and eliminate the curriculum that is not necessary anymore.

She continued with her ideas of deepening and expanding the partnership to include classroom teachers as instructors:

> We could have the master teachers help teach the methods classes if they had that master's or Ph.D. That would be ideal, so there's a lot we can do in the future to make this work, but it takes a while to get everybody on board.

Dr. Bernstein noted the importance of securing a formalized agreement for ATRP among all three partners in the form of a Memorandum of Understanding, along with getting more widespread support across organizations, including financial commitment. "We want to broaden the number of people who know about it [ATRP] and care about it within each organization. We should have an official budget for this program."

Dr. Florez summed up the major challenges this way:

> The interesting part about [how to institutionalize ATRP] is that it's up to us as people to make it happen. It totally is in our control. Just figuring it out. This is really something we want to make sure that it works, so what do we have to do to make it work and then just move forward with it.

She concluded with this comment about what it would take: "It's a willingness. It's going to take a will to want to do it."

What Changes Should ATRP Make?

In connection to these challenges, partners cited specific changes they would make in order to meet these challenges. All partners stated that they would increase the level of university involvement, and the necessity of recruiting stronger master teachers as mentors for the residents. As part of this recruitment, partners wanted to improve the screening process for master teachers to include interviews and classroom observations. To address these challenges, the Design Team has expanded ATRP to an additional elementary school in order to have access to more potential master teachers. To increase university involvement, the faculty members on the Design Team now have a designated agenda item on each faculty department meeting agenda to discuss what is happening with ATRP and answer faculty questions regarding the partnership.

Dr. Florez continuing with her comments about the importance of faculty involvement as an important change necessary for continued success:

> How do we bring [the faculty] in so that they understand what is going on and help us expand it? There's no reason in the world why, if we had faculty who were really committed, that they couldn't be a part of this ... at different schools. ... Just like we've been involved with these three [residency] schools, we could have faculty involved with three other schools. ... That's where the ownership comes in; institutionalizing it where they all feel a part of something.

Dr. Bernstein connected with her involvement as AFT president to the importance of strong master teacher selection:

> I would ask for an interview, possibly a classroom observation. I would want a pool of people who are interested, and I would want more support for them, as well as clear expectations of their roles, how they learn about co-teaching, how they do the gradual release of responsibility.

Dr. Florez expanded this to include selection of future residency schools:

> The point is to find schools that really help our students understand what it means to be high-quality teachers. The culture of the school is important. The leadership of the school is important. ...So that [the master teachers] have some rich experience in working with the residents and working with each other as professionals within the school .... So how we select our schools is really important.

What Is the Hope for the Future of ATRP?

Even though there are challenges and changes that need to be made to ATRP, all partners expressed positive beliefs about the future of ATRP, and continue to hope to secure funding sources, sustainability, institutionalization, and increased enrollment.

Ms. Rudys from APS expressed her hope for sustainability "above and beyond all the people that are connected with it now." She expressed the importance of expanding ATRP to special education and other high-need content areas. She connected her hopes for ATRP to the need for change along the way. ATRP should be a "permanent change of how teacher ed prep programs develop their curriculum and prepare students for the classroom, because it has to change." She connected the need for this change to the changing demographics of school populations in general:

> Our student population has changed through the years. It's just not the same. We all know that. The [teachers] are dealing with so many different things, social issues, for whatever reason didn't exist fifty years ago, even thirty years ago, so we have to change our mindset.

Dr. Bernstein echoed this hope for sustainability in the future, especially for "ATRP to be embedded and institutionalized as a post-bac prep program at the College of Education." She expressed hope for funding sustainability also by stating,

> I would like it to be funded so that it's not a question of, "Do we have enough will?" but it's automatic—it's part of the business of the College of Education to have a residency program for post-bac students.

Dr. Florez concurred in her comments about the hope for sustainable funding. She explained that ATRP was an extension of other grant-funded teacher preparation initiatives that developed strong partnerships with high-need schools to meet district needs for well-qualified teachers, prepared to teach in such high-need schools. She stated, "We've learned a lot over the last four years" through other such grant-funded projects. Dr. Florez continued,

> All of this contributed to us knowing that having students out in the classrooms with strong mentoring and supervision is very important. So I think that sustaining it is the way to go for the future in preparing teachers for the teaching profession. I really think this is the way of the future—teacher residencies.

Partners' Concluding Thoughts

All partners indicated they were glad they have been a part of ATRP, especially designing it from the beginning. Ms. Rudys stated, "I'm proud to be a part of this. I feel like it's really quality work and it's making a difference for the students in Albuquerque Public Schools and the state of New Mexico." Similarly, Dr. Bernstein lauded the value of the partnership by stating, "When we work in partnership, we have more collective intelligence and do more good work than when we are alone. It perpetuates the goals of the organization on so many levels I probably can't even count them all." Dr. Florez concluded by looking toward the future of the residents' career paths in education. She stated,

> I just think that if we are able to sustain this, the teachers will be stronger, and they will become more involved in their own schools. And it could influence policy down the road. Because when people become stronger in their own self-esteem, they will take more risks. Then that brings about a different kind of change, especially from the political side, and they stand up for what they really think needs to happen in the schools and with children.

She continues,

> I can see the difference in the residents since they have been at the school as we move into the second semester. They are really much stronger. When I visit with the supervisors, they say there is a he difference between the students in the residency versus the students who have only been out just observing and are starting their student teaching. The resident teachers are way ahead of them, and it's because of their comfort level. . . . So I think they are going to be much stronger in their first year of teaching, and because of that they will make decisions to volunteer more in their first year, or second year of teaching than they would have otherwise. Because it takes teachers three years to find that comfort level and I see it already in some of them. Their confidence is just so much stronger.

All partners agree that the first year of ATRP has been a success, and that a major component of that success has been the partnership among the Albuquerque Public Schools, the Albuquerque Teachers Federation, and the College of Education at the University of New Mexico. Even so, all partners also see several areas for improvement in order for ATRP to be sustained, especially institutionalization with all organizations and secure funding sources.

ADVICE FOR SUCCESSFUL TEACHER RESIDENCY PARTNERSHIPS

In addition to the advice and recommendations stated by the partners above, our experience has taught us that there are many important aspects of creating a successful teacher residency partnership.

First, having the support of NCTR and its long-standing experience in assisting groups to create such partnerships helped us create a successful, sustainable teacher residency program. NCTR's team visits to our site and also the Design Team visits to NCTR headquarters to meet and learn from other residency programs was invaluable. The mentoring by NCTR kept the Design Team on track toward implementing our program. We were not starting from scratch.

Second, we had strong, dedicated, sustainable representation from each of our partner organizations: the school district, the teachers' union, and the university. We also had the support, in writing, from the leadership of these organizations through the creation and signing of a Memorandum of Understanding regarding the roles and responsibilities of each organization.

A third successful aspect of ATRP is having a strong faculty member, who is a full professor and former dean of our college, to lead the Design Team. Her leadership was imperative to gain the support of faculty at the university. Even faculty who questioned the initiative trusted this faculty leader, and thus, supported ATRP. In addition, her strong network of national leaders in teacher preparation assisted us in making connections to other funding sources available nationally.

Finally, our strong connection with the teachers' union, that leads the district's mentoring program, was a key level of support, so that there was a more seamless transition for the teacher residents into the district through the mentoring process. We will continue to study this induction process as our current residents continue into their first and second years of teaching. Ideally, part of the sustainability of this project is that our former residents will become successful master teachers in ATRP in the near future.

IN SUMMARY

Moving into our second year of ATRP, we have much to continue to learn and improve.

Our strong partnership will hopefully sustain us into the future, to institutionalize this teacher education preparation pathway for all three of our partner institutions. The most rewarding part of this work is being a part of a movement to support out students professionally and financially to help meet our goal of providing the children of New Mexico with high-quality teachers in every classroom every day. We continue to strive to achieve our ATRP Mission: "To recruit, prepare, and retain what every student deserved: A competent, caring, and qualified teacher" (Albuquerque Teacher Residency Partnership 2019).

BIBLIOGRAPHY

Albuquerque Public Schools. "About APS." Albuquerque Public Schools. 2019. https://www.aps.edu/about-us.

Albuquerque Teachers Federation. "Our Mission." Zocoloco Studies. 2019. https://atfunion.org/your-union.

Center for Collaborative Researcher and Community. "Research Proposal Boilerplate." The University of New Mexico. 2019. https://coeresearch.unm.edu/for-researchers/pi-toolkit/research-proposal-boilerplate.html.

Guha, R., Maria E. Hyler, and Linda Darling-Hammond. "The Power and Potential of Teacher Residencies." *Phi Delta Kappan* 98, no. 8 (2017): 31–37.

June, Ana. "The Albuquerque Teacher Residency Partnership: Mission and Vision." Albuquerque Teacher Residency Partnership. 2019. https://www.abqteach.org/who-we-are.

New Mexico Public Education Department. "School Data: Achievement Data." New Mexico Public Education Department. 2018a. https://webnew.ped.state.nm.us/bureaus/accountability/achievement-data/.

New Mexico Public Education Department. "NM PED 2017–2018 Student Assessment Results." New Mexico Public Education Department. 2018b. https://webnew.ped.state.nm.us/wp-content/uploads/2018/07/PARCCBriefingPacket2018.pdf.

Wallin, Amber. "New Mexico Kids Count Data Book." New Mexico Voices for Children. 2017. https://www.nmvoices.org/wp-content/uploads/2018/01/NMKC-DataBook2017-Web.pdf.

Chapter 2

Identifying and Recruiting Quality Residents

Ashley Clark, Sarah B. Glover, and Jessamyn Lockhart

Colorado is known for many things—soaring mountains, vast amber fields of grain, and high desert plains. The diversity of the landscape is paralleled only by its diversity of people and places. Across the state, communities of 5 to 500,000 live in small rural towns, high mountain villages, and bustling cities. This dynamic landscape has attracted hundreds of thousands of people to the state over the past decade and with it has brought a booming economy, job growth, and housing rates that outpace earnings.

As higher-paying jobs have become more plentiful and the unemployment rate has fallen, fewer and fewer people are turning to more traditional careers like teaching. Every year, more than 3,000 new teachers are needed to fill open spots in schools across Colorado (Whaley 2017). Since 2010, there has been a 24 percent drop in graduates from traditional teacher prep programs at Colorado's colleges and universities (Colorado Department of Higher Education 2017). These declining numbers have caused a crisis-level teacher shortage in the state with the most acute shortages felt in rural areas. Compounding the issue is the fact that Colorado funds schools at one of the lowest rates in the country—about $9,700 per pupil (Vermont, the highest, funds at a rate of $20,795) ("Per Pupil Spending" 2018).

This lack of funding impacts not only the students in their classrooms but also the teachers who teach them. In Colorado, 77 percent of the state's districts are considered rural. The average salary for teachers in those districts is about $23,000 (Trafficanda 2018), less than a living wage in most communities in which teachers live. On top of that, teachers work under extreme stress and challenging conditions, making them more and more likely to leave the profession before five years. To respond to the growing need for educators in

Colorado, the Public Education and Business Coalition established a teacher residency program.

In partnership with the Boettcher Foundation, a Colorado-based philanthropic organization, the Public Education and Business Coalition (PEBC) founded the Boettcher Teacher Residency in 2003 to provide high-quality teacher preparation, and since its inception has developed a proven track record of recruiting, training, and retaining people in the profession at a rate that outpaces the national averages. In 2018, program census data showed that 92 percent of graduates are still in the field of education five years post residency. The PEBC Teacher Residency is now one critical solution to Colorado's teacher shortage, and our unique model prepares teachers in both urban and rural communities. But, as with most things in life, we cannot do it alone—partnerships are a key element in PEBC's residency model. Our residency was founded as the result of a partnership between PEBC and the Boettcher Foundation, and the success of the residency can be attributed not only to this continued partnership but to other collaborative efforts with organizations, government entities, and school districts.

HISTORY OF PEBC

PEBC's origins date back to 1983 and the release of the *Nation at Risk* report by the National Commission on Excellence in Education. The commission indicated that the public education system was failing to meet the national need for a competitive workforce. With funding from the Ford Foundation, several communities nation-wide created local education funds to concentrate efforts on quality teaching initiatives. Initially, PEBC's focus was on supporting teachers with literacy and reading comprehension instructional practices. In 1997, PEBC staff, Ellin Oliver Keene and Susan Zimmerman, published the ground-breaking book *Mosaic of Thought: Teaching Comprehension in a Reader's Workshop* which drew thousands of teachers to Denver wanting to work with and observe PEBC staff applying literacy best practices in their own classrooms. The organization expanded its efforts to coach teachers nationally, and created its highly respected PEBC Lab Classrooms. In 2004 PEBC expanded its focus to include professional learning in Science, Technology, Engineering & Math (STEM) instructional best practices.

In 2002, the Boettcher Foundation made the decision to invest in a teacher residency program in recognition of the 50th anniversary of the Boettcher Foundation Scholarship Program. The Scholarship Program awards merit-based undergraduate scholarships to Colorado's best and brightest students to be used at four-year accredited colleges and universities based in Colorado. The Foundation and PEBC recognized the important role teachers played in the lives of past, present, and future scholars. The residency was created to provide a high-quality preparation experience for teachers in the state of Colorado.

The first residency cohort began at PEBC in 2003 with eleven residents. The primary goal of PEBC's Boettcher Teacher Residency was to recruit, prepare, and retain exceptional teachers to serve in low-income, high-needs communities, where students were least likely to have highly qualified teachers. In addition, the program sought to recruit and train science and mathematics candidates, as well as teachers of color, in percentages higher than the national average, and in response to needs of the state. The design of the residency model was grounded in research showing that teachers are the most important factor in the achievement of K-12 students, and the quality of teachers are not equitably distributed across various populations of students (Berry 2010). To further compound the risks for students in high-needs contexts, teachers in these schools are significantly more likely to leave the profession (Ingersoll 2001).

In 2004, PEBC's Boettcher Teacher Residency along with other pioneering residency programs in Boston and Chicago created an informal partnership to share best practices in residency design and teacher development. In 2007, the National Center for Teacher Residency (NCTR) launched to develop, support, and promote teacher residencies at a national level, and the PEBC Teacher Residency continues to thought partner with existing and new residencies to offer lessons learned and expertise.

In 2013, PEBC's residency work expanded to rural regions in Colorado. The initial rural cohort was based in the San Luis Valley, the state's most fertile valley and an area rich in the spiritual and cultural histories of Indigenous populations and Hispanic settlers. The rural cohort grew to include the southwest region, and to date teachers have been prepared to teach in larger towns like Durango and small rural communities like Dove Creek and Ignacio, both of which are towns with populations of less than 800 people. In 2015, PEBC's Boettcher Teacher Residency merged with Stanley Teacher Prep, the first designated agency to license alternatively certified teachers in the state of Colorado. The Stanley Teacher Prep program was founded in 1972 by former First Lady of Colorado, Bea Romer, and founding head of Stanley British Primary School, Carolyn Hambidge, both of whom had a vision for a school that would not only teach children but would serve as a model for teaching teachers as well.

Today, the PEBC Teacher Residency continues to be a national leader in teacher preparation and is actively working with multiple schools and districts to develop a statewide pipeline of urban and rural teachers to address economic and workforce development issues across the state of Colorado. During the 2018–2019 school year, PEBC's Teacher Residency partnered with eighteen districts and forty-four schools to provide high-quality teaching experiences. After completing the residency year, alumni have access to differentiated professional development as well as further coaching support during their post-residency years. To date, residency graduates have impacted the lives of over 300,000 students ECE through Grade 12.

The PEBC Teacher Residency partners with many organizations across the state to sustain the high-quality programming of the residency. We strategically partner with private and public entities to secure funding and work collaboratively to address the state's need for high-quality teachers. Those entities include the Boettcher Foundation, the Colorado Department of Education, the Colorado Department of Higher Education and schools and districts statewide. We also partner with seven public and private institutes of higher education that represent diverse regions of our state to offer masters degrees to our residents. Specifically, we partner with University of Northern Colorado; University of Colorado, Denver; University of Denver; Colorado State University, Global; Fort Lewis College; Metro State University; and Western State Colorado University.

In order to maintain our reputation for providing high-quality educators who remain in the profession, we begin by screening for our core dispositions: learning orientation/reflectiveness, efficacy/agency, identity, complexity and difference, and professionalism. We screen for these dispositions during the interview and selection process, and we develop these dispositions during the residency year through intentional reflection time and coaching conversations. Our residency model blends theory and practice, so that after a careful selection process the resident is given a rich and relevant classroom-based learning experience guided by a skilled mentor teacher and enhanced by instruction from expert clinical educators.

IDENTIFYING AND RECRUITING QUALITY RESIDENTS

PEBC's Teacher Residency has developed its recruiting model through intentional planning, structured systems and building deep relationships with districts, community partners, and residency candidates.

Intentional Planning

PEBC's recruitment team is comprised of leadership that sets vision and strategy and staff from across the organization that supports with implementation. The recruitment team engages in internal bi-yearly planning meetings to identify the varied opportunities available to connect with potential teaching candidates and reflect on the systems and structures that support the execution of effective candidate recruitment. Specifically, the systems and structures that support recruitment include the recruitment strategic plan, the interview process and the acceptance process. Aligned to PEBC's core values and residency dispositions, the meetings utilize data from previous recruitment cycles to reflect on attempted efforts and inform future recruitment initiatives. The data also allow the team to make more informed decisions around event attendance, marketing efforts, selection process, and candidate management systems.

Data Utilization

During the recruitment and admissions cycle, data are collected to help guide both the current cycle and future recruitment cycles. These data include number of candidate inquiries, number of completed applications, number of accepted residents, number of deferred candidates, and number of waitlisted candidates. These quantitative data are housed in our client relations management system so that they are easily and quickly accessible for weekly analysis. In addition to tracking candidate level data, the recruitment team also collect data on the number of attendees at career fairs, information sessions, and other outreach events. These data inform decisions about the efficacy of recruitment strategy and guides decision-making about future strategy.

Although there are intentional planning structures in place, the team remains flexible to meet the needs of our partners. Prioritizing events, pre-planning informational meetings, and selection interviews has been critical to maintaining a schedule that is prepared to include unanticipated opportunities such as an opportunity to speak with a school's parent-teacher association or an invitation to join a community event. This flexibility due to intentional planning yields the space to be responsive to the needs of the various partners and candidates. The team is then able to use the data from new opportunities in the following planning meeting.

GROW YOUR OWN

These relationships are most evident in Grow Your Own initiatives. Grow Your Own initiatives have been defined as recruitment practices that help districts and schools identify individuals within their community that have the potential to serve as a future teacher-of-record through intensive training and coaching that prepare them for the classroom. Prior to implementing our Grow Your Own strategy, we focused more of our recruitment efforts on national recruiting. Our experience was that it was more difficult to attract candidates to teaching, especially in rural areas, if they did not have some connection to the state.

In Colorado, candidates who have not yet completed a licensure program are able to obtain an Alternative Teaching license by passing the PRAXIS exam in their given content area. Once the Alternative License is obtained, the candidate can be hired as a teacher-of-record in a classroom while they complete a licensure program to obtain their initial teaching license.

PEBC's residency recruitment team begins implementing Grow Your Own Initiatives by having initial meetings with school leaders to better understand their capacity needs, school culture, and community dynamics. This helps the team better understand the diverse needs of all their district partners and informs the team's recruitment strategies. More often than not, the recruitment team leaves these initial meetings with soft leads on individuals to follow up with, marketing opportunities within the community, and potential community partners that will aid in generating new leads. For example, one such meeting might lead to a connection with a paraprofessional in the district who has expressed interest in pursuing his teaching license. Or, in the case of a marketing opportunity, these meetings might yield a chance to post the residency opportunity in the school's weekly newsletter to parents. These meetings also provide an opportunity for the recruitment team to educate school leaders on the program model and application process candidates experience.

Lead Generation

Residency candidates are mostly generated from individuals within the school community or greater regional community. Often, candidates learn about the residency through word of mouth, either from alumni or other members of the community. The concerted efforts of community-based, targeted advertising in local newspapers and on local radio stations, and even flyers in school buildings also assist in publicizing recruitment efforts. Candidates may include but are not limited to paraprofessionals, substitute teachers, and after-school program leaders. Paraprofessionals, for example, have been a successful route for residency recruitment because these individuals are integrated members of the school community and are committed to the success of the students they support.

Christina* was a paraprofessional in rural Colorado who completed her bachelor's degree at a local university. Christina was a psychology major who obtained a position in a school as a paraprofessional, while she completed her degree. After working with students for a few years, Christina realized that working within a school as a classroom teacher was her passion. When PEBC's recruitment team met with her school principal, he identified that she would make a great teacher but was unsure of what steps to take to complete her license. After better understanding the program model, the principal helped Christina connect with the recruitment team prior to them leaving the school. The team was able to invite her to an upcoming information session to learn more about how she could obtain her Colorado Teacher's License. The team's willingness to make initial contact with Christina, connect with her at the information session, and routinely follow up while she completed enrollment steps is what helped Christina begin her new career. Christina completed her residency placement in the same school where she was employed as a paraprofessional. Christina's relationship with her school and successful residency year led to her employment as an elementary school teacher in the same district. The district was eager to hire Christina and continue to recommend leads to the residency recruitment team because of the support that was provided to Christina throughout the recruitment process and residency year.

Another successful paraprofessional story began in an urban school that identified a paraprofessional, Nancy,* as a teacher residency candidate. This school had a commitment to recruiting diverse teachers that reflected the students they served. Nancy obtained her bachelor's degree in Elementary Education but had not obtained her license upon graduation. Nancy was unable to afford the residency experience because of personal financial obligations. By working closely with Nancy's school, the recruitment team and residency staff were able to allow Nancy to remain a part-time paraprofessional while completing the residency. This school and resident candidate required PEBC's residency to be flexible in their processes to meet her needs. The uniqueness of Nancy's situation allowed the residency to create an access point for candidates of various backgrounds to obtain their license.

Stories like Christina and Nancy's are vast. It is imperative for residencies to be responsive to the needs of both the candidates and partner schools. Responsiveness includes connecting with candidates in their communities, recognizing the unique assets diverse candidates bring to their schools and providing access points for them to obtain their license.

Developing Community Partnerships

Community organizations have aided the residency in identifying individuals who have a deep understanding of the cultural needs of various communities and exhibit a level of commitment to stay in those communities. These organizations may have a direct or indirect connection to education and tend to generate successful teacher candidates. To deepen these partnerships, the recruitment team builds a relationship with organization staff, develops marketing campaigns tailored to organization affiliates and customizes the application process to attract more candidates.

Just as PEBC's recruitment team makes an effort to engage with district and school partners, annual meetings are scheduled to engage with organizations that serve partner school communities. Annual meetings serve as a space to share information and to strategize about both the efficacy of the partnership and the desired outcomes for all parties. These organizations may include Americorps programs, Troops to Teachers, After School Programs, and the like. Meeting with organization staff to identify their services, their affiliate demographics, and opportunities to engage with their network is critical to reaching a broad audience that may not be aware of the opportunity to join a teacher residency. Upon learning more about the organization and understanding their alignment, the recruitment team works to develop an action plan to market the residency. Marketing initiatives may include newsletter engagement, alumni highlights, and information sessions that allow the partner organization to engage with the residency. Residents like Harold* would not have known about the residency had it not been for the recruitment team's commitment to learning about the organizations present in the community he served.

Harold majored in Outdoor Leadership and found his way to rural Colorado after joining a service program upon college graduation. Harold quickly became enamored with his community when he was placed in a school to serve as an elementary math interventionist. After learning more about the residency from PEBC staff at his service program's annual retreat, he found his opportunity to remain in his new community while continuing his work with students. Harold is now a second year teacher and has become an advocate of the residency for others completing the service program where he was once a member. Individuals like Harold and others who have extensive classroom experience have inspired the recruitment team to establish a customized application process to support their entry into the residency.

Application Process

The PEBC Teacher Residency has a competitive application process for teacher candidates entering the residency. This process includes an online application, a phone screening, and a final interview that entails both a group and an individual component. The residency dispositions are deeply integrated into the selection process as a way of introducing candidates to the dispositions and remain a framework for the selection team's decision-making. For example, candidates are asked to reflect on a past experience and what they learned from that experience. The reflective nature of this task is critical to being a successful teacher and is central to the residency's core dispositions.

For individuals who hold ample experience working with students, they are accelerated to the final interview. This added track creates an accessibility point and honors the experiences of applicants. The recruitment team has also made a commitment to identify opportunities to highlight aspects of the residency within the application process. This includes readings that educate candidates about inequities within the education system, time to reflect on the communities where they would like to teach, as well as an opportunity to advocate for and obtain feedback. This comprehensive experience allows PEBC staff to engage with teacher candidates and evaluate them under a common language to ensure selection of the right candidates for the program.

LESSONS LEARNED

The recruitment and selection process is an ever-evolving one. What worked last year or last week might not work tomorrow and as such, we are continually reflecting, learning, and growing. Intentional planning and the ability to be flexible have been two of the greatest assets in the recruitment process. Given the diverse nature of our program (we serve large urban school districts of 90,000 students and small rural districts of 25 students), recruitment needs vary greatly. Close relationships with school and district leaders allow us to be flexible in our recruitment efforts and to intentionally plan the recruitment cycle to support the needs of our partners.

Despite intentional efforts to be responsive to school and district needs, our recruitment efforts do not always meet the demand for new educators. Because of this, we continue to think about how to engage more and different groups of people. In the future, we hope to continue to engage with diverse local community groups as well as national organizations to fill the Colorado pipeline. This effort requires dedicated time and more intentional strategy to effectively engage potential candidates.

From its inception, PEBC has been a mission-driven organization with a focus on preparing and retaining high-quality, effective teachers. Part of the success of the work has been in the intentional identification and recruitment of preservice teachers who become those highly effective teachers later in their career. While the recruitment process is thoughtful and inclusive of myriad perspectives of diverse partners, what remain as critical components are the use of data, the establishment of cooperative, trusting relationships and reflective practices to continually refine the process.

There is not one right answer or way to implement effective recruitment strategies. Rather, this chapter should serve as a launching point for thinking about how to leverage data, relationships, and structures in one's own context. Who are the players that should be at the table? What is the data you need to make informed decisions and to shape the strategy you implement to find high-quality candidates? How did the strategy work? What should be different tomorrow? Next month? Next year?

BIBLIOGRAPHY

Berry, Barnett, Alesha Daughtrey, and Allan Wider. "Teacher Effectiveness: The Conditions that Matter Most and a Look to the Future." *Center for Teaching Quality*, March 2010. http://www.ncsl.org/portals/1/documents/Educ/2010EdFinMtgBerry-Daughtrey-Wieder.pdf.

Cole, Cynthia, and Robert Mitchell. "Teacher Shortages Across the Nation and Colorado: Similar Issues, Varying Magnitudes." *Colorado Department of Higher Education*, December 2017. https://highered.colorado.gov/Publications/Reports/teachereducation/2017/TeacherShortages_Nation_Colorado_Dec2017.pdf.

Editorial Projects in Education. "Quality Counts 2018: Grading Scale and Methodology." *Education Week*, vol. 37, no. 34 (June 2, 2018), pp. 19–21. https://www.edweek.org/ew/collections/quality-counts-2018-state-finance/map-per-pupil-spending-state-by-state.html.

Ingersoll, R. "Teacher Turnover and Teacher Shortages: An Organizational Analysis." *American Educational Research Journal*, vol. 38, no. 3 (Fall 2001), pp. 499–534. https://www.gse.upenn.edu/pdf/rmi/TeacherTurnoverTeacherShortages-RMI-Fall-2001.pdf.

Keene, E. & Zimmerman, S. (1997). *Mosaic of thought: Teaching comprehension in a reader's workshop*. Portsmouth, NH: Heinemann.

Trafficanda, J. "Colorado's Teacher Shortage: Get the Facts." *Colorado Succeeds*, March 26, 2008. https://coloradosucceeds.org/teachers-leaders/colorados-teacher-shortage-get-facts/.

Whaley, Monte. "Colorado's Teacher Shortage is a 'Crisis' that's Getting Worse, Educators Say." *Denver Post* (Denver, CO), April 13, 2017. https://www.denverpost.com/2017/04/13/colorado-teacher-shortage-crisis/.

Chapter 3

Identifying and Recruiting Quality Mentor Teachers

Tamara L. Sober

INTRODUCTION

Teacher preparation is on a path of continuous improvement. A foundational component in this trajectory is the embrace of teaching veteran teachers, who serve as mentors, how to coach future teachers. When I reflect on the teacher preparation I received in the mid-1990s compared to what our current residents receive, there is a stark contrast. I can say the same about my experience as a supervising teacher for two student teachers who conducted their internships in my classroom in that decade. Both scenarios were built on a significant amount of "watch and learn." Fortunately, an education professor introduced me to "discovery-learning," and set me on a path toward what is essentially today's inquiry-based learning. In 2019, teacher preparation is experiencing the positive results of applying Dewey (1923), Piaget (Piaget, Varmer, & Williams 1976), and Bruner's (2017) constructivist, inquiry-based approach beyond K-12 learning, and to the process of teaching mentor teachers how to coach preservice teachers. It follows that an inquiry-based coaching model sets a foundation for certain dispositions to seek and cultivate in a mentor. This chapter will share the experiences of how the Richmond Teacher Residency (RTR) program recruits and identifies quality mentor teachers who hold or are open to cultivating these dispositions.

Sharing RTR's successful identification and recruitment practices over the past nine years, this chapter includes:

- Concrete advice from three seasoned staff members (the mentors' mentors) whose primary role is to recruit, identify, and support mentor/resident pairs in the field;

- Tools and best practices adapted or developed by RTR for identifying, recruiting, and selecting mentor teachers;
- Insight from veteran elementary, exceptional education, and secondary mentors on everything from what attracted and motivated them to apply to how their teaching practice has changed as a result of mentoring; and
- Specific talking points for current teachers to help them understand a teacher residency and their important contributions in the mentoring and coaching of residents throughout the residency year.

The Richmond Teacher Residency

RTR began in 2010 as a partnership between Virginia Commonwealth University (VCU), the Center for Teacher Leadership at Virginia Commonwealth University, and Richmond Public Schools (RPS) and was funded through a $5.8 million Teacher Quality Partnership grant from the U.S. Department of Education. Located in the heart of Richmond, VCU is a large, urban-serving, community-engaged, research institution, focused on the retention of first-generation college students. The RTR model is a thirteen-month intensive, school-based teacher preparation model resulting in initial licensure and a Master's of Education, Master's of Teaching, or a Post-Baccalaureate Certificate. Residents are admitted to one of three tracks: elementary education, exceptional education, or secondary education and begin coursework the summer prior to their residency year, and then complete a full residency year co-teaching (Friend & Cook, 2016) alongside a mentor teacher in their content area while completing methods courses. Curriculum is contextualized to cultivate identified dispositions for teaching in high-needs classrooms, and incorporates restorative justice, trauma-informed care, and critical pedagogy. Our Values (Leading Educators, 2019) equity, service, community, growth and results, comprehensively address our program.

We have identified our RTR Values as follows:

- Equity: We challenge educational inequity. We work toward a more just society.
- Service: We listen to and prioritize needs of others. We put students first.
- Community: We support, challenge, and celebrate each other. We build a collective movement.
- Growth: We develop ourselves and others. We make our best better.
- Results: We work hard and purposefully to reach results. When there is no wind, we row.

From our inception we have built our coaching model on the New Teacher Center's (2019) (NTC) *Professional Learning Series for Mentors and Coaches* that focuses on the knowledge, skills, and understandings critical for those who work with beginning and veteran teachers to improve instruction. Research supports the positive impact the NTC model has on teacher retention and student achievement (Fletcher, Strong, & Villar, 2010). Once hired as teachers-of-record, RTR graduates receive one-on-one mentoring for at least one hour a week from a highly skilled, content-specific career coach who has been carefully selected and trained to observe instruction and student learning, collect observation data, and assist in the delivery of instruction.

As of 2019, RTR has prepared 141 teachers, and 82 percent of RTR graduates have taught in RPS for three or more years. Thirty-six residents will graduate this year, and we are recruiting sixty-one residents for our ninth cohort to begin in the spring of 2019. With a strong focus on local recruitment, we have continually increased the diversity of our cohorts, and 51 percent of our current cohort are residents of color. RTR alums serve in 36 schools and have reached over 11,800 students. We have prepared 106 mentors, and 98 percent of those mentors reported that being an RTR mentor made them a more effective teacher. We are fortunate to have received two additional federal grants and our state and school district partners are now investing in the residency program. As we expand into a neighboring urban district and to high-needs schools in surrounding counties, we are exploring a sustainable, shared investment model by stakeholders from local and state government and the business and philanthropic communities.

Programmatically, RTR is structured with two staff who support the mentor/resident team. While the two staff members work together as a team, meeting frequently and conducting certain responsibilities together, some of which overlap, others are individualized to their role. A university-funded, faculty member is allotted half-time to serve as the curriculum coordinator (CC), overseeing and teaching courses, conducting the weekly resident seminar, and advising and observing residents throughout the program. A part-time, grant-funded, resident coordinator (RC), serves as the liaison between school sites and the RTR program and in that role recruits and identifies mentors, and supports the resident/mentor partnership through regular observations and informal site visits, monthly mentor forums, and through the use of the NTC coaching cycle tools. The next section of this chapter contains a description of our identification and recruitment process, details about our unannounced observations and follow-up conferences, essential qualities of high-impact mentors, and lesson learned. These details were drawn from RTR's three seasoned resident coordinators Elaina Martin (secondary), Angel Bartlett (exceptional education), and Shauntel Grassley (elementary). Throughout this chapter, mentors will be referred to as clinical resident coaches (CRCs) as they are referred to in our program. Following that section four veteran CRCs provide detailed insight on what attracted them to the program and what keeps them returning to mentor another resident.

MENTORING THE MENTORS: ADVICE AND RESOURCES FROM THE FIELD

"There are many important pieces to this conversation, but what I am looking for is for their ability to reflect and be metacognitive because as a coach that is a key piece."—Elaina Martin, Resident Coordinator

The three resident coordinators (RC) interviewed for this chapter each bring a wealth of breadth and depth to their work. Elaina Martin, our secondary program RC, is a white female who has nineteen years of experience teaching at the elementary, middle school, and university levels in both rural high-needs and suburban contexts, was a fully released mentor and then mentor coordinator of fully released mentors, for four years, and has served as a RC for eight years. Our exceptional education program resident coordinator, Angel Bartlett, is an African American female who has over twenty-five years of combined experience as an exceptional education teacher—having taught preschool to twelfth grade—as well as a building and district level administrator. Bartlett has taught in urban, rural, and suburban school districts and has been a RC with the RTR program for five years. Shauntel Grassley, a white female, and a graduate of the urban schools RTR serves, is our elementary education program RC. She is a former elementary school teacher with thirteen years as an urban educator and has served as a RTR RC for three years.

Identifying Mentors

RTR primarily uses a nomination process to identify new CRCs. The first recruitment year staff visited our four partner schools, made presentations at faculty meetings about the program to solicit mentor applicants, and relied heavily on central office staff and principal recommendations. After that first year veteran CRCs were invited to nominate their colleagues, often holding formal and informal meetings in their classrooms after school to explain and recruit for the program. Martin offers, *"These meetings were important because of the level of open conversation that took place and that may not have occurred in faculty meetings. We found that the teachers that met in those small groups knew what they were getting into—the real dirt on what this was all about."* We are intentional about soliciting nominations from past and present coaches via email and at our February monthly mentor forums. Our career coaches, who coach our graduates during their first year as teacher-of-record and have frequent exposure to a large number of teachers across the district, are also a dependable source for nominations.

We also recruit from the group of teachers who have completed our university's clinical faculty training, a modified and condensed version of the NTC model, and who have had successful clinical faculty experiences. At present the word of mouth network, heavily facilitated and supported by the work of our RCs, has provided an adequate applicant pool each year. However, we also use social media platforms and formal channels such as having our RPS liaison distribute information district-wide about the process, qualifications, and responsibilities of a CRC (see figure 3.1 for our informational recruitment flyer containing the description and qualifications of the role).

Below is the language we use for our CRC nomination letter that is sent to teachers who have been nominated to be our CRCs.

CRC Nomination Letter

Dear _____,

Congratulations! As an outstanding RPS teacher, you have been nominated by _____ as a candidate for a position as Clinical Resident Coach (CRC) in the Richmond Teacher Residency Program. _____ enthusiastic endorsement indicates you would be a great fit for our program!

This school-based teacher preparation program integrates the research and theory behind effective urban teaching with a year-long residency under the mentorship of an exemplary classroom teacher—the CRC. As a Clinical Resident Coach (CRC), you would provide year-long support for a talented, committed post-graduate Resident in a program designed to serve as a national model for teacher preparation.

You have been nominated because we believe that you have what it takes to be a role model for the Richmond teachers of tomorrow. Secondary Clinical Resident Coaches are distinguished by exemplary reflective practice, strong leadership, communication, organizational and critical thinking skills; sound knowledge of content, pedagogy, and adolescent development; and a curiosity and eagerness to learn. The year-long residency will allow Residents to scaffold their learning through an extended period of well-supervised clinical practice by both university faculty and master teachers—Clinical Resident Coaches—who jointly provide instruction which integrates theory and practice. In the classroom, Clinical Resident Coaches and Residents will embrace a team-based approach to teaching and learning including co-teaching, modeling lessons, and coaching to support Resident success.

If you are selected to participate in this highly competitive program, as a Clinical Resident Coach you will become a member of a growing network of Richmond teaching professionals who are committed to the development and support of Residents in high-need secondary schools. If selected, you will receive:

- *A $3500 honorarium for mentoring a Resident during the 2017–2018 academic year—with bonus potential;*
- *Re-certification points for participating in training and working with pre-service teachers;*
- *Training and experience that will enhance your own teaching skills; and*
- *Opportunities for further professional growth and leadership roles.*

Teachers consistently report that their student teaching experience was the most powerful and important part of their preparation program. Imagine the potential impact of a full year residency in the classroom! Upon successful completion of the residency program, these Residents will become your colleagues. Therefore, I hope that you will go online to complete an application to become a Clinical Resident Coach so that you can help shape the attitudes, dispositions, knowledge, and skills of tomorrow's teachers.

The application is available online at http://www.applitrack.com/vcu/onlineapp/. When you get to the website, select the first option, "View our Program Applications" and scroll down to Clinical Resident Coach (CRC), and click apply. For priority consideration, complete and submit the application no later than April 10, 2018.

Please call _____, the Richmond Teacher Residency Secondary Coordinator, _____ or email at _____ if you have questions. A detailed information flyer is also attached to this email.

CRC Recruitment Flyer
Richmond Teacher Residency

Attention: Accomplished Richmond Public School Elementary, Secondary, and Exceptional Education Teachers

The Richmond Teacher Residency (RTR) Program is a partnership between Richmond Public Schools (RPS), Virginia Commonwealth University (VCU), and the Center for Teacher Leadership at the VCU School of Education. The Richmond Teacher Residency Program recruits, prepares, supports, and retains extraordinary, inspiring teachers and teacher leaders who are committed to the students of Richmond Public Schools for the long term. This school-based teacher preparation program integrates the research and theory behind effective urban teaching with a year-long residency under the mentorship of an exemplary classroom teacher—the Clinical Resident Coach (CRC). Current secondary content teachers (middle and high school) and special/exceptional education teachers (elementary, middle, and high school), and elementary teachers (non-departmentalized) are eligible to become CRCs.

Become a Clinical Resident Coach

POSITION: A Clinical Resident Coach (CRC) is a classroom teacher who provides year-long specialized coaching support for a Resident--an individual with a bachelor's degree, seeking initial licensure--who is assigned to that teacher's RPS classroom.

JOB DESCRIPTION: The Clinical Resident Coach (CRC) will:
- Form a year-long trusting and reflective professional partnership with a Resident
- Embrace a team-based approach to teaching & learning including co-teaching, modeling lessons, & coaching to support a Resident
- Coach and assist with lesson planning, classroom management, instructional strategies, analysis of student work, curriculum development, and all aspects of the RTR experience;
- Document coaching support using specific New Teacher Center formative assessment tools & logs
- Conduct regular classroom observations and provide prompt data-based feedback with each observation
- Participate in ongoing professional development including New Teacher Center Trainings:
  August 6-9: Instructional Mentoring for Equitable Learning & Using Data to Inform Instruction
  August 20: Secondary Residency Launch
  October 2-3: Observing and Giving Feedback
  December 4-5: Assessing Growth and Deepening Practice
- Attend monthly professional forums after school
- Participate in a monthly coaching sessions with the Residency Coordinator at the coach's school site
- Accommodate the Resident's scheduling needs including early morning and late afternoon hours (beyond the regular contractual hours for teachers)
- Assume a variety of leadership roles within the program
- Participate in a program evaluation process

STIPEND: $3,500 per Resident for the RPS academic year.

QUALIFICATIONS: The Clinical Resident Coach must have:
- Valid Virginia Collegiate/Postgraduate Professional License with a minimum of three years recent teaching experience
- Full-time teaching assignment in elementary education (not departmentalized), exceptional education (K-12), or secondary education (math, science, English, social science/history)
- Strong interpersonal and communication skills
- Exemplary classroom practice and leadership capacity
- Credibility among teachers and administrators
- Commitment to personal and professional growth and learning
- Experience mentoring/coaching pre-service, novice, and/or veteran teachers (preferred)

APPLICATION: Upon completion of a successful application, an unannounced classroom observation and reflective conference will occur. To apply, go to: http://www.applitrack.com/vcu/onlineapp/. Note: To apply, select the first option, View our Program Applications, scroll down to Clinical Resident Coach (CRC), and click apply.

Share your expertise and passion for teaching by applying to become a Clinical Resident Coach!

Applications due: [rolling selection date]

Figure 3.1 CRC Informational Recruitment Flyer.

While we accept nominations from colleagues, principals, and central office staff, our experience has been that classroom teachers are the most informed about who among their colleagues would be a good fit for our program.

As we promote the program and recruit CRCs, we make it known that this is an opportunity for teacher leadership growth. Teacher leadership paths that don't require leaving the classroom are often limited. Being a coach provides teacher leadership opportunities for teachers explicitly seeking those avenues as well as for those who may not view themselves as teacher leaders. As Grassley relates, *"Once they start doing this work, it transforms them."*

As nominations are received, resident coordinators begin scheduling unannounced observations and tracking the CRC candidate recruitment process. Below is the checklist we use to track our follow-up communication with our potential candidates.

___CRC Candidate Email Address
___Email Sent
___Candidate Expressed Interest
___Nominated by _____
___Content Area/Grade Level _____
___School _____
___Application Complete
___Observation Scheduled for _____ (date)
___Reflective Phone Call/Meeting held
___Matching Party Invite
___Match (with _____)

The Unannounced Observation, and Post-Observation Conference

Once we have a list of nominees we contact the teachers, let them know that they have been nominated and explain the online application process. The application consists of basic questions such as: subject, grade and number of years taught, as well as questions about experience they have supporting teachers. Open-ended essay questions require candidates to write about why they are interested in mentoring and solicit their thoughts about what mentoring might look like for them. One particularly fruitful question asks: "If you were selected to work as a CRC what are some skills and strategies that you would like to learn?" We include questions about language fluency and standardized testing results (if applicable to their content/grade level). Two references are required, one from a principal and one from a colleague. The next step for RCs is to coordinate unannounced classroom observations with teachers who complete the online application.

"Sometimes [the unannounced observation] stops them in their tracks because it is hard for teachers to open up their classrooms . . . even for the best teachers because they are often so hard on themselves and have such high expectations. I give them a two-week window and they give me a schedule of their classes. I want to know if they are honors, regular, or collaborative classes, because I am very strategic about what class I want to see. I make a master schedule and I go out and spend 30 minutes to one hour and sometimes within a half-hour I am in awe because they are so amazing and other times I see a diamond in the rough. Sometimes it is necessary to conduct multiple observations." ~ E. Martin

"We attempt to take a colleague with us for the unannounced observations, so that two of us can make observations and can check to see if we are on the same page in terms of knowing the teacher's strengths and their needs, and to get a better idea of whether they would be a good fit for the program. We use a checklist to look at the classroom environment, their classroom management, and their instructional practices, since we want to get a full picture of what their classroom is like. Even the condition of the classroom—how organized/ unorganized it is—can provide a lot of information about whether or not a resident is going to be successful in that environment." ~S. Grassley

During the observation, our RCs all use the CRC Candidate Observation Score Sheet shown in table 3.1, as well as other tools (NTC tools, standard selected scripting, etc.) for data collection purposes. In best-case scenarios RCs conduct the observation with a colleague, the curriculum coordinator, or an RTR career coach, but at a minimum there is data for use in the follow-up conversations with candidates, and to inform the decision-making process. In line with our coaching model, the RCs hold a reflecting conversation, either over the phone or in person, with the mentor candidates to discuss the observation data and create a collaborative log.

"Within 24 hours of the observation I make a follow-up call and create a collaborative log of our discussion. Some of the questions that are asked are how do you think the lesson went, and of course the great teachers go straight to the negative and I try to reel them back in to discuss the positive, the things that went well. We also talk about the challenges and I ask them to give me a context for the lesson, what happened before, what are you thinking about next, who are the kids in the class, what are their strengths/challenges . . . and it gives me a total picture of what happened in that class. There are many important pieces to this conversation, but what I am looking for is their ability to reflect and be metacognitive because as a coach that is a key piece. You have to be able to share what you did, why you did it, and the thinking behind it and be really clear about that. Of course with all these steps in place it helps me get at organization and one of the sad things that I discovered is that they can be a fabulous teacher

Table 3.1 CRC Observation Score Sheet

Clinical Resident Coach Candidate—Observation Score Sheet			
Candidate _____ School _____			
Subject/Grade _____ Date of Observation _____			
Observer _____			
Rubric: 1= Does Not Meet Expectations 2 = Minimally Meets Expectations 3 = Exceeds Expectations 4 = Exceptional			
Criterion	Indicators	Score	Comments
Interaction with Students	Draws students into the lesson		
	Motivates students		
	Uses a variety of teaching/ learning strategies		
	Aware of everything in the classroom: "with-it-ness"		
	Enthusiastic		
Student Responses	Rapport Evident		
	Students are engaged		
	Student responses are relevant to the lesson		
	Student responses demonstrate understanding		
Learning Environment	Postings are appropriate and timely		
	Age/Developmentally appropriate		
	Learner Centered		
Lesson Design	Clarity of directions		
	Objectives clearly stated		
	Objectives tied into broad goals		
	Organization is logically sequenced		
Rigor	High expectations of all students		
	Rich content focus		

Additional Notes

and have the potential to be a great coach, but if they don't have strong organizational skills they are not going to be successful. I even had some teachers that have been trying to come back multiple years and I am honest with them. If we don't invite them back for another year, and they wish to continue coaching, I sit down and meet with them and talk about why and have a really honest supportive conversation to identify all the wonderful things that they are doing and then talk about their organization and how that might impact their work as a coach so that they are able to identify it.

"Going back to the follow-up phone conversations, I ask two other questions, how challenging is it going to be for you to give up your classroom and to give up really authority to this potential resident? That's a struggle because if you're a great teacher it's hard to give up control if you see your students struggling. They might not be learning as much as they would with you. The other piece that I ask about is organization. What kind of organizer are you, what kind of systems do you have in place in your classroom? Organization is just one piece.

I don't eliminate them at that point, if everything else is great. I want to give them a chance, and I am going to support them with those organizational skills. In our program (and we didn't realize this when we started) we are all about growing amazing residents and now it's a dual purpose, we are growing amazing residents and improving the incredible teaching of our coaches. We don't call our coaches master teachers, we call them master learners, as that's what we are looking for . . . teachers who want to learn. In a challenging urban setting that's what it is all about, because it is hard, nobody's perfect, nobody has it figured out and that's how I promote the coaching role, we are looking for master learners." ~E. Martin

"We hold a follow-up conversation [after the unannounced observation] using a collaborative log. We talk about the lesson that we observed and ask the candidate, what do you think went well and why . . . very similar questions that you would ask after an observation of a resident. Did the students meet your objectives? How do you know? What challenges/ concerns did you experience? What are you going to do next? With student learning? With learning about your teaching practice? We ask questions that help us determine if they are reflective and/or if they are coachable and whether or not they really think about their teaching." ~S. Grassley

"Following the observation, we have a feedback conversation with the teacher. We ask questions such as: how did your lesson go, what were the challenges, what do you want to do moving forward, how would you change the lesson? Talking with the candidates helps me get a sense of their effectiveness in planning and implementing instruction for students with disabilities. I also let them know they will be held to high expectations, held accountable, and just as we expect them to support residents, that they will be valued and supported not only as CRCs, but as individuals with full plates and lives." ~A. Bartlett

Essential Qualities of a High-Impact Coaches

Over time our program has identified essential qualities of a high-impact mentor. The foremost, minimum criterion is that candidates must be strong practitioners in both content knowledge and pedagogy. Those qualities are the following:

- Strong practitioner
- Growth mindset, reflective, meta-cognitive
- Coachability
- Ability to give up control and *trust* the resident
- Strong relational and interpersonal skills
- System-oriented
- Commitment to the profession

We use multiple data points to assess this quality, such as the observation and reflecting conversation discussed above, the answers on their application, and letters of reference from colleagues and supervisors. We are also interested in their success as it relates to student learning outcomes, which may differ depending upon the grade and subject.

> *"I can bring you along as a coach but you must be an effective teacher. I don't want your teaching skills questioned at all. First and foremost we need highly effective teachers. A potential CRC should be able to reflect on their teaching practice—not what's right or wrong, but how they can grow, improve and how they can get there."* ~A. Bartlett

After meeting the strong practitioner criterion we look for candidates with a growth, versus performance, mindset. Having a resident in your classroom for a full-year, examining every step of your practice with a microscopic lens, as well as program staff and university faculty weighing in on your teaching practice and your coaching skills, calls for a high tolerance for vulnerability and openness to change. Effective coaches are reflective and meta-cognitive about all aspects of being a teacher, including planning, decision-making, instruction, student relationships and more. Moving toward this level of reflective practice inevitably shines a light on opportunities to grow in one's own practice, setting an example of growth for the resident.

> *"I look for coachability. The work of a coach is skill-based, skills that you can learn, but you have to have that willingness to learn, not be perfect. It's interesting that teachers that are new to this role act like students in that they want to make sure that they are doing things the 'right way.' Our coaching model is intensively cognitive. It takes practice and it takes a while, so for teachers that are not in a growth mindset and more in to performance, they need to be willing to give themselves some grace to grow and to do the work. I don't want coaches to go through the motions in a compliance mode. It's great when they do the work and are like 'wow, this really works.' The most successful coaches that I have worked with are ones that get in there and try it, learn it, embrace this model and look at this work as the support and tools to help both them and their resident grow and develop. The ones that aren't as strong have that performance/compliance mindset: 'I'm required to do these tools so I have to do them' then it becomes paperwork and then they just fill out the boxes because they think that's what they are supposed to do. Those are challenging situations."* ~S. Grassley

The learning curve for coaches who may not initially bring this growth mindset to their work requires *trusting* the process. Grassley relays, *"An experienced CRC tells her residents that they just have to trust the process, and she knows that, because she has experienced it herself."* To create a climate conducive to growth, resident coordinators must model what it takes to build the same type of trusting relationship with coaches that they encourage between their CRC/resident teams.

> *"I've been working on relationship building, building trust so that coaches that are working with me don't feel like that they have to comply with what I am saying. Some have been conditioned by their school climate and they have not had an opportunity to be trusted. They may be in positions where professional development has been done 'to them' so when they attend professional development with the NTC tools and come together for our forums, it's a different frame of thinking that they may not be used to."* ~S. Grassley

The importance of a coach being willing to *trust* their resident cannot be overstated. Successful coaches are willing to give up control of their classroom and give their resident real authority. Martin shares, *"Coaches have to be willing to turn over authority, because it is a disaster if they don't. One year I had a coach quit after a month because she could not turn over authority and that was definitely a lesson learned that we needed to vet for this when choosing coaches."* Grassley adds, *"It is hard work and working everyday with someone in your space, it's like a marriage, you can't get away from each other during the day."* In giving up this control and signaling real trust coaches develop a relationship with their resident that provides the context for open, honest dialogue and when needed, courageous conversations. Veteran coaches interviewed for the second part of this chapter echo the power of this approach. Coaches, who assume positive intent and have the ability to empathize without having walked in their resident's shoes, create a powerful learning environment that allows the coach/resident team to address whatever needs to be tackled.

Trust is a foundational component for a strong working relationship. Resident Coordinator Bartlett emphasizes that *"the CRC role is built around relationships and support. In the context of RTR's mission, vision, and values, those two pieces are clearly the most important."* Effective coaches begin by establishing a strong working, professional relationship and once that foundation is in place they begin the work of using data as a third, nonjudgmental voice in the room and begin collaborating to use that data to support and move the resident's practice. To successfully function in that third, nonjudgmental space, coaches must have strong relational and interpersonal skills. The role requires the ability to differentiate between the personal and the professional. Bartlett notes, *"Coaches can't take things personal."* Coaches who are able to make the personal/professional distinction, excel in the role.

A lack of organizational skills does not eliminate candidates from our applicant pool; however, we have found that teachers who have created their own systems for organizing the various pieces of the work (classroom management, lesson plans, student work, etc.) more readily adapt to the systematic use of the NTC tools for collecting and analyzing resident data. Highly organized teachers model for residents the benefit of creating their own systems to handle the multitude and variety of work required of today's teachers.

While it may not fall into the category of an essential quality, we have found that our most successful coaches have a strong commitment to the teaching profession. They opt to coach in order to have a hand in molding future colleagues and making a difference beyond their immediate classroom. Many coaches express the desire to mentor because of the strong support they received from a cooperating teacher, whereas others had the opposite experience and want to provide what was not present and what would have helped them succeed.

> *"Once the word is out, it's such an easy sell because many teachers did not have the support that they needed when they became teachers. Every teacher remembers their first year of teaching. If you talk to teachers in high needs settings, they can give you a moment-by-moment, blow-by-blow account of what it was like when they had no support—no one to turn to. They know just how critical that is. If the opposite is true and they had great support, then they already know how important it is." ~E. Martin*

> *"What I consistently hear, is that teachers feel they have a responsibility to give back to the profession and it usually stems from an experience they had when they first started out with an outstanding cooperating teacher that brought them on and they feel like it's their turn to give back. That compels a lot of teachers to do this work, and to keep doing it because once you get in, there's a certain satisfaction in seeing someone that you have coached, supported, nurtured, and taught become a successful teacher. The responsibility to make sure that tomorrow's teachers are prepared and the intrinsic rewards of giving back to the profession, seem to be an essential motivator for many of our coaches." ~S. Grassley*

Bartlett intentionally vets for this commitment when meeting with potential CRCs: *"I want to know what drives them to want to serve as a coach. I don't want to get a sense that this is just something to add to a list of accomplishments."* Whether or not the coach's stance entails a commitment to the future of the profession, it *is* essential that the coach understand they are making a firm commitment to prepare their resident to succeed on day one as a teacher-of-record. She follows up with a key point, noting that although there are common, essential qualities we seek in potential coaches, these qualities may manifest themselves in very different ways: *"We each bring our unique selves to the process. What's important to one person and how that's presented may look different in the colleague next door, and that is okay."*

What may be noticeably absent from our recruitment, vetting, and selection of CRCs is heavy reliance on annual teacher evaluation data (such as data based on student test scores). As we firmly believe, have experienced, and have confirmation through the research-based evidence cited above, use of the NTC model improves the practice of the mentor teacher as they are engaged in reflecting on their own practice throughout the residency year. Our program is committed to improving student achievement, and therefore we value the opportunity to foster growth in the mentor teacher's practice, as well as to support the mentor teacher's individualized student remediation efforts. The latter is a benefit we encourage CRCs to take advantage of while the resident is solo teaching. And while all our CRCs' students have been successful on the required standardized tests, our comprehensive and intentional approach to recruitment has proven effective without using student test scores as a litmus test.

Next Steps: Beyond Recruitment

Once candidates have been vetted they are notified of their selection status. If they have not been selected to coach, upon request, RCs offer to provide feedback on the rationale for their decision, and encourage interested applicants to apply in future years. Candidates who qualify to coach are notified that RTR will begin the "matching process" to pair coaches with residents during the summer. Over the summer, the three programs (secondary, elementary, and exceptional education) hold separate "Matching Parties" at our Center for Teacher Leadership headquarters, complete with light refreshments, where they invite the pool of potential coaches to a meet and greet with residents.

> "What we are doing is creating a pool of potential clinical resident coaches. They're invited to the matching party, they meet by content [where applicable], and the time is structured with conversation starters such as: 'If given a full day of free time, how would you spend it?' At the end of the matching party both the resident and the coach complete a matching party reflection. I have tried other tools, but this is it. This is what works. Then we also consider the context of the school, the administration of the school, the coach, their personality, the knowledge they bring, the resident, their personality, and the knowledge they bring. We also have to get to know the residents prior to making the matches. We've improved this process by holding individual meetings with residents prior to the match, to get a sense of who they are as a person; much more effective than group 'get to know you' meetings." ~E. Martin

After the matching party, the RCs and the curriculum coordinator—who has been teaching residents throughout the summer—separately review the potential coaches' and residents' documents and propose coach/resident pairs. They come together as a team and review their recommendations, noting that the RC may have more perspective on the coach and the school context and the curriculum coordinator may have more perspective on the resident. Neither residents nor coaches are asked to provide us with their desired "match" due to the multiple variables that are being considered (school context, grade/subject matter, grouping residents at a particular school, potential let down for not receiving their "first" choice and more). We stress to both residents and coaches that all residents are high-caliber and all coaches are, or will be, highly prepared to coach. Decisions are made and coaches and residents are jointly notified of their pairing and of the date when the pair will be brought together for a launch prior to the start of the year.

Below is a sample of the CRC and Resident Match Notification letter we send out.

Congratulations, (resident) and (coach)!

You have been matched as a Richmond Teacher Residency partnership for the 2018–2019 school year. Your contact information follows:

   CRCs:
   Resident:

Work will begin with both CRCs during teacher work week with (resident) co-teaching in both classes beginning the first day of school. CRCs should feel free to reach out to their Residents. Residents, please understand that this is your CRCs summer break, so they may well be on vacation. Please be patient and know that you will be connecting!

~~~~~~

Congratulations to our newly selected CRCs for 2018–2019! The special knowledge and skills that our CRCs bring to this important work will be instrumental in helping to launch the teaching careers of our talented group of RTR Residents. Our CRCs will be giving back to their chosen profession in very important ways, and for that, we thank you!

~~~~~~

Important Dates

As a NEW coach, please plan to attend the following New Teacher Center workshops:

- *August 6–9, 2018: 8:00 a.m.–3:30 p.m. Instructional Mentoring for Equitable Learning and Using Data to Inform Instruction*
- *October 2–3, 2018 Observing and Giving Feedback*
- *December 4–5, 2018 Assessing Growth and Deepening Practice*

   Please note that there is no cost to you for these professional development opportunities. You will need to make arrangements for subs during the school year, and RPS will pay for your sub.

As a VETERAN coach please plan to attend the following workshops:

- *October 2–3, 2018: 8:00 a.m.–3:30 p.m. Observing and Giving Feedback*
- *December 4–5, 2018 Assessing Growth and Deepening Practice*

RESIDENTS ONLY

- *Sunday, August 19, 2018: RTR Launch! 4:00 p.m.–7:30 p.m.*

ALL COACHES and RESIDENTS

- *Monday, August 20, 2018: RTR Launch! 10:00 a.m.–4:00 p.m.*

CRCs, we welcome you to a select group of teacher leaders and look forward to working with you as we prepare tomorrow's Richmond Public School teachers! Please don't hesitate to contact either of us should you have any questions. ~ Resident Coordinator: _____ and Curriculum Coordinator: _____.

We encourage coaches to reach out and contact their resident prior to that date if they chose to do so and often we find many teams have met prior to the official launch. Coaches then begin the NTC Professional Learning Series in early August.

Lessons Learned

When reflecting on lessons learned about identifying and recruiting quality mentor teachers, our RCs shared that they have learned not to rely on administrators or central office for recommendations because of the potential politics involved in those recommendations. Letters of reference yes, recommendations, no.

"Some principals can really point out teachers that are not only great teachers but who also have the possibility of becoming a great coach as well. However, other principals looked at it differently and in fact I had one principal come up to me and say 'So I have the perfect coach for you.' He went on to tell me 'because she's a really weak teacher and the students desperately need two teachers in that classroom,' which was not quite the vetting we were looking for."

"Sometimes with the specificity of secondary content, I could not identify, for example, a strong math teacher who could be a potential coach, so I went to the content specialist for a recommendation. That is a tricky piece to negotiate because I received a recommendation for someone who was really weak and it was obvious, due to what was being taught. After several observations, I realized she was not a good fit. I went back to the specialist and said that I really appreciated the recommendation and explained that we are just having a tough time and I indicated several reasons why she was not a good fit." ~E. Martin

While briefly mentioned above in regard to the matching process, identifying and recruiting coaches cannot be carried out in isolation of considering resident placement. In the early years RCs and curriculum coordinators wrestled with the question of whether to place residents in schools that closely mirror both the accreditation status (warning or nonaccredited) and student demographic (highest need among the high-needs schools) where they are likely to be hired, or whether to place them in a school with fewer challenges. As may be expected, principal turnover is quite high in the highest-needs schools and unstable leadership adds strain to the social and policy context. We have come to believe that while there is value for residents to experience that setting, there is ultimately *more* value in placing a resident in a school where they have the maximum opportunity to learn to teach, which often means a school with stable leadership and one that, at worst, may be in "accredited with warning" status. Ultimately, we have found that in school-site selection stable leadership trumps accreditation status. However, as with many of our programmatic processes and policies, we consider each situation on an individual basis, and have not set hard-and-fast rules against placing a resident with a strong coach in a school that faces a multitude of even the toughest challenges. In relation to tough challenges, as much as we recognize the inherent problems associated with today's high-stakes testing policy context, we also caution against accepting a coach who has not been successful in having their students pass mandated standardized testing. It creates a stressful environment for both the coach and the resident and doesn't allow for the flexibility and risk-taking that optimizes the resident's growth.

> *"Candidates have to be successful with getting their students through standardized testing, even though I hate that, but if they do not know how to do it, how in the world will they support their resident to be successful in this high-pressure environment?"* ~E. Martin

Bartlett candidly shares the ambiguities inherent in this human-centered work:

> *"The only lesson that I have learned is that you really don't know if someone will be a successful CRC. You just have to look at the data and if you think it is a go then go with it. The lessons are not necessarily learned until after you begin working with the coach. Even once you learn a lesson, the question is how to screen for the lesson that you learned. For example, an extremely, soft-spoken teacher applied to be a coach. I hesitated because he was so soft-spoken and he struggled to speak with confidence about his effectiveness as a teacher. But we accepted him and he grew as a coach, became more outspoken and assertive. It took him a while to get adjusted, but he was very invested in making sure his resident got the best experience. Based on his demeanor, I was about to make a mistake."*

Grassley agrees, *"It's not a prefect process and there's only so many variables you can control in recruiting and working with mentor teachers. You learn from the process!"*

Throughout the year, the RCs continue to "coach the coaches" through formal professional development, scheduled opportunities for coaches to interact for peer-to-peer discussions and sharing, and individual meetings RCs schedule with the coaches and hold in their schools. The number of the latter varies based on the individual coach and their progression in using the NTC model. If problems arise between the resident/coach pair, both RCs and CCs step in to facilitate, mediate, and address issues.

MENTOR VOICES

"A CRC is a mentor, an advocate for the mentee, a resource . . . you must be reflective, transparent. Being willing to share your knowledge because there are many levels, parts and pieces of yourself that teaching requires, other than just the actual instructional piece. Mentoring is showing the resident what works for me but being collaborative to help them develop what will work for them."
~K. Rogers

Four veteran CRCs were interviewed for this chapter. Each has served as a mentor for a minimum of three different (not necessarily consecutive) years. Each has a different story about their recruitment path and their mentoring style. However, shared perspective emerged in their descriptions of what they appreciate most about mentoring and what keeps them returning to mentor another resident.

Attracting Mentor Teachers

The four veteran and very successful CRCs interviewed for this chapter all came to RTR through different recruitment paths. Kayla Rogers began coaching through the Clinical Faculty pipeline, and shared that after she was exposed to a taste of the coaching language and the process, she recognized that she was ready for the next level and wanted more. As a reminder, VCU's Clinical Faculty training is a modified and condensed version of the New Teacher Center model. While all cooperating teachers are not required to become clinical faculty certified, it is highly encouraged, and increasingly all VCU's student teachers (outside the residency program) are placed with cooperating teachers with clinical faculty status.

"I said to my resident coordinator that the clinical faculty process should be a pre-requisite to the CRC role, because it really worked in my favor to have that experience. Being a CRC is a real commitment, so you need to know what you are getting into and clinical faculty gives you a solid introduction. When recruiting coaches staff should seek teachers who have a commitment to the profession and to the process. You can be trained to coach, but to be a good coach you have to have a heart for this work. ~K. Rogers

Thomas Hughes was nominated by his content specialist.

"It was my 5th year of teaching and I think my content specialist for RPS nominated me to be a coach. At the time, I wasn't feeling very challenged. It was a relatively easy year; it was starting to feel boring because I was doing things the same way as I have always done them. It was something that I wanted to do

to push my career forward, and I was always interested in prepping, mentoring, and teaching teachers. So it felt like a very logical step for what I wanted: to grow as a teacher without actually leaving the classroom." ~T. Hughes

Danella Vargas was recommended by a resident in her building.

"Whenever young, new teachers come into the building, I try to be a positive role model, so it was a young lady that was already in the RTR program and she recommended me because I would always help her. I was her collaborative teacher so I would talk with her, offer strategies and suggestions. We became close and she nominated me to be a coach." ~ D. Vargas

In her third year of teaching, Shafton received an email from central office containing the recruitment flyer. She recalled witnessing how closely a CRC/resident pair in her building worked together during her first year of teaching.

"The resident was known for being a good teacher, so that was definitely something positive that stayed in my mind, and after three years I was ready for something new, another challenge. I was always meeting teachers who were working with new teachers. I have always felt that was something that was incredibly important and I was interested in what I could share and what I could learn. And when I read there was a stipend, I knew that was definitely something that I could use." ~ J. Shafton

The Role of a Mentor

When asked to describe the role of the CRC, our coaches used words such as "guide," "mentor," "advocate," and "resource." Their words capture the extent of what it takes to do this work well. In their own way, each CRC emphasizes the use of their interpersonal skills, and how they approach the wrap-around work of being a teacher, and mentoring residents in "everything else," beyond the clinical and instructional work of teaching and learning.

"Guides. We are guides and co-teachers that want to get someone through this incredibly challenging experience. Each day there is a layer of challenges that we are trying to get through and the goal is to make it to the end. We share our expertise and our own challenges and we help navigate a system that is different from what some of us may have experienced growing up. For example, how to navigate a system where you may find out only 30-minutes before you have to do something . . . that is not exactly the professional experience we may have been trained for. It's a different experience then when I went through my own educational program, and what I imagined the professional world being like. This year two kids were shot and killed and that is something that impacts the school and our students. Last year my resident and I went to a funeral for

a student . . . this role means being able to be a whole person in front of your resident, not limited to the role of reviewing their lessons and looking for standard alignment. That human connection is incredibly valuable. CRCs are here to help residents feel safe and secure and take on the challenges while using as many best practices as possible." ~ J. Shafton

"A CRC is a mentor, an advocate for the mentee, a resource . . . you must be reflective, transparent. Being willing to share your knowledge because there are many levels, parts and pieces of yourself that teaching requires, other than just the actual instructional piece. Mentoring is showing the resident what works for me but being collaborative to help them develop what will work for them." ~K. Rogers

"The number one role of a coach is you have to be very honest and fair, caring, reflective, not judgmental. You have to take people where they are, whatever that is on the spectrum of teaching, and continue to build them and you do it in a positive way. What has helped me is using the coaching language: for example, what I am hearing you say . . . . You just don't give them the answer. You let them come up with their own answers and strategies. You need to be a good listener. You have to show them that you are human and that you make mistakes too, that you are not perfect. And of course you have to be up on your readings and use research-based strategies. Also, to be a good coach you have to instill in the resident to always strive to become a better teacher." ~D. Vargas

"The role of a CRC is to mentor/coach a pre-service teacher throughout the year and not only show them how to be an effective teacher, but how to address, meet, tackle problems that will arise, especially in their first year of teaching, and ultimately how to persist through those first years of growth. There's a lot of reflection that takes place and what's nice is that as a coach we are given a lot of training and tools to really lift up our pre-service teachers to get them to understand how to do their job effectively." ~T. Hughes

Mentoring Styles

The *New Teacher Center* coaching model suggests a coaching stance that moves progressively along a continuum from instructive to collaborative, to facilitative, and at times it is an iterative process. VCU's conceptual framework emphasizes developing critically reflective practitioners. Therefore, it is no surprise that this language surfaces when CRCs describe their coaching styles.

> "I would say my style is reflective. When I think about my current year of coaching it is definitely reflective . . . and my style of coaching has changed over the years. I am definitely more open and willing to let go and willing to see a lesson through and allow the resident to try out their own ideas. When I began coaching I just needed to take more steps back and just say 'try it' and I am also much

warmer to developing a friendship now than when I first started coaching. I think the most beneficial part of coaching isn't necessarily when you pull up the laptop and fill out the forms, but it's more of the conversations that occur right after a resident teaches a lesson, to stop and ask how did it go? I have found, especially with my resident this year, that the better the relationship, the more reflective the conversations have become. I have seen a lot of growth in my own residents in just being willing to reflect and say: 'I could have done this differently.' " ~ J. Shafton

"My style is very collaborative, but it also depends on what the resident needs. I tend to adapt very early on . . . I can tell if they need me to be more instructive or more facilitative. That's why I go in being collaborative because I learn a lot as well, so I want to get their input and fresh ideas that they bring to the classroom and to the profession. I'm both collaborative and reflective, because I put a lot of those 'how am I doing' questions back on the resident." ~K. Rogers

"My goal early on is to give my residents a lot of agency. I give them active roles in the classroom right from the beginning of the year and try very intentionally to give them gradual responsibilities as it progresses." ~T. Hughes

Tips for Success: Advice from the Frontline

For groups starting a residency program, for new coaches embarking on the role for the first time, or for existing programs seeking input from the field for growth and improvement purposes, our CRCs offered their advice for success.

> "Be willing to let go. I mean you are the star of your own show, you have created the classroom and your environment, but be willing to share the stage and know that it will be beneficial for your resident. That was truly a challenge for me. Be prepared to be humbled and while that is a benefit it can be a true challenge for a new coach to step back . . . ultimately it is going to be something incredibly impactful for your own practice. I also recommend making time to meet with and get to know your resident before the school year actually starts. It allows you to hit the ground running. Having that time to together, away from the scheduled meetings, to just grab coffee and check in, or maybe even to begin outlining your curriculum . . . that has been incredibly helpful for my last two residents. I didn't have the opportunity to do that the first time, and I can see the difference and how it helped to ease some of our nerves and get to know each other and that was also very helpful." ~J. Shafton

The ability to let go is a reoccurring theme with resident coordinators and with coaches. Hughes resounds the importance of this approach,

> "A coach has to be willing to let go and let the chips fall where they may at some point. Very little learning from the resident's perspective takes place when

you as the coach are constantly putting out fires and rescuing them. That is a best practice that I know has benefited the residents I've coached." ~T. Hughes

"Buy into the mission of the New Teacher Center and the coaching model. Ask yourself: do you believe in this work? Do you trust the process? In the beginning it is very hard to see, but after a year's time in doing the work and being committed to the work, it's awesome to see how the residents have blossomed. . . . Residents are like little butterflies. . . . Now you have two fully equipped educators in the room. The impact that this program has on teaching and learning is phenomenal. Be a committed professional that is willing to do the work." ~ K. Rogers

"Programs should provide coaches the explicit license to be instructive. When we were first trained in the NTC model of coaching and the Instructive, Collaborative, Facilitative Continuum, the collaborative and facilitative modes were emphasized as more effective. The takeaway for many coaches was that we should avoid the instructive mode. It took a little time to realize that these are preservice teachers with little to no experience and that the NTC model is actually focused on first and second year teachers and adapted for our residency program. Basically once we were given permission to be more instructive as an effective best practice for supporting preservice teachers it gave a lot of coaches the license to say the things we wanted to say, but at first felt like we were not allowed to do so or we would be working against the model's best practices. Coaches should also take the license to be creative and change things up especially if you as the coach can see that something is not working or that the resident is not getting the experience that they need to be getting. In that vein, residency programs should give the coaches as much agency as possible and make sure the lines of communication between the coach and the residency staff stay open. Not only will this create conditions for more effective coaching, but it will keep coaches coming back and help retain coaches." ~T. Hughes

"Learn to lean on the residency program staff and other CRCs for support. The monthly CRC forum is always positive because I get good feedback from my colleagues doing this same work, in terms of what is working for them and I can apply some of the same strategies with my residents. Being in that common space and mindset and having those conversations at the CRC Forum is super helpful." ~K. Rogers

CRCs were aligned and clear on their belief that residency program staff should be explicit with coaches about the need to build trust in the mentor/resident relationship. They also stressed the importance of intentionally having a conversation with new mentors about the necessity and value of letting go and providing residents with autonomy. They suggested that these conversations be incorporated into the program's mentor forums. CRCs reiterated the importance of the monthly mentor forums that create opportunities for mentors to come together and brainstorm, share, and be vulnerable, ultimately increasing their self-efficacy in the coaching process.

Growth and Lessons Learned as Recruitment Tools

CRCs were asked about the mistakes they made as a coach, what they learned from those mistakes and how, over time, they have grown as a coach. A commonality in their responses was the move toward trusting their professional expertise and judgment in numerous facets of the work and differentiating and adapting to meet their resident's needs. For example, all four coaches mentioned the importance of moving beyond strategic compliance with the coaching tools to identify which tools best meet their resident's needs.

> *"I also had to learn to use the tools and give myself grace for using the tools because I wanted to do it right. Through training I began to understand that it is about what works for your resident, and you find what fits. It was helpful to hear that language from the resident coordinator. I realized it was not about using the tools for the sake of completion, but about identifying how a given tool would impact my resident's practice."* ~K. Rogers

> *"I have become more collaborative. My first three years, before I began coaching, I taught in a silo. I was rarely, if ever, observed. Our school is relatively small so we did not have many teachers teaching the same subjects. When I became a CRC I had room to grow and I had to explain why I was doing everything that I was doing. I had to justify it, and I felt if I couldn't justify it I didn't want to teach that lesson. I grew because I had to be more critical of myself. I wanted to grow because of my students but there is also a pride piece that drives the growth. As a mentor, I am keenly aware that when my resident observes me and when I walk them through a lesson, that I want to model the practices that they will adopt one day. It really does push you to grow in your own practice. I feel like I am now more open-minded and I want my lessons to reflect the needs and experiences of the needs of my students. There was a time where I was talking with a resident and they brought up, for example, that we had not incorporated a female author in a while. I had not realized that. I think the residency program makes you slow down, because you can't rush through the program."* ~ J. Shafton

> *"The mistake I made the first year was wanting to be like I am with colleagues with my resident. I was very collaborative, but that decision depends on the personal maturity level of the resident as well. I had a very young resident that was not very mature and I was treating her very much like a colleague and she needed me to be more instructive. I had to adapt and adjust quickly to keep the lines separate . . . so she would understand that we were not there to be friends but that we were there to do this work together in order to get her to the next level."* ~K. Rogers

Providing more agency and freedom has created the space for one coach to be more direct when direct instruction is needed. When residents are given the freedom to plan their own lessons, the direct feedback is focused on the lesson's impact on student learning as opposed to whether the lesson was delivered and taught as the coach would have taught it.

> *The one area I have for sure improved in gradually over the years is giving my residents more agency and freedom to do what they want to do. I am direct in my feedback when I need to be but I also approach it as a team effort when we encounter problems or challenges. I use the pronoun "we" more often than I use anything else because I want the residents to feel supported and validated in their decision making. At the same time I want them to understand that I still have a very active role in whatever decisions we are making and directions we are going in the classroom. I try and put my feet in their shoes as often as possible and recognize that they have a lot of other responsibilities. I know that some coaches have a sink or swim mentality, I don't adhere to that necessarily. For instance, I will offer to help grade assignments and prepare activities, just because I recognize that a) they are still in school and b) they are really early in their careers and not only do I want them to feel supported, I also want to make sure that my students aren't suffering due to a resident's lack of experience.*
>
> *I have learned to be more direct at times. Early on as a coach if I saw a problem I was hesitant to be evaluative. I've gotten better about being hesitant and now I just rip the band-aid off and address it right then and there. That may seem counterintuitive to what I have said about giving my residents more agency but it actually goes hand in hand with giving up more control. With my first resident I had a heavy hand in a lot of the planning. As the years progressed I have taken further steps back and have allowed my residents to make more decisions and hopefully become more of the teachers they want to become as opposed to carrying out my directives and my plans. That has come with finding a little bit of humility and recognizing just because it is the way I like to do doesn't necessarily mean it's the most effective way or the only way of teaching. ~T. Hughes*

Our CRCs always mention the growth in their own teaching practice. Specifically, they point to growth in formative assessment and becoming more data driven. Hughes shares, *"Rather than telling residents they were doing something wrong, I have to use assessment data and this forces me to approach the conversation with evidence (or lack thereof) of student learning."* Technology is always mentioned as a growth area, Hughes relays, *"I have learned about so many new resources from my residents, especially when it comes to technology and integrating it into our lessons."* Coaches express growth in differentiating and in student engagement,

> *"Coaching makes you a better teacher. I have grown more in the last 4 years than I did the first five years that I was teaching because there's never a day*

that you can phone it in. Someone is always watching so it forces you to be more attentive and reflective about what you are doing in the classroom. Having a second teacher in the room really gives you a chance to collaboratively teach in an effective manner, and that opens up a world of possibilities in terms of differentiation, scaffolding, and other teaching strategies that maybe you wanted to try in the past but were not able to find the time to make it happen. For example, I have become better at finding strategies that allow us to differentiate. Before becoming a coach I used a lot of direct instruction. There was a lot of lecture, it was almost a joke amongst students and even though I was good at it, there was a lot of it. Over the last 4 years I have replaced a lot of that with strategies like gallery walks, online interactives, and strategies that keep students engaged . . . I'm learning to focus on those micro engagement opportunities.

"All the formal NTC professional development and tool training that we have received, is not only applicable to coaching but definitely to teaching in general. Before stepping into this program, I wasn't analyzing student learning to the degree I am now, after being introduced to the Analysis of Student Learning tool. That is definitely something that I will continue to use, probably even more so if I have a year that I won't be coaching, because it is such a quick and effective strategy to assess student learning." ~T. Hughes

Why Coaches Value the Residency Program

Coaches are ideal ambassadors for the residency program as they have a close-up lens on how the program moves teaching practice and impacts student learning, as well as a wider lens for how the program builds capacity, school and district wide. As teachers in high-needs schools, they experience the strain that unfilled teaching positions place on their schools. They witness the impact of high teacher turnover on student performance and on the climate and culture of the school. The residency program provides them with an opportunity to be a part of the solution to these very real problems that routinely face their schools and their profession. Shafton shares, *"I see so much teacher turnover in high-needs schools. It's pretty cool that I have been able to help bring quality teachers into an awfully neglected system and our kids deserve that."* Rogers reveals,

> *"I'm a parent of children in RPS so what I value the most is that I know this program is developing quality educators. I always measure it as whether I would want my child to be in this person's class. I think the program is attracting and retaining quality teachers . . . people that are really passionate about education and willing to adapt to the needs of the kids and not just do things the way they have always been done."*

All four veterans expressed their satisfaction and pride in having residents they mentored hired in their own buildings, and being able to pop in their classroom and see amazing teaching and learning taking place. Coaches recognize the impact of their work beyond their own classroom or building,

> *"We know that we are making an impact here at our school but we are also well aware that there is a huge need elsewhere in the district where, without this program, we only have so much influence. This is one way to start building that critical mass and make an impact on other buildings that need well-equipped, highly-effective teachers that are going to stick around for a long period of time. I am getting older and I want to pass the baton on, and by coaching I am not only helping children but I'm helping teachers. When I began coaching I said to myself, if I can help them become a better teacher in any way, then I will to do it."* ~T. Hughes

Coaches appreciate a career ladder for teacher leadership, growth and professional development that doesn't require leaving the classroom.

> *"As teachers we often do not have the opportunity to grow in our field. You're either a teacher or an administrator or maybe a department chair. I think we lose teachers for that reason. I love the idea of how coaching meets a need in between those options. I hope in the future that school districts begin to see mentors as incredibly valuable in sustaining teachers. It has been rewarding and beneficial for me. I take pride in being a teacher coach and it was particularly rewarding when there weren't many leadership opportunities."* ~J. Shafton

> *"I value the chance to have supervisors and superiors outside of the RPS district that have the time to give me meaningful feedback. Along those lines, I really value getting the chance to work with and network with like-minded and thoughtful educators. The time that we have spent in forums, especially in the breakout areas where we get to work with the other secondary teachers, those are some of the best conversations and professional development that I have ever had. A big piece of why I keep coming back is because I get a lot of professional satisfaction out of working with RTR staff. It's one of the best parts of my year and without that I would feel much more like an island. For those teachers that like to collaborate and work with other adults, even though coaching is more work, it's meaningful work and it feeds that need to collaborate and engage with other teachers."* ~T. Hughes

Finally, CRCs provided numerous stories of capacity building, such as having time to pull students out for remediation while their resident continued with the group lesson. They spoke of how coaching frees teachers up for building-level leadership opportunities, more active roles in grade-level or department teams, or even to work with administration on providing and implementing suggestions for building-level changes. And while coaches spoke at length about the intrinsic rewards of the work, they also clearly identified the stipend as recognition that they are valued as professionals.

CONCLUSION

The RTR program has numerous forms of evaluative feedback. Our federal Teacher Quality Partnership requires a formal evaluation each year which includes a qualitative, longitudinal study consisting of interviews with our residents and coaches. In our work with the National Center for Teacher Residencies, we survey our coaches and residents on an annual basis. We have had two formal evaluations by the Teacher Prep Institute (TPI) (Teacher Preparation Institute US, 2019). During each evaluation, a four-member TPI Team, comprised of teacher preparation faculty members from across the country, spent a week heavily immersed in our program to make recommendations for expanding our promising practices and to identify areas for improvement. Members of the team observed our program across all three tracks in the schools and in the university. They reviewed syllabi, attended methods classes, observed residents teaching and CRCs coaching, and interviewed residents, coaches, resident coordinators, curriculum coordinators, and faculty members. The team evaluated the evidence they collected against four judgment areas:

1. Quality of selection addresses the program's responsibility to select candidates who show potential to become successful teachers;
2. Quality of content knowledge and teaching methods focuses on how well the program ensures teacher candidates acquire content knowledge and key teaching methods and skills needed to be an effective educator;
3. Quality of clinical placement, feedback, and candidate performance analyzes the key elements of the clinical experience in which candidates must apply the knowledge acquired through the program; and
4. Quality of program performance management examines whether and how program leadership—at all levels—utilize data to continually improve the quality of teacher preparation and outcomes for all teacher candidates.

One of four key strengths cited in the formal TPI report was our CRC selection process: CRCs are selected through a rigorous process that ensures their ability and commitment to supporting residents' growth as a classroom teacher.

We also routinely conduct informal surveys and solicit feedback from our residents and coaches. We have received very rich data from these methods, evaluations, and inspections. However, sitting down individually with our three resident coordinators, and then individually with four veteran coaches to capture their thoughts on the work, the value, and the impact of the residency program has given me renewed zeal for our work. The discussions surfaced much alignment in our attempts to build a firm foundation of trust between the resident and the coach, to allow the authentic vulnerability for the resident to be honestly reflective, as well as firm ownership of the value in our instructive, collaborative, and facilitative coaching model. It was affirming to hear coaches describe the intrinsic rewards they receive in giving back to their profession. After all, as Hughes so aptly captured it, *"It's a lot of work . . . but it's meaningful work!"*

BIBLIOGRAPHY

Fletcher, Stephen, Michael Strong, and Anthony Villar. "An Investigation of the Effects of Variations in Mentor-Based Induction on the Performance of Students in California." *Teachers College Record* 110, no. 10 (2008): 2271–2289.

Friend, Marilyn, and Lynne Cook. *Interactions: Collaboration Skills for School Professionals*. White Plains, NY: Longman Publishing Group, 2016.

Glazerman, Steven, Eric Isenberg, Sarah Dolfin, Martha Bleeker, Amy Johnson, Mary Grider, and Matthew Jacobus. "Impacts of Comprehensive Teacher Induction: Final Results from a Randomized Controlled Study. NCEE 2010-4027." National Center for Education Evaluation and Regional Assistance (2010).

Leading Educators. "Our Mission and Values." Accessed May 3, 2019. http://www.leadingeducators.org/values.

New Teacher Center. Accessed May 3, 2019. https://newteachercenter.org/.

Schmidt, R., V. Young, L. Cassidy, H. Wang, and K. Laguarda. *Impact of the New Teacher Center's New Teacher Induction Model on Teachers and Students*. SRI International, Menlo Park, California, 2017.

Strong, Michael. "Does New Teacher Support Affect Student Achievement." *Research Brief* 6, no. 1 (2006): 1–4.

Strong, Michael, and Linda St John. *A Study of Teacher Retention: The Effects of Mentoring for Beginning Teachers*. Santa Cruz: University of California, Santa Cruz, 2001.

Teacher Preparation Institute US. "Better-Prepared Teachers Mean Better Outcomes for Our Students." Accessed May 3, 2019. https://www.tpius.org/.

Chapter 4

Residency Year Curriculum
Marisa Bier

INTRODUCTION AND BACKGROUND

Developed in 2012 and launched in 2013, the Seattle Teacher Residency (STR) is a teacher residency preparation program designed and implemented by four partners:

- Seattle Public Schools (SPS)
- University of Washington College of Education (UW COE)
- Seattle Education Association (SEA)
- Alliance for Education (AFE)

STR draws its strength and continuity from this partnership, which includes representatives from each of these four organizations who play critical roles in the success of the program. Aside from the UW COE as the degree granting and credentialing institution and the district (SPS) hiring graduates of the Seattle Teacher Residency, the local nonprofit (AFE) and the teachers' union (SEA) play unique roles for fundraising, community convening, and advocacy of teacher development. The four partners came together to focus on a common goal of improving the quality and retention of teachers in schools that serve students impacted by poverty, and collectively saw the residency model as a way to achieve this goal.

Based on an interest across the partner institutions, the organizations envision STR as an innovative solution to the ubiquitous problem of teacher retention, which inherently affects student achievement. More specifically, we know that when teachers are prepared in contexts unlike where they're hired, their effectiveness is impacted (Guha et al., 2016). Typically, new teachers are hired in the hardest-to-fill positions, often in high-poverty schools, and their lack of success in meeting the needs of their students results in a low sense of efficacy and high attrition (Carver-Thomas & Darling-Hammond, 2017). Teacher ineffectiveness due to misaligned preparation and lack of continuity in the school environment because of teachers leaving both have negative impacts on student outcomes (Ronfeldt et al., 2013). In addition, continued instability in the school environment can negatively impact performance. Students from low-income communities are often impacted by trauma caused by factors such as poor nutrition and food insecurity, homelessness, family instability, and resource scarcity. Those traumatic experiences can affect the student's ability to learn and regulate emotions and as a result, classroom behaviors escalate when these students are triggered by secondary stressors in school (Australian Childhood Foundation, 2010; Cole et al., 2005). For teachers who may not have the tools to recognize and address the root causes of these behaviors, teaching and learning becomes secondary to efforts of trying to manage a classroom. These challenges of feeling unsuccessful, frustrated, and even intimidated by certain behaviors can be overwhelming and cause teachers to leave the school or the profession. Through our residency model, we are attempting to recruit and prepare people to teach in the contexts in which they get hired and address the problems suggested above by offering an innovative approach to recruiting and retaining high-quality teachers for hard-to-fill positions that is grounded in deep clinical training (Guha et al., 2016).

THE SEATTLE TEACHER RESIDENCY (STR) MODEL

The residency model is centered on intensive preparation of a diverse cohort of aspiring educators who receive master's level coursework integrated with a full-year classroom residency alongside an experienced mentor (Berry et al., 2008). Success relies on preparing teachers who are trained in and understand the contexts in which they will be hired—specifically, Seattle Title 1 schools. In addition, residencies are touted as a promising practice for recruiting and retaining teachers of color in order to build a diverse teacher workforce (Carver-Thomas, 2018). Research clearly demonstrates that when children have teachers who reflect their cultures and backgrounds, they are more successful in school (Carver-Thomas, 2018; Vercelletto, 2018). The commitment to high-quality, context-specific preparation along with diversifying the educator workforce are central components of the goals of STR.

Once in the STR program, residents are immersed in SPS schools that are rich in culture and diversity and are also impacted by poverty. Through coursework, residents engage in deep exploration of their own identities and how power and privilege impact the biases and assumptions that individuals make about others. They specifically explore and experience what this means in the classroom. For example, residents visit the Monroe Correctional Complex to engage in conversations with the Black Prisoners' Caucus and reflect on the school-to-prison pipeline with men who have had this experience in order to better understand how to interrupt the effects of that pipeline in their own classrooms. Residents are charged with challenging their own assumptions and are supported to leave STR with the belief that not only can all children learn and be held to high expectations, but that our students, their families, and their communities are partners in their education, bringing rich resources and assets to the classroom.

STR AND ITS IMPACT ON TEACHER PREPARATION

A team of members from across partners designed STR. These team members understood the need to view teacher preparation and support across a continuum that spanned traditional roles. For the institutions most directly impacted by the program—university-based teacher preparation and K-12 school district—there needed to be a paradigm shift in the way each institution thought about the role it plays that continues today. That is, the teacher preparation program needed to consider revisions to curriculum that aligned with district practices as well as attend to the performance of graduates and the role the institution played in induction support to foster retention. For the school district, hiring practices shifted to a much earlier part of a teacher's preparation and the investment in the recruitment of a pipeline became more focused and intentional such that district human resources personnel became more closely tied to the identification and support of residents who would intern in their schools and subsequently be hired into the district. The residency model drove this paradigm shift.

SUPPORT FROM NCTR

We enlisted the support of the National Center for Teacher Residencies (NCTR) in the development of STR, working closely with the program director and design team to explore existing residency practices and combining what the team understood about innovative teacher preparation with those practices. This resulted in creating a program that was both district-responsive and context-specific. Our work with NCTR has evolved in that STR now serves as a model for other developing programs and plays an active role in the network of residencies to review and improve upon our local and national work.

The remainder of this chapter will take an in-depth look at how STR approaches the combination of teaching methods instruction with the residency field experience, and how this experience also relies on the expertise of the mentor teachers. This includes cross-course collaboration as well as specific professional development for mentor teachers in order to increase the coherency of theory and practice and maximize residents' classroom skills and knowledge as they enter their own classrooms.

STR PROGRAM DETAILS

Seattle is the largest K-12 school system in the state of Washington and is committed to eliminating opportunity gaps to ensure access and provide excellence in education for every student (Seattle Public Schools, 2019). The district serves approximately 53,000 students and 53 percent of those students are nonwhite and 32 percent are low income. In the district's Title 1 schools, those percentages are much higher (62 percent), as reported by SPS. STR was designed to address the teacher retention issues that are evidenced in those schools.

The STR Design Team, led by the program director, was organized in 2012 and comprised of individuals from both the school district and the university. The group developed a mission and plan for the program in alignment with the district's strategic plan and in response to the needs of SPS. The mission of the STR is "to accelerate student achievement through the preparation, support, and retention of exceptional teachers who reflect the rich diversity of the student population in Seattle Public Schools" (Seattle Teacher Residency, 2019). Graduates of STR commit to teaching in the district's Title 1 elementary schools and special education classrooms. The program's theory of change puts student outcomes at the forefront and relies on our strong partnership to support teacher effectiveness along a continuum from recruitment of candidates to retention of early career teachers to teacher leadership development. We not only focus on the recruitment and preparation of teacher candidates but also the preparation and support of the teachers who mentor them throughout their residency and induction for the graduates of the program.

A new cohort of twenty to thirty carefully selected candidates begins the fourteen-month masters in teaching program each year beginning in June. Residents receive a $16,500 stipend that is typically used for living expenses and/or to offset the cost of tuition. The teacher training program includes a combination of direct curricular instruction and classroom observations with residents working alongside SPS teachers carefully selected as mentors. Residents are educated as either elementary teachers in K-5 settings with an English Language Learner or Special Education (SPED) endorsement, or as Special Education teachers with General Education training in K-8 settings.

To receive Washington state teacher certification and a Masters in Teaching from the University of Washington, Seattle, each resident completes the practicum experience in a classroom of a school identified as high poverty and participates in graduate-level courses. Upon the start of their training, STR residents sign an agreement with the program making a five-year commitment to teach in SPS, taking on the hard-to-fill positions in Title 1 and SPED environments.

Residency Year Curriculum

STR delivers a comprehensive elementary school level and special education curriculum that is rooted in culturally responsive and trauma-informed practices (described in a later section entitled "Equity-focused Curriculum") and is closely tied to the specific demands of teaching in SPS and Title 1 environments. Multiple players are responsible for the curriculum. Coursework is designed and delivered by a combination of University of Washington faculty, SPS district staff, SPS mentor teachers and Seattle Teacher Residency staff.

STR mentor teachers (SPS classroom teachers hosting residents) receive instruction and opportunities for collaboration to ensure they are effective and supported in their work with residents through professional development provided throughout the year by the STR team. The tie to mentor teachers is critical to providing a cohesive, relevant program that is directly applicable to the contexts in which residents will ultimately be hired. Mentors become well informed of the curriculum during professional development days where instructors share coursework content and assignments and engage mentors in thinking through how to support residents to apply what is learned. Mentors are also trained in effective coaching techniques derived from resources such as Mentoring Matters (Lipton & Wellman, 2017) and Leverage Leadership (Bambrick-Santoyo, 2012) so that they can provide direct support to residents' planning and instruction and participate in assessing on resident effectiveness.

The Residency Year Curriculum was designed so that residents have ongoing opportunities to connect theory with practice. Research-based teaching methods in elementary math and literacy instruction, special education, culturally and linguistically diverse students, and classroom management are delivered and closely aligned to assignments that are directly applicable to classrooms in which residents complete their practicum. Coursework is woven into the residents' experiences throughout the year and is tightly integrated with both the progression of responsibilities expected of residents as well as their schools and community contexts.

In many cases, courses are delivered in modules so that instructors can break up learning experiences over time and give residents opportunities to enact certain practices, be assessed on those enactments, and then use the lessons learned to apply to new pedagogical practices and connect to other course content. That is, courses do not exist within parts of the year but are offered over time so that content is chunked and aligned with the practicum's gradual release. Below is an example of a curriculum map for a course that occurs across several quarters of the program describing the progression of residents learning practices for supporting culturally and linguistically diverse students(see table 4.1).

After two months of full-time summer content area methods and classroom management courses, residents spend an entire academic year in a

Table 4.1 Culturally and Linguistically Diverse Students STR Curricular Map 2018–2019

	WINTER
Know	
• Determine the language demands of a content area lesson	
• Assess and analyze language data gathered about a specific ELL student	
• Use content objectives and student data to develop appropriate language objectives	
Do	
• Collect language samples from specific students during classroom instruction and activities	
• Use a lesson template to plan and deliver a language-focused small group lesson based on assessment of students' language needs in specific content area lesson	
Where	What/How (Learning Experiences/Instructional Activities/Assessments)

CLD studio prep day and ELL math studio day (@Van Asselt)	In studio prep day:
	• Residents review the process of determining language objectives based on student data and content area language demands
	• Residents view and debrief a language lesson and determine components of explicit language lessons
	In ELL math studio:
	• In the preliminary classroom visit, residents observe math lesson and gather language samples from focal student/s as they participate in an instructional activity
	• Residents review and analyze the data they collected about their focal student/s. They use the data, in concert with the content objectives, to determine a reasonable language objective for particular student/s based on specific activity.
	• Using a lesson plan template, residents collaboratively plan a small group mini lesson focused on explicit instruction around the particular language objective they identified.
	• In a second classroom visit, residents teach small group lesson to their focal student/s.
	• Residents reflect on their learning regarding:
	  ○ The performance and participation of their focal student/s
	  ○ The relationship between language and content learning
	  ○ The challenges and necessities of formative assessment and data analysis for the work of effective instruction and differentiation

SPS classroom teaching alongside an experienced teacher who is carefully selected to be their mentor. During the academic year, residents typically spend four days co-planning and using various approaches to co-teaching in their school site. They simultaneously take coursework in content area methods (math, literacy, science, and social studies), classroom management, child development and learning theory, culturally responsive pedagogy, special education, and linguistic diversity across the year. These classes are held on Fridays and Wednesday evenings, plus one Saturday per month. Ongoing coursework creates opportunities for residents to link classroom experiences to current education theory and research, all within the context of the local education environment and in alignment with district-specific programs and initiatives. The curriculum map below demonstrates how the teaching of classroom management practices and the theories behind it are scaffolded throughout the year from resident learning (see table 4.2).

The following represents key program components that contribute to the quality of developing residents' pedagogical content knowledge and teaching practice:

Table 4.2 STR Classroom Management Curricular Map 2018–2019

	SPRING
Know	
	• The fundamentals of designing and teaching differentiated small group lessons that incorporate language objectives, bridge to students' experiences and build background, scaffold comprehensible input, explicitly teach language in meaningful contexts, foster interaction, and utilize ongoing formative assessment
Do	
	• Utilize formative assessment to determine next instructional steps for differentiated small group of ELL students
	• Design small group lesson to address content and language needs of ELL students based on assessment, students' English language proficiency, and content area standards
	• Enact and videotape lesson, and reflect on lesson's effectiveness with special attention on essential ELL practices, students' engagement, and evidence of student learning
Where	What/How (Learning Experiences/Instructional Activities/Assessments)
CLD	In CLD session #1:
	• View and debrief small group differentiated lesson for ELL students
	• Co-plan and/or collaborate with colleagues on upcoming small group lesson
	In placement classroom:
	• Teach small group lesson with explicit language focus based on assessed needs of ELL students
	• Videotape lesson to share with colleagues
	In CLD session #2:
	• Share videotaped lessons and feedback on lessons
	• Reflect on strengths, areas for growth, and next steps

- Implementation of the co-teaching model and support from an experienced teacher who serves as the resident's mentor, with intentional periods of lead teaching scheduled throughout the academic year.
- Friday classes held in STR partner school sites (placement-based math and literacy methods), taught by university faculty in collaboration with classroom teachers (often STR alumni); courses are designed to offer additional classroom experience and to facilitate multiple passes through a Learning Cycle,[1] which guides residents through a process of Planning, Rehearsal, Enactment, and Reflection. (Enactment takes place in the context of a host classroom where residents collaboratively apply learning with instructor support.)
- Field-based internship for an entire school year, providing residents with significant and authentic work experience and connections within a school community as well as the district.
- Studio Days: at least two day-long professional development sessions that focus on either elementary math instruction for students with specific focus on those identified as English Language Learners or literacy instruction for students with focus on those identified as receiving Special Education services; lead instructors are ELL and SPED faculty with support from math and literacy methods instructors.
- Strong emphasis on equity and social justice preparing candidates to work with youth in poverty-impacted communities.
- Exploration of residents' own identities as individuals and teachers in diverse, poverty-impacted learning communities and how one's own biases and assumptions impact teaching practice.

Program Design

The residency year is specifically designed to prepare graduates to teach in the SPS system, which includes elements of the district's evaluation framework used in the resident evaluation tools as well. The STR program director and STR Curriculum and induction manager collaborate with the SPS chief of Curriculum, Assessment and Instruction and with SPS program managers to learn about the goals and vision for content areas in SPS. SPS program managers were included in STR's planning process and subsequent meetings have followed up over the years of STR implementation. The goal is to create alignment between the STR curriculum and the SPS vision, to best prepare the residents to teach within the context of SPS. STR trains residents in curriculum planning such that they can access the district's Math in Focus and Collaborative Literacy programs. SPS educators serve as course instructors in our "Working in Schools" equity strand, Elementary Science methods, and Health and Physical Education. Elements of the district's training on trauma-informed teaching are also integrated into the residency year in order to tie together residents' understanding of their students. In addition, residents are educated in the Common Core State Standards and the SPS teacher evaluation framework.

The scope and sequence of STR is unique in that most courses, including Math, Literacy, Classroom Management, Special Education, Culturally and Linguistically Diverse Students, and Working in Schools (our cultural competency and equity thread), are held across three or four quarters throughout the year. Coursework is offered in modules so that residents are not experiencing instruction in silos, but rather have opportunities to cycle through content and explore how it is interconnected and applicable to practice. STR integrates modules across the year for the following content: Social Studies methodologies, Next Generation-Based Science instruction, Using Data to Inform Instruction, Differentiation specific to English Language Learners and Students with Special Needs, Trauma-Informed Instruction, and Learning Theory.

STR tries to ensure that coursework does not exist in isolation by capitalizing on the deep expertise and knowledge base of each of its stakeholders, that is, mentor teachers, university faculty, university instructional coaches, resident graduates, hiring principals, and SPS consulting teachers (district-based induction coaches). For example, science is taught by a mentor teacher who has been a lead teacher for the district's initiative to roll out instruction addressing the Next Generation Science Standards. Her instruction for the residents (and also for the mentor teachers) mirrors the launch of the district's professional development work.

In order to foster alignment across the curriculum, STR instructors, including SPS staff (program managers, instructional coaches, teacher leaders), attend several full-day instructional team retreats throughout the year, facilitated by STR's curriculum manager. These retreats give them the opportunity to collaborate, share best practices, align content, and learn about others' courses in greater depth. Mentors who support residents for the yearlong internship attend a three-day workshop in the summer and monthly professional development lead by STR's program director and director of clinical practice, often in collaboration with other team members as well as district and community partners. This time is specifically designed to develop mentors' coaching skills, collaborate on program curriculum, and review processes and tools for resident evaluation. By intentionally integrating STR curricular content into mentor professional development, mentors have the ability to learn alongside their residents and to grow their own professional practice, while allowing the STR staff to calibrate the program based on their feedback. Throughout the year, in these targeted professional development sessions, mentors are provided tools that position them as teacher educators and prepare them for the responsibility of coaching residents with effective feedback and delivering content and instruction to residents.

The instructional team recognized a need for alignment and common language across courses and lead by the curriculum manager, developed curriculum maps for all courses. Standards of the program are articulated through these curriculum maps, which are shared among course instructors, mentors, residents, and other stakeholders to communicate what residents will know and be able to do by the end of each quarter, and cumulatively, by the time they graduate. Instructors use these curriculum maps to connect their content to other courses. For example, this summer, the math methods instructor used the main principles highlighted in the learning theory class (prior knowledge, sense-making, and deep understanding) to make explicit connections to the instructional activities the residents were learning as a way to foreground those principles. Instructors also use the curriculum maps to align and coordinate assignments.

Program Pedagogy: Curriculum Integration with Practicum Experience

A particular strength of the STR program lies within the pedagogical philosophy of the program embedded in rigorous graduate-level university-based instruction. All residents complete three quarters (summer, fall, winter) of placement-based methods for research-aligned literacy and math instruction that guide residents through the Learning Cycle (defined in previous section) to practice methodologies in the context of a partner classroom. This gives residents an opportunity to apply new learning with immediate feedback from the university instructor, the partner teacher, and peers. Through this placement-based methods model, STR supports teachers' development of enactable episodes of teaching, or instructional activities,[2] couched within a set of core practices.[3]

Throughout the year, residents participate in a number of learning cycles to gain instructional practice through modeling, video, lesson planning, enactment, analysis of video, and analysis of student work. This learning cycle is supportive in developing residents' enactment of STR's Core Practices of Equitable Teaching by embedding their practice within authentic and meaningful instructional activities where they engage in intellectually rigorous content with K-5 students. For example, residents learn the instructional practice of guiding students through choral counting activities. The university math methods instructor will take them into a partner classroom and model the practice with students. Residents will debrief with the instructor and then, for groups of students they have been assigned to as "Husky Buddies" in mind, they will plan small group activities for reinforcing choral counting and perhaps challenging students. Once residents have planned and rehearsed their teaching, they will reconnect with students in the partner classroom to teach their lessons with some residents designated to teach and others to observe and capture video. This is followed by reviewing video, analyzing student data, and sharing observations and reflections in order to understand what went well, what they would do differently, and how they will apply this learning to the next time they work with their students. While the opportunities to learn in practice for residents is great, another invaluable opportunity with this method of teaching coursework is that the teacher educator gets to give immediate feedback as well as understand and observe how residents are taking up the practices taught. In addition, the classroom teacher who partners with them has the opportunity to receive a multitude of data on their students as well as have math practices modeled in their classrooms.

To the extent possible, STR attempts to align program content with district curricula. Though STR's instructional team works to streamline the coursework and assignments so that a significant degree of resident learning takes place in placements alongside veteran mentor teachers, there is ongoing program review and reflection such that we can identify ways to increase alignment and coherency. This will ensure that residents can focus on the work that is most important—or what we've determined with district partners to be nonnegotiable—for a first-year teacher to be proficient in as they enter their first year as a teacher-of-record. These criteria are drawn from districts teacher evaluation framework as outlined by Washington State's Teacher Principal Evaluation Program (TPEP) (State of Washington Teacher Preparation, 2019).

Supporting residents to meet expectations is accomplished in two ways:

1. Residents are embedded in a school community that reflects the context in which they'll be hired, and
2. Relationships and collaboration with partners build STR's understanding about the district context so coursework is aligned with school initiatives and residents can more readily apply learning both in the residency year and as early career teachers.

The STR curriculum manager who is on staff at the nonprofit partner also meets with SPS content program managers, including math, literacy and social studies, science, and special education. Quarterly meetings focus on understanding highlights of district efforts related to content, strengthening partner relationships, and sharing goals, priorities, and dispositions that we collectively believe are vital for novice teacher preparation. This regular communication gave us a direct connection in particular to developing our science methods coursework aligned with the district's curriculum adoption.

COURSEWORK CONNECTIONS
TO CLINICAL PRACTICE

STR makes specific attempts to connect curriculum to practicum evaluation. Teachers interested in serving as mentors to residents, for the full year, participate in a robust selection process. This process consists of submission of an application, observation by the STR director of Clinical Practice for new mentors or approval from coach for returning mentors, and identification of a suitable resident match. This is part of our resident/mentor matching process that occurs in the spring quarter, which allows us to have placements finalized at least eight weeks before the school year starts. As a result, mentors and residents can ideally spend time together over the summer getting to know each other and planning for a successful start to the residency year. Mentors and residents are encouraged to do this informally through most of the summer, and then have time to formally co-plan during summer Mentor Professional Development that launches mentors into the year.

Once the school year begins, residents are regularly observed and given feedback by instructional coaches (from our university-based team) and mentors through our Gateway process. Gateways are the benchmark assessments that evaluate resident progress in teaching practice and professionalism and are the mechanism for residents to receive credit for their quarterly Field Experience course. This process includes mentor and coach both completing formal observations. These experiences provide detailed data to the resident, involve a discussion of resident performance related to particular Danielson rubrics as defined in TPEP, and help residents set action steps in their practice. For all formal observations, residents must demonstrate content knowledge, use classroom management strategies, implement formative assessments, and differentiate for a variety of students. This lesson plan was originally developed by the STR team in 2013 and has been revised to include input from coaches based on resident growth that provides evidence of resident progress in coursework and edTPA. The most updated version in use this quarter has also been aligned to the edTPA rubrics and includes specific language residents are exposed to in coursework(see figure 4.1).

Mentor Support

Mentors receive support throughout the year on mentoring and coaching practices. Professional development is provided (with required attendance) both in the summer and for full days once a month. Mentors learn about and enact mentoring moves such as charting, teacher time-outs, and huddling in both a lab setting during PD and with their resident in the classroom. Specifically, these activities are designed to do the following:

4. Materials: What do I need to teach this lesson effectively?
Name all materials needed for this lesson. Include any coursework or curricular resources as applicable.

5. Implementation of the Lesson: What will learners and I *do* during the lesson? How will I support learners to meet the objective?
Script below exactly how each part of your lesson will go. Use relevant *Instructional Activity Planning Templates* from methods coursework (guided reading, quick image, etc.). Remember that a lesson block will have the following components: a lesson *opening*, *exploration/application*, and a *closing* that are tied to the lesson objective. You may add boxes to account for additional activities if needed.

Time Location Grouping	Activity & Purpose (Press Points)	Script & Notes for Myself (Key Questions and Directions)	Caution Points & Listen/Look Fors

STR Formal Observation Guide; Spring Gateway 2019
Adapted from the Boston Teacher Residency; University of Washington's Secondary Teacher Education Program; Washington Teacher/Principal Evaluation Project (http://tpep-wa.org); 2018 edTPA handbook. Board of Trustees of the Leland Stanford Junior University.

Figure 4.1 STR Formal Observation Guide.

Charting: Charting is one way in teacher education in which mentors and coaches can provide concrete, quantitative feedback on a novice's practice. It gives the teacher educator and the novice a chance to isolate a particular practice or "behavior" and simply watch for and tally its presence or absence. Charting can focus on teacher behavior (creating opportunities for children to participate during group instruction, questioning towards goals, building on children's ideas, orienting children to one another) or child behavior (participation, hand-raising, off-task behavior). It provides a way for teachers to share explicit information on a novice's current instruction while addressing ways he or she can improve.

Teacher Time-Outs: In a Teacher Time Out, a mentor or a novice can pause instruction to puzzle aloud over what they are hearing from students and what they might try next. Teacher Time Out can be useful for helping beginners decide which move in their repertoire to use in a given moment in order to advance student's ideas. It can provide an opportunity for a mentor and a novice to work on responsive decision-making around important elements of teaching practice such as eliciting student thinking, representing students' ideas, and making sense of content ideas. Either the person leading instruction or the person observing can initiate a time out. A Teacher Time Out can give a mentor and a novice a chance to slow down momentarily to think through what is happening together. And Teacher Time Out is best used as a moment to share genuinely puzzling or interesting moments in teaching rather than to correct one another.

Huddling: This mentoring activity asks mentor teachers to make visible to novice teachers how to carefully monitor students' learning during independent or small group work. The task requires that mentor teachers choose a specific principle that guides their practice when monitoring students during small group work. The mentor teacher articulates this principle to the novice, describes how s/he puts this principle into practice, and then has the novice observe them using this principle as a lens while they work with one small group. After a short debrief, the mentor and the novice switch places: the novice works with a small group, while the mentor observes. The two teachers huddle and then continue monitoring for learning.

Mentors bring data from the use of those tools to mentor professional development sessions to share and debrief collectively to discuss usefulness and ensure that they are being used in ways that support resident growth.

By integrating program course content into mentor professional development, mentors have the opportunity to understand the expectations of residents, learn alongside their residents, and grow their own professional practice. The STR team also collects mentor feedback in order to calibrate and align program expectations with classroom realities. This is evidenced in many ways, but most recently through our social studies and science methods coursework. In social studies methods, residents and mentors learn two specific methods over the course of the year (Inquiry and Structured Academic Controversy). They learn how to connect those methods to civic engagement and participation. Over the course of the year, mentors participate in two social studies workshops. Workshops include readings, discussion and rationale for the method, as well as modeling of the method for mentors. Mentors are provided lesson planning templates and grade level exemplars to use while co-planning with residents. Possible topics for a lesson could include a specific school, neighborhood or community issue that affects students. Residents, after learning the method during a workshop session, teach the lesson and submit the lesson and reflection as part of their seminar grade. For example, a mentor in a kindergarten class and his resident designed a series of inquiry lessons engaging students in constructing what they believed to be "fair." Rather than stop at completing the assignment, they found that both the engagement of their kindergarteners and the learning that took place was reason to continue developing the concept of fairness using the inquiry method through the rest of the year. The mentor and resident became a model for demonstrating the method in our program.

It is a priority that we strive to increase the calibration of feedback between mentors and university instructional coaches through co-observations and discussions of observation data across coaches. Residents receive regular feedback from both individuals, and it is important that messaging is consistent with both mentors' practice and content, as well as pedagogy from resident coursework. Mentors and coaches are conducting co-observations when possible to increase alignment of feedback. As in previous years, the team analyzes resident observation data at coaches' meetings to help increase the effectiveness of feedback and trends we see in the data.

This information is used to plan future mentor professional development topics and activities in the Field Experience Seminar course. We are also continuing to review and analyze examples of resident lesson plans and teaching with our coaching team to help calibrate the feedback provided.

Equity-Focused Curriculum

STR actively works to develop a common language of equity across course content by putting STR's Core Practices for Equitable Teaching at the heart of all aspects of the curriculum. STR's eight Core Practices stem from the values of our program and describe what the work of teaching looks like (as defined by the STR team and program mentors). The Core Practices are what we *do* as teachers, the actions we take that make the vision and values real and tangible. To that end, the STR instructional team uses these

Core Practices to plan coursework and makes these practices transparent within their instruction. In addition, the Core Practices are grounded in the coaching model. Residents are expected to identify Core Practices in planning for their own instruction and will be evaluated throughout the year with a framework that incorporates these elements. Core Practices include the following:

- Establish a Community of Learners
- Teach Toward Instructional Goals
- Position Students as Competent Sense Makers
- Teach with Each Student in Mind
- Orient Students to the Content
- Assess Student Understanding to Guide Instruction
- Invest in the School Community to Support Student Learning
- Reflect on Teaching Practice

These core practices, developed by district and university partners, are aligned with the district's framework (TPEP) as well as the state of Washington required teacher performance assessment, edTPA (Pearson 2019).

Racial equity work in STR is comprehensive and partially based on the work of Hammond (2014)—the text that the SPS Department of Equity and Race Relations uses in their work with Equity Teams, and Emdin (2017). Instructors of the course focused on race and equity dive deep into personal identity work that leads to understanding one's own position and power in relation to students as well as the importance and relevance of building family and community partnerships.

Residents learn various methods of teaching elementary math (such as math talks, counting collections, quick images) and literacy (such as guided reading, read alouds, literacy development), along with other content areas, such that connections are made to setting up an equitable learning environment as well as working with students who receive special education services and/or are English language learners. Related to classroom management, the learning of content methods is associated with the ways in which residents learn to set up routines and procedures and build classroom community through their Culturally Responsive Classroom Management course. Because the residents are working in SPS classrooms, instructors help them make direct connections to district curricula in teaching particular content area methods. Assignments and evaluation structures are designed to be enactable in placement classrooms. The intentional focus on classroom context sets residents up to be well prepared for day one as teachers-of-record in their own SPS classrooms.

OUTCOMES/ACCOMPLISHMENTS

Since the first cohort of residents began their training in 2013, STR has prepared over 100 new teachers now serving 2,200+ students in 30 Seattle schools. We continue to provide resources and services to our graduates through STR's post-residency support. In addition, twenty-six residents are currently enrolled in STR's Cohort Six, and admissions for Cohort Seven to begin in summer 2019 are underway.

Outcomes for the STR program as of the 2018–2019 school year:

- *Hiring*: In summer 2018, seventeen Cohort Five residents completed their fourteen-month training and were hired by SPS to teach elementary or special education in Title 1 schools for the 2018–2019 school year. Over the last four years, STR has made up an average of one-third of total hires in SPS Title 1 elementary classrooms, which is a significant resource to both Human Resources and school-hiring teams.
- *Induction*: To extend the first-year support provided by the district's Professional Growth and Educator Support Consulting Teacher program, STR graduates in years two through five as teachers-of-record received professional development opportunities through post-residency support from the STR program in the 2018–2019 school year.
- *Teacher Retention*: An average of 83 percent of STR graduates from 2014 to 2016 are in years three through five of teaching in SPS for the 2018–2019 school year. According to SPS, this compares to 55 percent overall 2018–2019 retention for those in years three through five. One hundred percent of graduates of Cohort Four have entered their second year of teaching. Almost one-third of graduates of Cohort Five were hired in the school in which they completed their residency (five out of seventeen).
- *Diversity*: STR graduates have on average included 40 percent people of color, compared to the district average of 20 percent of people of color among teachers of record.
- *District Recruitment*: STR intentionally recruits from the classified staff pool of SPS and admits residents through the district's Classified to Certificated program. The launch of Cohort 6 in June 2018 includes twenty-four residents, six of whom are part of the district's Classified to Certificated program, and who serve as paraprofessionals during their residency. Since Cohort Three in 2015–2016, STR has prepared a total of sixteen paraprofessionals who are now teaching in SPS, averaging one-quarter to one-third of all those in the Classified to Certificated program each year.
- *Funding*: The STR program has been able to secure diverse and sustainable funding, especially in recent years. STR was a sub-grantee of the Bill and Melinda Gates Foundation Teacher Transformation project awarded to

the National Center for Teacher Residencies, and in conjunction with that project, the program successfully received a perfect score on the Teacher Preparation Inspection conducted by TPI-US. The Seattle School Board unanimously supported a $250,000 contribution to STR in the 2018–2019 academic year. Private donors, both individuals and foundations, have also supported the program with five- and six-figure multiyear contributions.
- *Shared Practice*: Since its inception, STR has hosted multiple NCTR network events and participated in biannual network convenings. We have convened learning communities and both share and access network program resources. Each visit and collaborative activity contributes to ongoing program improvement.
- *Climate Survey Data*: Initial analysis of the district's student perception survey data indicates positive outcomes (https://secure.panoramaed.com/seattle/understand)
  - For schools as of September 2018 with five or more STR graduates, SPS 2017–2018 student climate survey data shows:
    - Overall: S68 percent favorable overall percentage compared to 62 percent for other Title 1 schools with less than five graduates
    - Classroom Environment: Over 49 percent favorable percentage compared to 41 percent for other Title 1 schools with less than five graduates
    - Healthy Community: 60 percent favorable percentage compared to 50 percent for other Title 1 schools with less than five graduates
    - Student Motivation and Inclusion: 78 percent favorable percentage compared to 69 percent for other Title 1 schools with less than five graduates

Supporting Retention through Induction: Extending the Curriculum to STR Graduates

STR offers ongoing support, training, and guidance to graduates of the residency program, including targeted curricular offerings designed to increase teacher success, sense of efficacy and, ultimately, positively affect retention. A priority is to align and augment this support with the district's Professional Growth and Educator Support Program. SPS Consulting Teachers (those who provide individualized coaching and instructional support to new to profession teachers) and the STR curriculum and induction manager collaborate with two main goals: (1) SPS consulting teachers gain a specific understanding of the preparation work of the residency graduates, and are able to reinforce and reconnect graduates to that learning in their mentoring work with them in the first year of teaching; and (2) SPS consulting teachers give the STR team critical feedback regarding trends they see in STR graduates' strengths and challenges, allowing STR staff the opportunity to continue to hone curriculum and program elements to best prepare graduates for SPS Title 1 schools.

The SPS professional growth and educator support program manager works closely with the STR Curriculum and induction manager in ongoing reciprocal learning and refinement of both programs. The STR team leverages feedback to continually strengthen coursework and the resident experience to ensure best-prepared graduates. Additionally, the SPS professional growth and educator support program has adopted some aspects of STR induction strategies, extending them to the broader new teacher cohort. An example of this integration is the incorporation of an STR classroom management plan into the SPS August New Teacher Orientation (NTO). The STR assignment was adjusted to create a classroom procedures checklist that is used at the NTO and with new teachers, both in the first weeks of work with them, as well as over the course of the year.

STR's induction services have evolved from providing residency graduates support that supplements that of SPS Consulting Teachers' during the graduates' first year of teaching to extending induction services for an additional four years. Given the multiple ways STR maintains connections with graduates, induction support is responsive to cohort and individual need, and can extend and deepen the support offered by the consulting teachers. Induction activities may include classrooms visits, problems-of-practice sessions, content lab days, wellness sessions, and surveys to assess induction effectiveness.

Other alumni opportunities are supported by the STR Alumni Board which serves to build community among residents and graduates by providing information and support to current residents as they navigate the residency year, supporting and connecting with alumni as new to the profession teachers, and representing STR through participation in events both within the program and externally, including playing key roles in fundraising and communication. The group meets monthly to plan ways to support current residents, build the alumni community, and engage in collaborative work with STR leadership (such as approving use of discretionary funds).

The STR curriculum and induction manager has begun Induction Collaborative Walks with the administration of partner schools. Principals join STR in classroom walk-throughs of STR graduates. These walks have four goals: (a) develop and/or strengthen the relationship between partnership schools and STR, (b) ensure STR graduates are meeting school leadership expectations through co-observations with principals and program staff, (c) calibrate observation feedback between school principals and program staff in relation to the Danielson Framework and STR's Core Practices, and (d) use feedback to communicate graduate performance to stakeholders and to inform the ongoing improvement of STR's coursework experience and induction support programming. This experience with school leaders gives STR the opportunity to both recognize strong practices of our graduates as well as potential challenges that we can help support in collaboration with school leadership. Through these methods of collaboration, the STR team works closely with administrators and SPS Consulting Teachers, who lead district's induction work, to determine the skills that are most important for proficiency for a first year teacher as they enter their first year as a teacher-of-record.

STR's Path Forward

The STR program director is currently developing a three-year Strategic Plan for STR and has met with partner leadership to confirm priorities. To date, the following outline has been proposed for the future of STR:

- Priority 1: Diversify educator workforce/Address hiring needs of district
  - Explore possible expansion/scale—grow cohort size, develop middle/high school program
  - Recruitment—particularly African American males
- Priority 2: Retention of teachers in high-poverty schools/high-needs positions (i.e., Special Education)
  - Continue development of a robust, relevant induction program
  - Provide opportunities for teacher leadership development
  - Implement strategies and programs for teacher retention, particularly for teachers of color
- Priority 3: High-quality preparation
  - State and national development—continue to host and consult with other programs to improve STR programming as well as support new program development locally and nationally
  - Data analysis/research—work closely with district to monitor teacher effectiveness, retention, and contribution to teacher diversity; build our research on program effectiveness based on resident performance and perceptions

Considering the success of the program thus far in meeting partnership goals, STR is positioned to continue to grow and have a broader impact on the district's Title 1 schools. We hope to continue modeling best practices, contributing to innovation in teacher preparation, and strengthening the profession through leadership development, improved teacher retention, and building a strong sense of efficacy, particularly among a growing diverse teacher corps.

NOTES

1. Learning Cycle see McDonald, M., Kazemi, E., & Kavanagh, S., 2013, Core Practices and Pedagogies of Teacher Education: A Call for a Common Language and Collective Activity, *Journal of Teacher Education*, 64(5) 378–386.
2. En-actable episodes of teaching ... The use of instructional activities is one way to construct authentic episodes of teaching around core practices for the purpose of novice learning. (McDonald et al., 2013).
3. McDonald et al., 2013.

BIBLIOGRAPHY

Australian Childhood Foundation. "Making Space for Learning: Trauma Informed Practice in Schools." Australian Government Department of Families, Housing, Community Service and Indigenous Affairs. 2010. https://www.theactgroup.com.au/documents/makingspaceforlearning-traumainschools.pdf.

Bambrick-Santoyo, Paul. *Leverage Leadership: A Practical Guide to Building Exceptional Schools.* San Francisco: Jossey-Bass, 2012.

Berry, Barnett, Diana Montgomery, Curtis Rachel, Mindy Hernandez, Judy Wurtzel, and Jon Snyder. "Creating and Sustaining Urban Teacher Residencies: A New Way to Recruit, Prepare, and Retain Effective Teachers in High-Needs Districts." 2005. https://eric.ed.gov/?id=ED512419.

Carver-Thomas, Desiree. "Diversifying the Teaching Profession: How to Recruit and Retain Teachers of Color." Learning Policy Institute. 2018. https://learningpolicyinstitute.org/sites/default/files/product-files/Diversifying_Teaching_Profession_REPORT_0.pdf.

Carver-Thomas, Desiree and Linda Darling-Hammond. "Teacher Turnover: Why it Matters and What We Can Do about it." Learning Policy Institute. 2017. https://learningpolicyinstitute.org/product/teacher-turnover-report.

Cavendish, Marshall. "Math in Focus: Singapore Math." Houghton Mifflin Harcourt. 2019. https://www.hmhco.com/programs/math-in-focus/news-events.

Center for the Collaborative Classroom. "What is Collaborative Literacy?" NMC. 2019. https://www.collaborativeclassroom.org/programs/collaborative-literacy/.

Cole, Susan, Julia Landau, Thomas Mela, and John Mudd. "Helping Traumatized Children Learn: Supportive School Environments for Children Traumatized by Family Violence." Massachusetts Advocates for Children: Trauma and Learning Policy Initiative. 2013. https://traumasensitiveschools.org/wp-content/uploads/2013/06/Helping-Traumatized-Children-Learn.pdf.

Emdin, Christopher. *For White Folks Who Reach in the Hood...and the Rest of Y'all Too: Rality Pedagogy and Urban Education.* Boston, MA: Beacon Press, 2017.

Guha, Roneeta, E. Hyler, and Linda Darling-Hammond. "The Teacher Residency: An Innovative Model for Preparing Teachers." Learning Policy Institute. 2016. https://learningpolicyinstitute.org/product/teacher-residency.

Hammond, Zaretta. *Culturally Responsive Teaching and the Brain: Promoting Authentic Engagement and Rigor among Culturally and Linguistically Diverse Students.* Thousand Oaks, CA: Corwin, 2014.

Lipton, Laura and Bruce Wellman. *Mentoring Matters: A Practical Guide to Learning-Focused Relationships*, 3rd ed. Charlotte, VT: MiraVia, 2017.

Office of the Superintendent of Public Instruction. "Washington State Report Card." EDS. 2019. http://reportcard.ospi.k12.wa.us/summary.aspx?groupLevel=District&schoolId=1&reportLevel=State&yrs=2017-18&year=2017-18.

Pearson Education. "edTPA for Washington: Resources." Washington Professional Educator Standards Board. 2019. https://www.edtpa.com/PageView.aspx?f=GEN_Washington.html.

Ronfeldt, Matthew, Susanna Loeb, and James Wyckoff. "How Teacher Turnover Harms Student Achievement." *American Educational Research Journal* 50, no. 1 (2013): 4–36.

Seattle Public Schools. "Strategic Plan." SchoolMessenger Presence. 2019. https://www.seattleschools.org/district/district_quick_facts/strategic_plan.

Vercelletto, Christina. "Educators of Color bring Numerous Benefits to Students while Facing Daily Challenges." Education Dive. 2018. https://www.educationdive.com/news/educators-of-color-bring-numerous-benefits-to-students-while-facing-daily-c/524544/.

Washington Superintendent of Public Instruction. "Teacher/Principal Evaluation Project: Teacher Evaluation Criteria." TPEP. 2019. http://www.k12.wa.us/TPEP/pubdocs/TeacherCriteriaDescriptors.pdf.

Chapter 5

High-Leverage Resident Practices

Sherryl Browne Graves and Susan Gonzowitz

SETTING THE CONTEXT

In 2015, the East Harlem Tutorial Program (EHTP), a nonprofit educational organization, partnered with the School of Education at Hunter College, of the City University of New York, and AmeriCorps, to develop a teacher residency program, the East Harlem Teaching Residency (EHTR), for preservice elementary teachers. The residency was created to increase the number of well-prepared teachers to meet the needs of the East Harlem community with a large population of Black and Latino students. Many of the students are English language learners and are children of, or are themselves, immigrants and most live at or below the poverty line. During their fourteen-month residency in the East Harlem Scholars Academies, residents complete tailored graduate coursework, while working alongside experienced teachers to receive coaching, mentoring, and cohort-based learning. Residents also serve as lead teachers in an after-school program, which serves the East Harlem district public school students. Upon successful completion of the program, residents earn masters' degrees in Childhood Education and a New York State teaching license.

HUNTER COLLEGE

Hunter College of the City University of New York (CUNY) is a distinguished public university that values learning in the liberal arts and sciences as a cornerstone of individual development and a vital foundation for a more just and inclusive society. The Hunter College School of Education (HCSOE) is the largest and most selective education program within CUNY, and offers forty-one master's programs, eighteen post-masters certificates, an undergraduate program, and a doctoral program in Instructional Leadership. The school is accredited by the New York State Education Department (NYSED), and the Council for Accreditation of Educator Preparation (CAEP), with each teacher preparation program being nationally recognized.

Founded in 1870, Hunter College was New York City's first teacher-preparation school and continues its deep commitment to advancing understanding and practice of education in an urban context and to engaging teacher candidates as they prepare to enter increasingly complex and diverse communities as professionals in education. HCSOE prepares approximately 10 percent, or roughly 7,800 in any given time period, of New York City Department of Education teachers (Caballero, 2017). Graduates assume roles of responsibility and leadership in PreK-12 classrooms by using reflective practice and translating research into action; they are prepared to guide the academic, social, and emotional development of children, adolescents, and adults. HCSOE relies on strong partnerships with local schools to enhance the experiences of students. Faculty believe their work is built on the strengths and assets of the dynamic urban community in which we live. This happens through the use of evidenced-based practices, appropriate to meet the goal of educating all students, with the use of technology to enhance learning and integrated clinical experiences to provide strong, practice-based preparation. Through research, teaching and community engagement, HCSOE faculty, staff, and candidates make significant contributions to improving the lives of youth, families, and the community.

EAST HARLEM TUTORIAL PROGRAM (EHTP)

Founded in 1958, EHTP is a 501(c)(3) nonprofit organization in NYC dedicated to providing East Harlem children with the resources and opportunities they need for academic, social, and career success. EHTP operates multiple after-school and summer college preparatory programs for district public school students (these programs are called Out-of-School-Time, OST). Almost a decade ago, as a way to increase the reach to and impact on East Harlem youth, EHTP leadership designed and implemented public charter schools in the community to complement our existing work in after-school programming. EHTP founded and currently operates four charter schools serving over 1,000 youth from the community. In order to help East Harlem youth achieve their academic, career, and life goals, EHTP takes a comprehensive approach to youth development through out-of-school time (OST) programs that provide rigorous academic assistance and curricula; build social and emotional skills; and increase family engagement in student learning. Between OST programs and charter schools, more than 15,000 East Harlem youth and their families have participated in EHTP's free, year-long programs. While the East Harlem community claims only a 54 percent high school and a 13 percent college graduation rate, over the past five years, 95 to 100 percent of OST high school students graduate from high school and 95 percent have gone on to two- or four-year colleges and the college persistence rate for OST high school classes of 2014 and 2015 is 85 percent.

EHTR has quickly become a highly prominent component of EHTP's work. With the goal of producing a pipeline of quality teachers who are prepared to be leaders in the East Harlem community, EHTR is integrated into both OST programs and charter schools. Residents in the program work with Elementary Program students in OST classrooms after school and assist in Scholars Academies classrooms during the day. East Harlem Scholars Academies, two public charter schools founded and operated by EHTP, serve a combined total of 583 students in grades Pre-K-5 and Elementary Program serves 240 students in grades K-5, and their families in OST. In the afterschool programs, 40 percent of EHTP K-5 students are English Language Learners and 33 percent have individualized education plans (IEPs). Ninety-four percent of all OST students qualify for free or reduced price lunch. In terms of ethnicity, using US census categories, 67 percent of our students are Hispanic, 14 percent are African American, 3 percent are Asian, 2 percent are other, and 13 percent are undesignated. EHTP serves 48 percent males and 52 percent females. Many residents have shared identities with the student population, with a large majority of residents identifying as people of color and first-generation college students.

The Residency has enhanced the caliber of the instruction in our OST programs and public charter schools and thereby is helping students make even greater gains. The residency model allows us to attract and retain candidates who are committed to the education profession and who are eager to gain the content knowledge and instructional experience that will challenge and inspire students. Before launching the Residency, EHTP struggled to maintain a competitive and consistent pool of OST teachers. Due to the unique skills, atypical hours, and part-time nature of the OST roles, it was difficult to attract top-notch candidates to lead classroom instruction. It was also difficult to provide meaningful professional development (PD) within limited hours of service. Thanks to the Residency, OST classrooms have consistent, structured, quality instruction led by qualified adults who are committed to the East Harlem community. Addressing the need for quality instruction in local public schools as well as in OST programs, the Residency is building a pipeline of outstanding teachers ready to serve the East Harlem community.

EAST HARLEM TEACHING RESIDENCY (EHTR)

The residency is a fourteen-month program for aspiring teachers which includes enrollment in a subsidized master's degree program at Hunter, participation in a clinical residency in the classroom of a master teacher, and employment as a lead teacher in EHTP's OST programs. Throughout the year, residents receive extensive coaching support from two sources: a coach assigned by EHTP who is an experienced teacher, known as a clinical instructor (CI), and field supervisors from HSCOE for methods and practicum courses. While undertaking their residencies, candidates also complete course work at Hunter College that is explicitly designed to integrate with their field experiences, including videotaping and close analysis of practice teaching experiences. Upon successful completion of the program, each resident earns a master's degrees in education. Further, after residents pass three certification tests (Content Specialty Test, Educating All Students Test, and edTPA, a performance-based assessment of teaching), they receive their NYS initial teaching certification. CIs, mentor teachers at Scholars Academies, serve as model teachers and each supports two residents. CIs in turn receive ongoing coaching and professional development from a residency staff member, who trains CIs to go from being master teachers to teacher educators. This staff member meets with CIs biweekly, observes CI teaching and coaching sessions, and leads CI professional development. From a financial perspective, CIs are paid a small stipend of roughly $3,000 and residents receive approximately $15,000 cost-of-living stipend, tuition subsidies and awards, free health coverage, travel expenses, and some additional subsidies included state certification testing reimbursement. Their out-of-pocket cost for graduate school comes to roughly $6,000.

RESIDENT PREPARATION

The Teaching Residency year begins during Hunter College's first summer session with an induction period to acclimate teaching residents to the structure of the program and the organizational culture of EHTP (see figure 5.1).

The residents participate in Hunter College orientation and start coursework at Hunter College. They take six summer courses across two summer sessions. During these days, the residents engage in opening sessions that set the groundwork for being part of EHTP and working with one another.

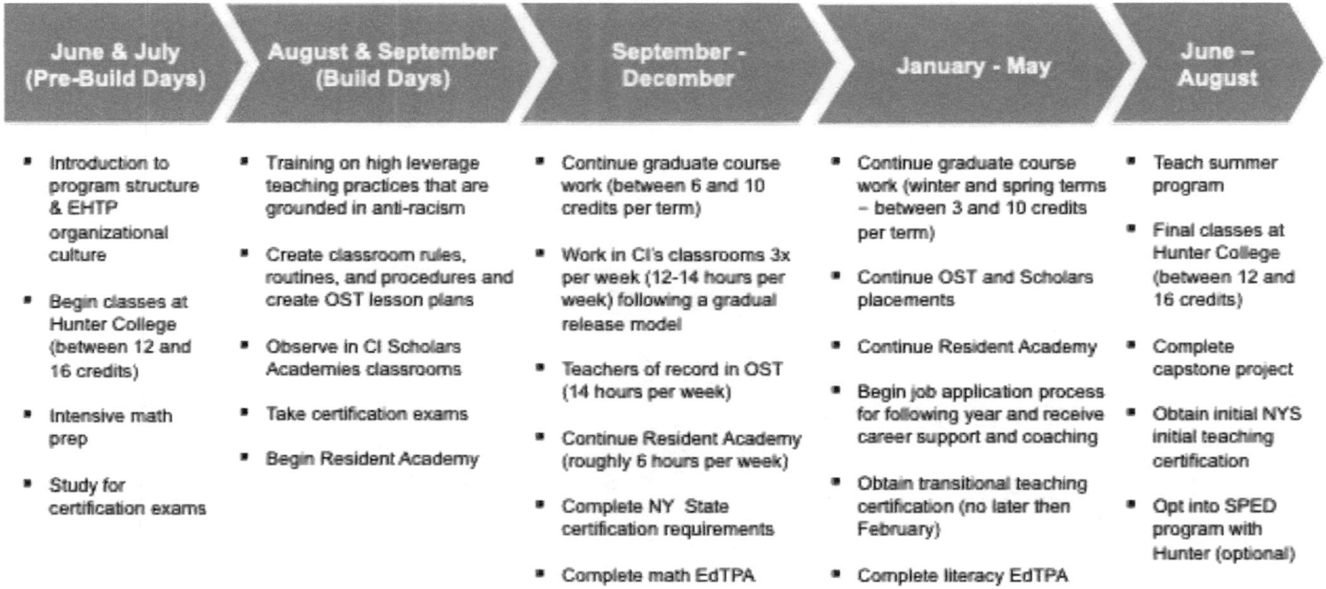

High-Leverage Resident Practices

EHTR Program Timeline

June & July (Pre-Build Days)
- Introduction to program structure & EHTP organizational culture
- Begin classes at Hunter College (between 12 and 16 credits)
- Intensive math prep
- Study for certification exams

August & September (Build Days)
- Training on high leverage teaching practices that are grounded in anti-racism
- Create classroom rules, routines, and procedures and create OST lesson plans
- Observe in CI Scholars Academies classrooms
- Take certification exams
- Begin Resident Academy

September – December
- Continue graduate course work (between 6 and 10 credits per term)
- Work in CI's classrooms 3x per week (12-14 hours per week) following a gradual release model
- Teachers of record in OST (14 hours per week)
- Continue Resident Academy (roughly 6 hours per week)
- Complete NY State certification requirements
- Complete math EdTPA

January – May
- Continue graduate course work (winter and spring terms – between 3 and 10 credits per term)
- Continue OST and Scholars placements
- Continue Resident Academy
- Begin job application process for following year and receive career support and coaching
- Obtain transitional teaching certification (no later then February)
- Complete literacy EdTPA

June – August
- Teach summer program
- Final classes at Hunter College (between 12 and 16 credits)
- Complete capstone project
- Obtain initial NYS initial teaching certification
- Opt into SPED program with Hunter (optional)

Figure 5.1 EHTR Program Timeline.

Residents are trained on EHTP's core value, mission, racial equity, identifying their leadership styles, understanding the community we serve, and utilizing technology across the organization, as well as other areas.

Year 1 Summer Preparation

The core goals of the summer work are to: (1) help residents become familiar with the curriculum and students they will be teaching in the upcoming year; (2) give mentors and residents the opportunity to cocreate a classroom management plan and establish shared expectations for classroom routines and procedures; (3) develop a plan for completing a baseline assessment of students; (4) orient residents to the school culture—building, resources, student population, policies; and (5) give mentors and residents time to get to know each other and develop an effective working relationship.

The Academic Year Preparation

HCSOE provides a rigorous master's degree component and certification pathway to the teaching residents. A team of HCSOE faculty has worked closely with EHTP staff to design a unique approach to teacher education. This team has created a learning experience for residents, which will help them face the challenges they will experience when they become full classroom teachers in fourteen months. Graduate classes are designed around the residents' field experiences and residents are given opportunities to regularly reflect on best practices and apply theory. Classes are also designed specifically to support program residents as they navigate New York City classrooms. The EHTR program offers residents a significant amount of time to explore identity, diversity, and privilege and how these concepts are present in the classroom; this experiential training greatly supports our residents in their success. Residents complete a unique capstone project, including a paper and presentation, that allows residents to reflect on how the theory they have learned and their teaching experiences can impact student achievement. HCSOE faculty and staff meet regularly with residents to ensure that they are on track for certification and graduation. When residents struggle either academically or financially, HCSOE staff work with EHTR staff to help residents find solutions through tailored improvement plan development that includes support from the writing center, math center, or other departments within Hunter College or EHTP. Additionally, HCSOE provides targeted workshops on topics related to teaching, state certification exams, the EdTPA, and career pathways; throughout the year, several workshops are offered exclusively to EHTR residents. For financial matters, HCSOE works with students, through the Office of Academic and Student Affairs to access Hunter College resources.

The Academic Year Clinical Experience

Residents have two types of clinical experiences. Residents are employed as lead teachers in OST classrooms at EHTP. They lead after-school classes of twenty to twenty-five district public school students four times per week. They plan and implement lessons and units by using data to drive student progress. Residents develop a classroom culture and form meaningful relationships with families and community members. They are observed by an instructional coach and a graduate school instructor. Residents also serve as assistant teachers to a CI. They are assigned to their CI working four days a week in a Scholars' Academy classroom. They receive real-time coaching and observation from a CI, master teacher. They partake in a gradual release clinical training model to eventually lead a school day classroom.

The staffing structure of the residency program is designed to ensure that all residents have the individualized support they need. The managing director of the program oversees the program vision, mission, and structure. This person is also responsible for designing professional development for residents and CIs and for coaching CIs. A program director is the liaison for all external partners, coaches residents in the OST program, and works closely with the Hunter team to ensure alignment. Additionally, EHTR employs one of the Hunter methods professors to coach residents in the OST program. Residents also have a dedicated faculty member at Hunter College who is responsible for supporting them through graduate school and state certification requirements. In the future, we will add an operations role that will support with grant maintenance and other program operations. Each team member works to manage his or her piece of the puzzle, but the team also meets regularly to ensure continuity in the residency experience.

SPECIFIC JOB DESCRIPTIONS

Managing Director, East Harlem Teaching Residency

- Serves as the lead hiring manager for residency program
- Drives/manages the clinical instructor program
- Manages planning and oversees execution for all professional development all resident and clinical instructor academies
- Develops and solicits buy-in of all long-term goals for residency
- Primary program liaison to all senior managers, partner schools/programs (i.e., Academies & OST) and EHTP Board
- Teacher of select graduate courses at Hunter College deputy director, East Harlem Teaching Residency (ideally in a practicum professor role)
- Instructional coach for target group of four to six residents at a time (shifting focus groups three to four times per year).

NARROWING OUR FOCUS

When we compared the college attrition and graduation rates of East Harlem to those of the neighboring community, the Upper East Side, we were left to draw one of two conclusions: either there was something fundamentally different between these two populations or there was something very different about the financial and public resources within these communities (Annenberg Institute for Educational Reform, 2012). When looking particularly at elementary school performance on state proficiency exams, broken down by district and race (New York State Education Department, ELA & Math Exams, 2018), we found a strong disparity between the performance of young people in East Harlem and those on the Upper East Side and, even within the East Harlem district, there was a clear divide along racial lines. Our research also suggested that teachers working in school communities of little poverty are more likely to be more experienced and stay longer than teachers working in communities like East Harlem that have higher rates of poverty (New York City Independent Budget Office, 2014). No matter how we reviewed performance data and school suspension rates (U.S. Department of Education, Office of Civil Rights, 2014), we kept arriving at the same conclusion: students of color, particularly Black students, were consistently underserved in public schools. This research was evidence of what we already felt to be true, that this country's legacy of institutionalized racism had negatively affected students of color.

Therefore, when we began EHTR, we knew our teaching candidates must be supported to face, honestly and directly, their own racial identities and their own conscious and unconscious biases. With the goals of self-realization and racial justice in mind, we worked to design all of our teacher training pedagogy and content. Through this commitment, we hoped to prepare our teachers to help affect educational outcomes in East Harlem and promote an equitable society in which students succeeded and challenged the world in and beyond their classrooms.

The Hunter College School of Education and EHTP planning team members hoped to create a program for preservice teachers that clearly connected theory and practice through a foundation of racial equity. The team decided that it was critical for residents in the program to consider dynamics of power and privilege and how those dynamics affect teacher/student relationships and student learning. The team was particularly focused on supporting residents to consider the ethical implications of each of their pedagogical and instructional choices and the impact of poor execution. All professional development provided to the residents include a focus on racial equity and several of the graduate school courses specifically work toward this goal.

In the first few years of our residency, we named the goal of racial equity for our residents and launched the program with a month-long course on race and identity. Through the course, *Diversity in the American Schools*, residents explored identity with a particular focus on their experiences in comparison to experiences of East Harlem families. The course required residents to complete a community ethnography, analyze popular perceptions of East Harlem, and consider their own educational histories as well as the educational biography of an East Harlem student. They also began to explore the history of white culture in this country and to study culturally responsive instruction. Residents would now be able to understand the assumptions they might have had about the students and families they were about to work with and how racism had affected both them and their students. The idea was that the residents could use the knowledge they gained in this course to make intentional choices to support East Harlem students in considering their own racial identities. To establish connections between learning and practice, the course was co-taught by a staff member of the East Harlem Teaching Residency and a college faculty member. Throughout the remaining thirteen months of the residency program, residents were periodically asked to reflect on race and racism and how it showed up in their work.

After training two cohorts of residents in this way, we found that most of them felt ill-prepared to engage with students in conversations of race and racism. A survey as well as anecdotal evidence suggested that residents could not define what anti-racist teaching practices looked like. It became clear that EHTR trainings and graduate school courses needed to be more intentionally tailored to the anti-racist focus of our program. We needed to more clearly define anti-racist teaching practices and how to measure those practices.

DEFINING OUR PRACTICES

It was at this time that we joined the National Center for Teacher Residencies (NCTR). NCTR had a two-year contract with TeachingWorks, a research center within the School of Education at the University of Michigan. We began receiving coaching from a TeachingWorks team member and attending regular TeachingWorks professional development. The TeachingWorks team had researched and developed a set of nineteen high-leverage teaching practices (HLPs) that they define as

> the basic fundamentals of teaching. These practices are used constantly and are critical to helping students learn important content. The high-leverage practices are also central to supporting students' social and emotional development. These high-leverage practices are used across subject areas, grade levels, and contexts.

They are "high-leverage" not only because they matter to student learning but because they are basic for advancing skill in teaching. (TeachingWorks, 2019)

The TeachingWorks team had *decomposed* each practice, which is a term they use to explain breaking down the practice into small actionable steps so that anyone attempting to implement or evaluate the practice would have a shared sense of what success looked like.

While all nineteen practices are critical for highly effective teaching, they were not fully aligned with our anti-racist vision nor did we believe that we could properly teach nineteen practices in a fourteen-month program. Keeping our mission and vision in mind, we prioritized the TeachingWorks HLPs into primary and secondary practices. We defined primary practices as those that residents should be evaluated in, with the secondary practices being practices that should be taught but not formally evaluated. During this process, we renamed several of the practices and added one, *managing bias and racism*, which needed to be more intentionally embedded in every practice as well as defined in its own measurable way. Once we had sorted and renamed some of the practices, we reworded the language in many of the primary practices (see table 5.1).

GETTING INPUT AND TAKING STOCK

After drafting an initial version of the practices, the management team and school leaders at EHTP, current residents, EHTR graduates, professors who had taught EHTR classes, Hunter College School of Education leadership, and clinical instructors (CIs) all participated in a review and revision process. At this stage, we were not asking stakeholders to adopt the practices; instead we were asking them to consider whether these practices aligned to our stated mission while meeting the needs of preservice teachers in East Harlem. During this phase, we missed a critical opportunity to receive input from school district leaders, principals at local district schools, and parents and guardians of East Harlem students. To remedy this situation, we are currently working to develop an organization-wide instructional leadership team that will define what anti-racist teaching looks like. In order to do that, we have begun to survey students, caregivers, staff, and school leaders; we will use this data to create a shared vision of anti-racist classrooms. We are working with NCTR staff to develop a system for collaborating with school and OST leaders.

Once the HLPs were drafted and stakeholders were bought in, we needed to ensure that they were present in all resident learning spaces. These spaces included the following:

Table 5.1 EHTR Version of TeachingWorks Adult Learning Cycle

HLP	TeachingWorks Definition (TeachingWorks, 2016)	EHTR Definition
Managing bias and racism	N/A	Teachers recognize the pervasive inequalities faced by people of color in this country and consider ways in which racism is at the core of the inequity that many students and families face. Teachers consider their own conscious and unconscious biases and their own internalized racial inferiority or superiority. Teacher identify dynamics of diversity, identity, power, and privilege and how those dynamics affect teacher/student relationships and student learning. Teachers consider the ethical implications of each of their pedagogical and instructional choices and the impact of poor execution. In order to do this, teachers consider how racism has affected themselves and their students, and make intentional choices to support their students in considering their own racial identities. Teachers foster an environment in which anti-bias language, asset-based thinking, protective practices, restorative justice, and therapeutic intervention are evident.
Leading a group discussion	In a group discussion, the teacher and all of the students work on specific content together, using one another's ideas as resources. The purposes of a discussion are to build collective knowledge and capability in relation to specific instructional goals and to allow students to practice listening, speaking, and interpreting. The teacher and a wide range of students contribute orally, listen actively, and respond to and learn from others' contributions.	In a group discussion, the teacher and students analyze and interpret specific content together, using content-based evidence, their own knowledge, and one another's ideas as resources. The purpose of group discussion is to build collective knowledge and capability in relation to specific instructional goals and to allow students to learn from one another while enhancing their listening, speaking, and interpreting skills. In effective discussions, the group collaborates to respond to a central question or theme that is appropriate to students' learning needs, prior knowledge, cultures, identities, and interests and the teacher facilitates as students build on one another's ideas and learn from one another.

(Continued)

Table 5.1 EHTR Version of TeachingWorks Adult Learning Cycle (Continued)

HLP	TeachingWorks Definition (TeachingWorks, 2016)	EHTR Definition
Explaining and modeling content, practices, and strategies	Explaining and modeling are practices for making a wide variety of content, academic practices, and strategies explicit to students. Depending on the topic and the instructional purpose, teachers might rely on simple verbal explanations, sometimes with accompanying examples or representations. In teaching more complex academic practices and strategies, such as an algorithm for carrying out a mathematical operation or the use of metacognition to improve reading comprehension, teachers might choose a more elaborate kind of explanation that we are calling "modeling." Modeling includes verbal explanation, but also thinking aloud and demonstrating.	secondary practice (introduced and taught, but not evaluated)
Eliciting and interpreting individual students' thinking	Teachers pose questions or tasks that provoke or allow students to share their thinking about specific academic content in order to understand student thinking, including novel points of view, new ideas, or misconceptions; guide instructional decisions; and surface ideas that will benefit other students. To do this effectively, a teacher draws out a student's thinking through carefully chosen questions and tasks and considers and checks alternative interpretations of the student's ideas and methods.	Teachers pose questions or tasks that provoke or allow students to share their thinking about specific academic content in order to understand student thinking, including novel points of view, new ideas, or misconceptions; guide instructional decisions; and surface ideas that will benefit other students. To do this effectively, a teacher draws out a student's thinking through carefully chosen questions and tasks and considers and checks alternative interpretations of the student's ideas and methods. When teachers effectively interpret student thinking, they consider the students responses in the context of their own biases and what they know about students as learners and people.

(Continued)

Table 5.1 EHTR Version of TeachingWorks Adult Learning Cycle (Continued)

HLP	TeachingWorks Definition (TeachingWorks, 2016)	EHTR Definition
Diagnosing particular common patterns of student thinking and development in a subject-matter domain	Although there are important individual and cultural differences among students, there are also common patterns in the ways in which students think about and develop understanding and skill in relation to particular topics and problems. Teachers who are familiar with common patterns of student thinking and development and who are fluent in anticipating or identifying them are able to work more effectively and efficiently as they plan and implement instruction and evaluate student learning.	secondary practice
Implementing norms and routines for classroom discourse and work	Each discipline has norms and routines that reflect the ways in which people in the field construct and share knowledge. These norms and routines vary across subjects but often include establishing hypotheses, providing evidence for claims, and showing one's thinking in detail. Teaching students what they are, why they are important, and how to use them is crucial to building understanding and capability in a given subject. Teachers may use explicit explanation, modeling, and repeated practice to do this.	secondary practice
Coordinating and adjusting instruction during a lesson	Teachers must take care to coordinate and adjust instruction during a lesson in order to maintain coherence, ensure that the lesson is responsive to students' needs, and use time efficiently. This includes explicitly connecting parts of the lesson, managing transitions carefully, and making changes to the plan in response to student progress.	secondary practice

(Continued)

Table 5.1 EHTR Version of TeachingWorks Adult Learning Cycle (Continued)

HLP	TeachingWorks Definition (TeachingWorks, 2016)	EHTR Definition
Specifying and reinforcing productive student behavior	Clear expectations for student behavior and careful work on the teacher's part to teach productive behavior to students, reward it, and strategically redirect off-task behavior help create classrooms that are productive learning environments for all. This practice includes not only skills for laying out classroom rules and managing truly disruptive behavior, but for recognizing the many ways that children might act when they actually are engaged and for teaching students how to interact with each other and the teacher while in class.	Teachers must work with students to define, establish, affirm, and maintain clear, consistent, and developmentally appropriate expectations for students' and teachers' actions. Teacher must model and support these expectations, differentiate for individual students' needs, and redirect, in a manner that takes student and teacher identity into account, when necessary. Effective reinforcement of productive student behavior is designed around students' emotional and physical needs, provides space for students to recognize their own needs and the needs of their peers, and provides students safe space to rehearse, reflect on, reinforce, and build (or restore) expectations.
Implementing organizational routines	Teachers implement routine ways of carrying out classroom tasks in order to maximize the time available for learning and minimize disruptions and distractions. They organize time, space, materials, and students strategically and deliberately teach students how to complete tasks such as lining up at the door, passing out papers, and asking to participate in class discussion. This can include demonstrating and rehearsing routines and maintaining them consistently.	**Renamed:** Implementing organizational norms, routines, systems, and structures Teachers work with students to implement routine ways of carrying out classroom tasks in order to create a safe learning environment for all students and to maximize the time available for learning and minimize disruptions and distractions. Time, space, materials, and students must be strategically organized and students must learn how to complete tasks according to these routines. Successful implementation of routines, systems, and structures includes working in collaboration with students to establish expectations, making transparent the reasons for each expectation, identifying how these expectations are (or are not) aligned with students' cultural norms, demonstrating and rehearsing routines, and maintaining these systems consistently.

(Continued)

Table 5.1 EHTR Version of TeachingWorks Adult Learning Cycle (Continued)

HLP	TeachingWorks Definition (TeachingWorks, 2016)	EHTR Definition
Setting up and managing small group work	Teachers use small group work when instructional goals call for in-depth interaction among students and in order to teach students to work collaboratively. To use groups effectively, teachers choose tasks that require and foster collaborative work, issue clear directions that permit groups to work semi-independently, and implement mechanisms for holding students accountable for both collective and individual learning. They use their own time strategically, deliberately choosing which groups to work with, when, and on what.	secondary practice
Building respectful relationships with students	Teachers increase the likelihood that students will engage and persist in school when they establish positive, individual relationships with them. Techniques for doing this include greeting students positively every day, having frequent, brief, "check-in" conversations with students to demonstrate care and interest, and following up with students who are experiencing difficult or special personal situations.	**Renamed:** Building respectful relationships with and among students Teachers establish positive, individual relationships with and between students. Techniques for doing this include greeting students positively every day and establishing systems for students to greet one another, having frequent, brief, "check-in" conversations with and among students, following up individually or in structured group settings with particular students when needed, providing opportunities for students to share experiences and listen to one another, recognizing academic competency, and establishing clear systems and structures for students to reflect on their own identities and on similarities and difference with one another and how those affect their experiences.

(Continued)

Table 5.1 EHTR Version of TeachingWorks Adult Learning Cycle (Continued)

HLP	TeachingWorks Definition (TeachingWorks, 2016)	EHTR Definition
Talking about a student with parents or other caregivers	Regular communication between teachers and parents/guardians supports student learning. Teachers communicate with parents to provide information about students' academic progress, behavior, or development; to seek information and help; and to request parental involvement in school. These communications may take place in person, in writing, or over the phone. Productive communications are attentive to considerations of language and culture and designed to support parents and guardians in fostering their child's success in and out of school.	secondary practice
Learning about students' cultural, religious, family, intellectual, and personal experiences and resources for use in instruction	Teachers must actively learn about their particular students in order to design instruction that will meet their needs. This includes being deliberate about trying to understand the cultural norms for communicating and collaborating that prevail in particular communities, how certain cultural and religious views affect what is considered appropriate in school, and the topics and issues that interest individual students and groups of students. It also means keeping track of what is happening in students' personal lives so as to be able to respond appropriately when an out-of-school experience affects what is happening in school.	**Renamed:** Learning about students' cultural, religious, family, intellectual, and personal experiences and considering those aspects in instruction Teachers must be deliberate about understanding their own cultural and racial norms and how those are the same and different from the norms of each of their students. Teachers must recognize student behaviors and expectations for communication, collaboration, and learning within the context of each student's individual and community culture. Teachers need to learn how cultural views affect what is considered appropriate in school, and the topics and issues that interest individual students and groups of students. Teachers must communicate with students, caregivers, and other important people in the students' lives. Teachers must learn students' personal stories and the events in their lives so as to be able to respond instructionally and interpersonally.

(Continued)

Table 5.1 EHTR Version of TeachingWorks Adult Learning Cycle (Continued)

HLP	TeachingWorks Definition (TeachingWorks, 2016)	EHTR Definition
Setting long- and short-term learning goals for students	Clear goals referenced to external standards help teachers ensure that all students learn expected content. Explicit goals help teachers to maintain coherent, purposeful, and equitable instruction over time. Setting effective goals involves analysis of student knowledge and skills in relation to established standards and careful efforts to establish and sequence interim benchmarks that will help ensure steady progress toward larger goals.	secondary practice
Designing single lessons and sequences of lessons	Carefully sequenced lessons help students develop deep understanding of content and sophisticated skills and practices. Teachers design and sequence lessons with an eye toward providing opportunities for student inquiry and discovery and include opportunities for students to practice and master foundational concepts and skills before moving on to more advanced ones. Effectively sequenced lessons maintain a coherent focus while keeping students engaged; they also help students achieve appreciation of what they have learned.	Teachers design and sequence common core and anti-biased standards aligned lessons and units. Successful lessons and units explicitly include clear teacher modeling and explicit explanations of what, how, and why students are learning as well as opportunities for students to demonstrate mastery of new skills and strategies. Lessons and units are created with an eye toward providing differentiated opportunities for student inquiry and discovery. Successful planning provides students with opportunities to practice and master foundational concepts and skills before moving on to more advanced ones. Effectively sequenced lessons maintain a coherent focus for all learners, while keeping students engaged and allowing for adaptation based on anticipated student reactions and based on real-time assessment of student understanding. In planning effective lessons teachers must consider students' learning needs, prior knowledge, cultures, identities, possible misconceptions, and interests.

(Continued)

Table 5.1 EHTR Version of TeachingWorks Adult Learning Cycle (Continued)

HLP	TeachingWorks Definition (TeachingWorks, 2016)	EHTR Definition
Checking student understanding during and at the conclusion of lessons	Teachers use a variety of informal but deliberate methods to assess what students are learning during and between lessons. These frequent checks provide information about students' current level of competence and help the teacher adjust instruction during a single lesson or from one lesson to the next. They may include, for example, simple questioning, short performance tasks, or journal or notebook entries.	secondary practice
Selecting and designing formal assessments of student learning	Effective summative assessments provide teachers with rich information about what students have learned and where they are struggling in relation to specific learning goals. In composing and selecting assessments, teachers consider validity, fairness, and efficiency. Effective summative assessments provide both students and teachers with useful information and help teachers evaluate and design further instruction.	secondary practice
Interpreting the results of student work, including routine assignments, quizzes, tests, projects, and standardized assessments	Student work is the most important source of information about the effectiveness of instruction. Teachers must analyze student productions, including assessments of all kinds, looking for patterns that will guide their efforts to assist specific students and the class as a whole and inform future instruction.	secondary practice

(Continued)

Table 5.1 EHTR Version of TeachingWorks Adult Learning Cycle (Continued)

HLP	TeachingWorks Definition (TeachingWorks, 2016)	EHTR Definition
Providing oral and written feedback to students	Effective feedback helps focus students' attention on specific qualities of their work; it highlights areas needing improvement; and delineates ways to improve. Good feedback is specific, not overwhelming in scope, and focused on the academic task, and supports students' perceptions of their own capability. Giving skillful feedback requires the teacher to make strategic choices about the frequency, method, and content of feedback and to communicate in ways that are understandable by students.	secondary practice
Analyzing instruction for the purpose of improving it	Learning to teach is an ongoing process that requires regular analysis of instruction and its effectiveness. Teachers study their own teaching and that of their colleagues in order to improve their understanding of the complex interactions between teachers, students, and content and of the impact of particular instructional approaches. Analyzing instruction may take place individually or collectively and involves identifying salient features of the instruction and making reasoned hypotheses for how to improve.	Learning to teach is an ongoing process that requires regular analysis of instruction and its effectiveness. Teachers study their own teaching and that of their colleagues in order to improve their understanding of the complex interactions between teachers, students, and content and of the impact of particular instructional approaches. Analyzing instruction takes place individually and collectively, following particular protocols, and involves identifying salient features of the instruction and student learning and creating reasoned and research-based plans for improvement

Clinical Experience

Scholars Academies Charter Schools: Twelve to sixteen hours per week

- Residents received real-time coaching and more formal observations from a master teacher/clinical instructor.
- Residents participated in a gradual release to eventually lead a school day classroom.

EHTP Out-of-School-Time (OST): Fourteen hours per week

- Residents led after-school classes of twenty to twenty-five district public school students.
- Residents planned and implemented standards-based content lessons/units.
- Residents received observation from an instructional coach and a graduate school instructor.

Professional Development

Whole group: Four hours per week

- Residents received whole group professional development grounded in the evaluation rubric and observed needs.
    Small Group: One hour per week

- Residents participated in co-planning meetings with their OST grade team partner and an EHTR staff member.
    One-on-One: One to two hours per week

- Resident received professionalism coaching from an EHTR staff member.
- Resident received lesson planning and observation feedback from CIs and coaches.
    Graduate School

- Residents completed tailored graduate coursework at Hunter College to learn the foundations of teaching.
- Residents learned to apply theory and pedagogy into practical classroom experience.

We began by taking stock of already existing resident courses and training materials. We created an audit tool for course syllabi and professional development plans that allowed us to determine where our HLPs were already being taught in practice-based ways. We reviewed the syllabi of the math and literacy methods courses, two pedagogy and research courses, all resident professional development, and a yearlong field-based course called *practicum*. It would have made sense, at this stage, to review all course syllabi with the professors, but in order to establish faculty investment we started with only a handful of courses that were taught by the same professor year after year. For classes in which different faculty taught the courses each year, we created a system to introduce the HLPs during each semester's welcome meetings, which we held with professors new to our program; they could use that time to reimagine syllabi as appropriate.

As part of the auditing process, we looked to see if our primary HLPs were taught in the phases of the TeachingWorks Learning Cycle which "lays out pedagogies that might be appropriate for novice teachers at different stages in the process of learning a particular practice" (Lambert, Franke, Kazemi, Ghosseini, Turrou, Beasley, Cunard & Crowe, as cited by TeachingWorks, 2019) (see figure 5.2).

Conducting this audit allowed us to do a comprehensive review of our program and to determine how to move the work forward. We discovered that our methods courses needed to be adapted and our professional development

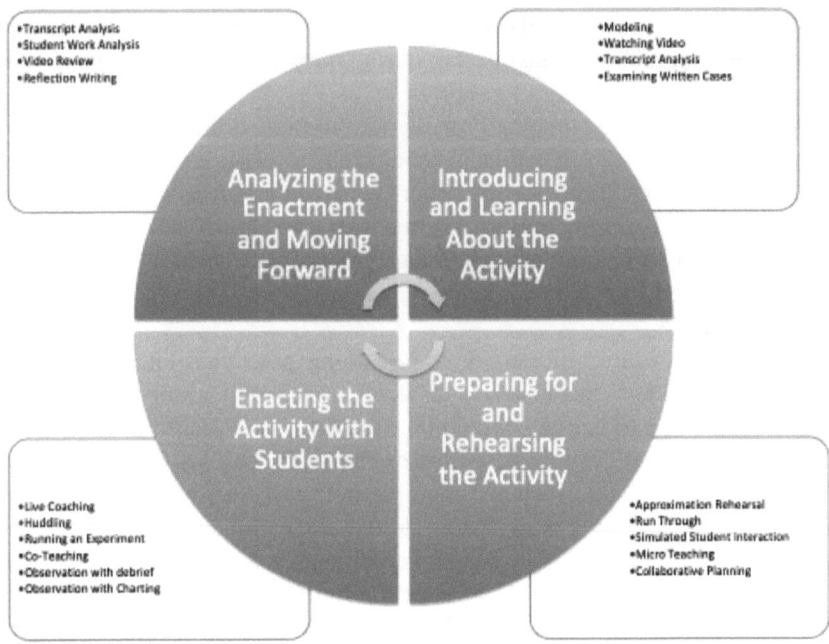

Figure 5.2   TeachingWorks EHTR and HLP Comparison.

offerings needed to be fully reimagined. Ideally, we wanted every primary practice to be taught through the cycle of learning a minimum of two times throughout the fourteen-month residency year and we wanted all instructional coaching to be grounded in the practices.

DESIGNING EVALUATION METHODS, COURSES, AND PROFESSIONAL DEVELOPMENT

Before beginning the program redesign, in order to ensure it would yield measurable results, we cross-walked the teacher effectiveness rubric we had been using, the Danielson Group Framework for Teaching Clusters, with the new HLPs (Dallas Teacher Residency personal communication 2018; Danielson Group, 2017; TeachingWorks Library, 2019). Even as we coached residents in HLPs, we wanted to evaluate them using a tool that was recognized nationally. As a part of this crosswalk, we considered what evidence we could use to evaluate resident growth in each HLP and cluster.

With the HLPs written and an evaluation tool in place, we thought were ready to reimagine resident professional development and coursework. In retrospect, the redesign might have gone more smoothly if we had created decompositions for each HLP in advance. Instead, because we did this work as we introduced each new HLP to residents, there was some lack of alignment between professors and coaches during our initial attempts to teach and coach to the HLPs.

After creating the evaluation process, we redesigned resident professional development offerings. Residents participated in whole group professional development every Friday for four hours per week and received small group and one-on-one coaching for one to three hours per week (see table 5.2).

We decided to restructure the Friday professional development time to align with the HLPs and then asked coaches and CIs to support HLP development in the field.

Working with the professor of the yearlong practicum class, who also served as an instructional coach to residents, we created a timeline for when the first full cycle of learning would take place for each HLP. We rebranded Friday professional development time as the "Resident Academy" and created a full syllabus that included multiple field tasks for each HLP. At the same time, we recreated the syllabus for the practicum course so that HLPs were being taught in a parallel way. By coordinating with the professor of the course, we ensured that the HLPs were reinforced through multiple content and classroom structures and that HLPs were revisited several times throughout the course of the year so that residents' understanding could be deepened as they advanced their teaching skills.

Table 5.2 EHTR Coaching Structure

Danielson Component Cluster Rubric Areas (THIS IS DANIELSON GROUP LANGUAGE)	EHTR High-Leverage Practices	Evidence (For use with EHTR Evaluation Tool)
Clarity of Instructional Purpose and Accuracy of Content • To what extent does the teacher demonstrate depth of important content knowledge and conduct the class with a clear and ambitious purpose, reflective of the standards for the discipline and appropriate to the students' levels of knowledge and skill? • To what degree are the elements of a lesson (the sequence of topics, instructional strategies, and materials and resources) well designed and executed, and aligned with the purpose of the lesson? To what extent are they designed to engage students in high-level learning in the discipline? • To what extent did the teacher make adaptations to the lesson? • To what extent did the teacher use formative assessment to check for student understanding?	Managing bias and racism Designing single lessons and sequences of lessons Analyzing instruction for the purpose of improving it Leading a group discussion Eliciting and interpreting individual students' thinking	Planning documents: learning outcomes/objectives, instructional activities • published ELA, math, science, and SS units • Unit planning around anti-bias standards • Family meeting plans that address race and identity • Unit plans that include race and identity • Observation/Video Submission: • Statements to students about purpose, conversation with students • Accuracy of content • Alignment of questions, activities, and assignments to purpose

(Continued)

Table 5.2 EHTR Coaching Structure (*Continued*)

Danielson Component Cluster Rubric Areas (THIS IS DANIELSON GROUP LANGUAGE)	EHTR High-Leverage Practices	Evidence (For use with EHTR Evaluation Tool)
Safe, Respectful, Supportive, and Challenging Learning Environment • To what extent do the interactions between teacher and students, and among students, demonstrate genuine caring and a safe, respectful, supportive, and also challenging learning environment? • Do teachers convey high expectations for student learning and encourage hard work and perseverance? • Is the environment safe for risk taking? • Do students take pride in their work and demonstrate a commitment to mastering challenging content?	Managing bias and racism Implementing organizational norms, routines, systems, and structures Building respectful relationships with and among students Learning about students' cultural, religious, family, intellectual, and personal experiences and considering those aspects in instruction Leading a group discussion Eliciting and interpreting individual students' thinking Analyzing instruction for the purpose of improving it	Observation/Video Submission: • Interactions of students and teacher • Student perseverance and pride • Student surveys • Unit planning around anti-bias standards • Family meeting plans that address race and identity • Unit plans that include race and identity • culture plans that include restorative justice • lesson plans on accountable talk • lesson plans on active listening • evidence of peer feedback in the classroom • class roster with proof of knowledge of students • lesson plans designed around student interest • classroom artifacts that celebrate student culture • classroom matrix • classroom culture plan

(*Continued*)

Table 5.2 EHTR Coaching Structure (Continued)

Danielson Component Cluster Rubric Areas (THIS IS DANIELSON GROUP LANGUAGE)	EHTR High-Leverage Practices	Evidence (For use with EHTR Evaluation Tool)
Classroom Management • Is the classroom well run and organized? • Are classroom routines and procedures clear and carried out efficiently by both teacher and students with little loss of instructional time? • To what extent do students themselves take an active role in their smooth operation? • Are directions for activities clearly explained so that there is no confusion? • Do students not only understand and comply with standards of conduct but also play an active part in setting the tone for maintaining those standards? • How does the physical environment support the earning activities?	Managing bias and racism Implementing organizational norms, routines, systems, and structures Designing single lessons and sequences of lessons Specifying and reinforcing productive student behavior Analyzing instruction for the purpose of improving it	Observation/Video Submission: • Routines • Student conduct • Physical environment • Unit planning around anti-bias standards • Family meeting plans that address race and identity • Unit plans that include race and identity • classroom matrix • classroom culture plan • published ELA, math, science, and SS units

(Continued)

Table 5.2 EHTR Coaching Structure (Continued)

Danielson Component Cluster Rubric Areas (THIS IS DANIELSON GROUP LANGUAGE)	EHTR High-Leverage Practices	Evidence (For use with EHTR Evaluation Tool)
Student Intellectual Engagement • To what extent are students intellectually engaged in a classroom of high intellectual energy? • What is the nature of what students are doing? • Are they being challenged to think and make connections through both the instructional activities and the questions explored? Do the teacher's explanations of content correctly model academic language and invite intellectual work by students? • Are students asked to explain their thinking, to construct logical arguments citing evidence, and to question the thinking of others? • Are the instructional strategies used by the teacher suitable to the discipline, and to what extent do they promote student agency in the learning of challenging content?	Managing bias and racism Designing single lessons and sequences of lessons Leading a group discussion Eliciting and interpreting individual students' thinking Analyzing instruction for the purpose of improving it	• Planning documents Observation/Video Submission: • The nature of the work students are doing • The quality of teacher presentation of content • The nature of student discourse and class discussion • Student worksheets or activities • Unit planning around anti-bias standards • Family meeting plans that address race and identity • Unit plans that include race and identity • Samples of student work • published ELA, math, science, and SS units

(Continued)

Table 5.2 EHTR Coaching Structure (Continued)

Danielson Component Cluster Rubric Areas (THIS IS DANIELSON GROUP LANGUAGE)	EHTR High-Leverage Practices	Evidence (For use with EHTR Evaluation Tool)
Successful Learning by All Students • To what extent does the teacher ensure learning by all students? • Does the teacher monitor student understanding through specifically designed questions or instructional techniques? • To what extent do students monitor their own learning and provide respectful feedback to classmates? • Does the teacher make modifications in presentations or learning activities where necessary, taking into account the degree of student learning? • Has he or she sought out other resources (including parents) to support students' learning? • In reflection, is the teacher aware of the success of the lesson in reaching students?	Managing bias and racism Analyzing instruction for the purpose of improving it Eliciting and interpreting individual students' thinking	• Planning documents for formative and summative assessments • Observation: monitoring, feedback, adjustment • Reflection: comments on learning of individual • Artifacts documenting both record keeping and communication with families • Unit planning around anti-bias standards • Family meeting plans that address race and identity • Unit plans that include race and identity

(Continued)

Table 5.2 EHTR Coaching Structure (Continued)

Danielson Component Cluster Rubric Areas (THIS IS DANIELSON GROUP LANGUAGE)	EHTR High-Leverage Practices	Evidence (For use with EHTR Evaluation Tool)
Professionalism • To what extent does the teacher engage with the professional community (within the school and beyond) and demonstrate a commitment to ongoing professional learning? • Does the teacher collaborate productively with colleagues and contribute to the life of the school? • Does the teacher engage in professional learning and take a leadership role in the school to promote the welfare of students?	Managing bias and racism Analyzing instruction for the purpose of improving it	• EHTR professionalism rubric/indicators • Artifacts documenting: • Contributions to professional culture • Engagement with professional learning • Participation in other professional activities

To support clinical instructors to become teacher educators, we developed a "Clinical Instructor Academy." The syllabus for this CI Academy laid out a parallel timeline for how we would train CIs to coach to the HLPs. For example, during the first cycle for the HLP of *eliciting and interpreting student thinking (EIST)*, we trained coaches and CIs how to evaluate the practice, how to offer targeted feedback, how to set measurable goals, and how to model eliciting and interpreting by using it to make sense of resident thinking in feedback sessions.

The idea of having coaches and CIs model the high-leverage practices when they engaged with residents was critical. Before we explicitly taught an HLP in the Resident Academy, we began practicing it in our work with residents. For example, months before we introduced the practice of *leading group discussion (LGD)*, we spent time in the Resident Academy having article discussions in which the EHTR staff member leading the discussion modeled the practice of LGD. When the LGD decomposition and the LGD field task were presented to residents months later, they had experience as students participating the practice. We did this for most practices. At the very beginning of the year, well before we had residents completed their first field task of conducting a "check-in conversation," a part of the HLP *building respectful relationships with and among students*, EHTR staff conducted these types of conversations with residents. When we later made the practice explicit, residents had experiences to call upon when decomposing the components of a successful "check-in conversation" and were able to use those experiences during their rehearsal and eventual field task of the practice. The idea of having coaches intentionally model each HLP, which we believe is critical and has not been a focus of traditional teacher preparation, is one we are still developing. Ideally, CIs and professors will become so versed in the HLPs that the modeling will become intentional across all courses and all coaching conversations.

We also changed the way we acclimated new professors to the program. During our initial orientations with professors, we shared our high-leverage practices and told professors which HLPs the residents would be studying in the Resident Academy during the time they were enrolled in the professors' courses. As a result, methods professors have been able to adapt their syllabi to align with the HLPs. We are still working with content professors to determine the best way to align and ensure HLPs are represented. We also restructured the final graduate course that served as a culminating experience for the residents. In this course, residents create a capstone assignment in which they reflect on their growth in one HLP and the effect their growth had on student learning. Through a year of careful planning and implementation, we were able to adapt our program to offer much more targeted and mission-aligned teacher training that is more easily assessed.

CONSIDERING NEXT STEPS

We are still early in our process of implementing the HLPs. Many courses need to be more intentionally aligned with HLPs; we need to continue to ensure that it is clear to residents how receiving coaching in the HLPs will help them make progress in the evaluation rubric; we need to find ways to regularly review our HLPs to make sure they are the right practices to focus on; we need to ensure that CIs are modeling their HLPs in their own classrooms; and we need to create tools to assess if graduating residents can clearly define what anti-racist teaching practices look like.

Coaching around the HLPs can also be improved. For the Resident Academy, we are still thinking about how to balance being responsive to residents' needs as they come up while also implementing the preplanned HLP training. In the field, clinical instructors and coaches struggle to narrow their HLP feedback into achievable small goals that lead to greater resident mastery of the HLPs. Residents struggle to manage all of the feedback they receive around a given HLP. To avoid confusion, we are piloting a coaching tool that will help coaches and residents create and track specific HLP goals. The idea is that residents and coaches will input all of their feedback into one central location and set small, weekly goals, grounded in the feedback and focusing on one or two HLPs at a time. In the tool, each HLP is broken down into small, actionable teacher moves. For example, the practice of *leading group discussion* is comprised of seventeen teacher moves, including, "resident probes on student thinking by asking for connections, use evidence, or by connecting shared ideas" and "resident echos/amplifies student voice without stealing student agency by rephrasing." For whichever move the coach decides to support the resident on, she uses the tool to set a specific, measurable goal. The tools also guides the coach to think through the strengths the resident has that the coach will leverage as she coaches the new goal, the way in which the resident will demonstrate mastery of the goal, and the type of coaching the coach will provide to support resident growth. Residents can then track their progress toward HLP mastery.

As we continue to grow and develop our infrastructure, with HLPs and the Cycle of Learning central in the work, we will concentrate on making practice explicit, always maintaining a clear focus on developing anti-racist educators. We hope that our reimagining of traditional teacher training will graduate teachers who affect educational outcomes in East Harlem and promote an equitable society in which students succeed and challenge the world in and beyond their classrooms. We also hope that as EHTR discovers and implements successful techniques, we can become a model of change in the teacher training landscape.

BIBLIOGRAPHY

Caballero, M. Personal communication. 2017.

Danielson, Charlotte. "The Framework for Teacher Clusters." *The Framework: The Danielson Group.* https://www.danielsongroup.org/framework/.

Hough, Heather H., Susanna Loeb, and David Plank. "The Quality Teacher and Education Act: Second Year Report." *Annenberg Institute for Educational Reform.* http://www.annenberginstitute.org/publications/quality-teacher-and-education-act-second-year-report.

Lhamon, Catherine E. "Civil Rights Data Collection: Data Snapshot: School Discipline, Issue Brief No. 1." *U.S. Department of Education Office for Civil Rights*, March 2014. https://ocrdata.ed.gov/downloads/crdc-school-discipline-snapshot.pdf.

New York State Education Department. "English Language Arts and Math Exams for New York City." *Educational Design and Technology.* http://www.nysed.gov/edtech/3-8-english-language-arts-and-mathematics-tests.

Regents of the University of Michigan. "Our Perspective: Teacher Education." *TeachingWorks Resource Library.* https://library.teachingworks.org/our-perspective/on-teacher-education/.

Roy, Joydeep. "Demographics and Work Experience: A Statistical Portrait of New York City's Public School Teachers." *New York City Independent Budget Office*, 2014. https://ibo.nyc.ny.us/iboreports/2014teacherdemographics.pdf.

University of Michigan. "TeachingWorks: High Leverage Practices." *University of Michigan School of Education.* http://www.teachingworks.org/work-of-teaching/high-leverage-practices.

University of Washington. "Teacher Education by Design." *College of Education: University of Washington.* http://inspire.washington.edu/index.php/activities/teacher-education-by-design-tedd-org/.

Chapter 6

Alignment of Coursework to the Clinical Experience Bridging Theory and Practice

Brandon Ware, Holly Gonzales, and Harry Ervin

Teacher Preparation programs across the nation are pondering and searching for ways to improve programmatic structures that produce highly qualified teacher candidates. Understanding the various components and nuances of this tangled web requires grit, determination, and potential failure to break free from centuries of inadequate preparation. Thus, a lack of reform to misaligned teacher preparation is a threat to society. Educational systems have produced theoretically skilled individuals who lack practicum to facilitate daily teacher practice. Along the continuum, teacher candidates must navigate the unique correlation of theory and practice to understand the importance of becoming an effective educator.

Inhale slowly, take a moment, and reflect on the following questions:

- How is theory integrated into practice within your program's structure?
- Does your organization struggle to align university coursework to the clinical practice experience?
- How well is communication established?
- Is your feedback systemized?

After you have considered the questions above, note that they all center around one question:

How important is the teacher candidate clinical experience?

Context is important when discussing how to create systems and structures within an organization. It is the context that defines specific organization's need, as well as the desired outcomes. Provided below is a concrete example of the Kern Teacher Residency Program, along with contextual references that can be replicated to begin such processes within your teacher preparation program.

A RESIDENCY MODEL: THE KERN URBAN TEACHER RESIDENCY

Approximately 140 miles north of the greater Los Angeles area is Kern County, the "Country Music Capital of the West Coast." Bakersfield, California, is located in the Central Valley and is home to the Kern Urban Teacher Residency. The Kern Urban Teacher Residency (KUTR) is a partnership between California State University, Bakersfield (CSU Bakersfield) and the Bakersfield City School District (BCSD). Like pioneers during the westward expansion in the 1840s and 1850s paved the way for an unseen landscape of today's world, as we are striving to do the same for educators within our community. The KUTR program was established in 2016, fostered on a long-standing relationship between the university and the largest local school district. The core leadership team, which will be elaborated upon later in the chapter, created a shared mission and vision to guide all programmatic actions. In the words attributed to Jonathan Swift, "Vision is the art of seeing what is invisible to others." The KUTR partners thoughtfully composed a mission and vision statement with the goal of establishing a transformational teacher preparation program.

The Kern Urban Teacher Residency Mission:

> The Kern Urban Teacher Residency is dedicated to excellence in preparing educators with distinguished pedagogical skills, cultural competency, and connection to community for the Bakersfield City School District. The Kern Urban Teacher Residency will actively recruit talented and passionate future educators, provide systematic support, and foster a sustainable partnership between CSU Bakersfield and the Bakersfield City School District.

The Kern Urban Teacher Residency Vision:

> The Kern Urban Teacher Residency will be a model program for teacher preparation, committed to ensuring that students in the Bakersfield City School District will be provided with the highest quality educational experience and become successful and productive leaders that will impact positive change. (http://www.kernurbanteacherresidency.org)

The Strength of an Effective Partnership

What is a partnership? A partnership is a formal agreement between parties agreeing to manage and operate the daily workings of a given project. The Bakersfield City School District and CSU Bakersfield have a well-established partnership that has continued to flourish for nearly two decades and one in which partners support one another in preparing and hiring qualified teachers to serve students throughout Kern County. As a natural stepping-stone, while facing a teacher shortage, each partner recognized the opportunity to streamline systems of support. As a result, creative minds prevailed and established the KUTR program. The KUTR is a unique relationship that extends beyond a mutual agreement of parties. The foundation of the residency is built upon a collaborative model that is jointly guided and maintained by both organizations.

Due to the generosity of the S. D. Bechtel, Jr. Foundation, the residency program received $900,000 over a three-year period to jump-start the program. From the outset, the leadership from both organizations committed to create and provide a sustainable teacher residency model. This commitment evolved over the course of three years, working toward executing the program's mission and vision. In short, these partners collaborated to create a pipeline of educators highly prepared to meet the diverse needs of Bakersfield City School District. This commitment required breaking down long-existing statues of operations that had limited progress toward reinventing the way teachers are prepared. This systems change was paramount in the shift from a partnership to a relationship with vested individuals that promoted autonomy and creativity with all employees. This creativity was driven by working to establish new norms of operation for the partnership in regard to residency teacher preparation and the roles in which each organization would serve. For example, some of these new operating procedures included shifting the start date of clinical experience to begin prior to the start of BCSD's academic school year, revamping mentor training, and revising the structured phase-in process designed to support and prepare highly qualified candidates (see figure 6.1).

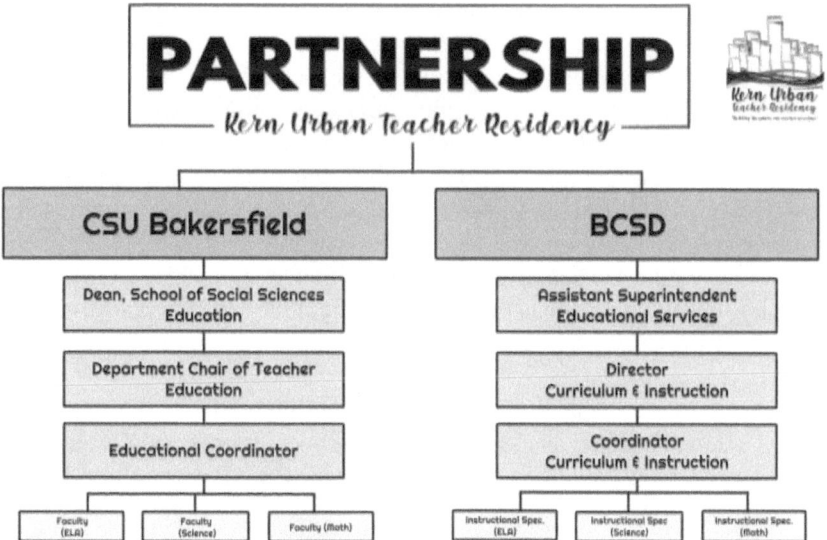

Figure 6.1 Organizational Chart for the KUTR Partnership.

In traditional student teaching structures, an Institute of Higher Education (IHE) provides a field supervisor assigned to a group of individuals to monitor the student teaching experience. The university and field supervisor would coordinate most decisions in regard to feedback, observation structure, and mentor development (if any). In contrast, the KUTR model includes a university program coordinator specifically dedicated to the co-facilitation of the residency alongside the local education agency (LEA) program coordinator.

With a dedication to paired personnel agreement, Bakersfield City School District restructured their curriculum and instruction department by placing the importance on hiring an LEA administrator to coordinate all programmatic decisions in conjunction with CSU Bakersfield. The joint coordination includes but is not limited to the following: observation and feedback procedures, mentor development, gradual release of responsibility of resident and mentor duties, state-mandated examination and certifications, and methods course alignment and scheduling. Also, the coordinators communicate and represent the residency as needed throughout their individual organizations.

Thus, autonomy and most importantly trust has been established to create systemic structures that aim to produce an ideal environment for teacher development. KUTR has adopted and provided the same structure throughout all factions of the program. The core leadership team of KUTR ensures that coordinators, mentors, residents, faculty, instructional specialists, and all parties involved are encouraged to be creative decision makers.

Let's narrow in on the bottom portion of the partnership chart. These individuals (faculty and instructional specialists) are directly involved with the content and pedagogical development of the residents, in tandem with the core leadership team. Each faculty member from the IHE is paired with an instructional specialist to co-teach the methods courses in order to align university and district initiatives. This is the foundation of creating a pipeline of well-prepared educators. In determining what it would take to co-teach a methods course, we ultimately landed on providing time and space for the team to develop a curricular model that is flexible, equitable, and rigorous enough to meet the demands of the partnership. Our methods courses define the essence of the program in totality, a creative partnership to shift the landscape of teacher preparation.

This type of partnership platform has begun to blossom around the country and even in our own backyard. Due to the local success of KUTR, local education agencies have recently partnered with CSU Bakersfield to launch two additional residencies.

FAILING FORWARD

Threats to an organization, partnership, individual, or situation can be perceived as a failure or unfortunate. We view threats as merely attention-getters than can result in failure if they are not turned into opportunities for growth. Take the commonly known creature of an octopus or cephalopod. The ocean-dwelling invertebrate develops in four critical stages: egg, larvae, adolescent, and adult. What is fascinating about this creature is the ability to adapt to perceived threats, analyze the situation, context, and surroundings to result in a desired outcome of successfully capturing prey or avoiding a predator. This provides a vivid analogy of the work ahead when adapting to potential threats and failures that surround teacher residency preparation (see figure 6.2).

The chart illustrates the cephalopod approach over the last three years of the KUTR. The importance of adaptation was paramount to fit the contextual framework to shift teacher preparation along with facilitating a sustainable partnership. Take a look at the 2016–2017 structural components, which were swiftly changed within four months into the program.

The design was to meet the needs of an original concept created by the initial grant proposal team prior to the launch of the program. For instance, one facet was the substitute teaching structure that was put into place. Due to the large number of classroom teacher absences on Mondays and Fridays,

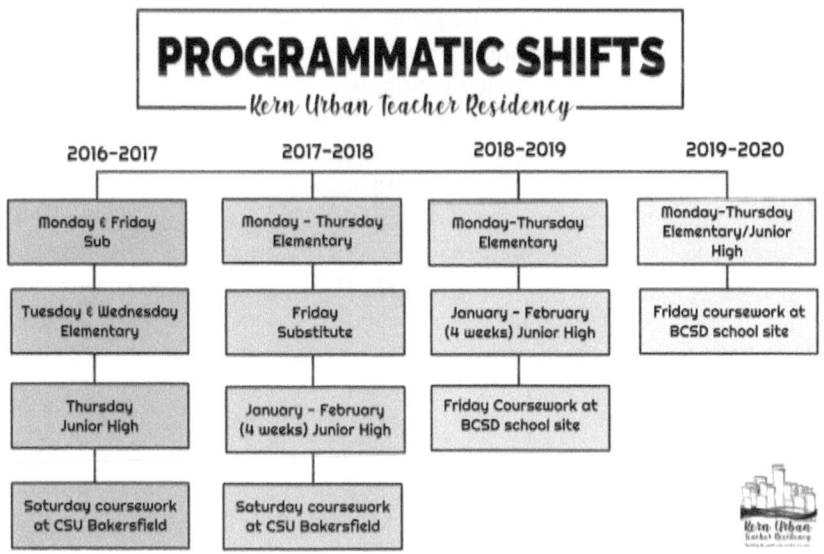

Figure 6.2 KUTR Programmatic Shifts over Time.

the idea of having residents substitute teacher on those days would alleviate the tension experienced by the district. Substitute teaching also provided residents an opportunity to offset financial hardships often experienced while earning their teaching credentials. On Tuesdays and Thursdays residents were in an elementary schools, and they spent Wednesdays within a middle school placement, followed by coursework on Saturdays. The derived notion was to produce a variety of clinical experiences for the residents and reduce the necessity of residents having to attend night classes throughout the course of the residency year. Also, the well-known teacher shortage in the areas of math and science was influential in having the residents select one of these two areas of focus to help solve the shortage of teachers in these areas. The organization and partnership allowed for structural changes illustrated above to occur smoothly and swiftly, with an input from all parties including mentors, residents, and students. As a result of the feedback from these groups, we have evolved to the Monday/Friday substitute teaching structure remaining the same, moving residents to their elementary clinical placements on Tuesdays and Wednesdays, and junior high school clinical experience on Thursdays. The "egg" stage of KUTR has officially commenced. Did we fail or progress?

Larvae may be the best comparative analysis of the year two implementation stage, in which we learned to become agile, develop a strength-based model, navigate the environment of a residency along with refinement of processes similar to an ability the octopus possess. Throughout the year, collaborating at partnership meetings and gathering countless forms of data helped us quickly realize the opportunity to restructure the clinical experience for the residents. After all, they were the reason for our partnership. This is a common threat facing many organizations in the world of teacher preparation: the ability to recognize a broken system and restructure to meet the diverse needs through a shared collaborative. Would we become the predator or the prey?

An overhaul heading into the 2017–2018 calendar year was needed. The residents and their clinical preparation experience drive the work of the program. Based on trends gathered during data analysis, mentors wanted more time with their residents to hone their content and pedagogical development. Quite honestly, many wanted a "do over." As many educators have voiced, they would enjoy with their first year of being a teacher of record. In short, what more can a partnership of teacher preparation ask of their mentors?

In year two of the residency, we obliged, removing the Monday substitute day and adding an $800 monthly living stipend to each resident, and a $300 a monthly stipend provided to the mentor teacher. This allowed for more ask of mentor and resident teacher for the increase in time spent moving forward. Keeping the substitute day on Fridays and coursework on Saturdays worked threefolds: allowing the residents to gain experience in other clinical settings, earning money to offset credentialing, and no coursework during the weekdays. One last shift in the structure was to provide the residents with an opportunity to earn or add a California single subject teaching authorization to their preliminary credential in the content of their choice. A California single subject teaching credential authorization can consist of up to four state exams, depending on the content area, and one additional course, which allowed residents to simultaneously earn a multiple (elementary) and single subject (secondary) teaching credential. Thus, the institution of the four-week middle school placement increased the rigor of the program for those who were willing to go the extra mile. There are many nuances that were enacted over the course of the restructuring stage of year two. We began to develop in a systemic way with an informed decision-making process, not only as partners but also as mentors and residents.

In 2018-2019, "The Adolescence Stage" involved progressing and establishing strong structures to challenge the conventional thinking in teacher preparation. Implementing change was a cyclical study process over the course of two years that was enacted by the residency and the push for continuous improvement as a whole. The Plan-Do-Study-Act (PDSA) cycle was the catalyst to establishing a systemized approach to reform. The PDSA developed by W. Edwards Deming explained,

> The Plan-Do-Study-Act (PDSA) cycle is part of the Institute for Healthcare Improvement Model for Improvement, a simple yet powerful tool for accelerating quality improvement. Once a team has set an aim, established its membership, and developed measures to determine whether a change leads to an improvement, the next step is to test a change in the real work setting. The PDSA cycle is shorthand for testing a change—by planning it, trying it, observing the results, and acting on what is learned. This is the scientific method, used for action-oriented learning. (2010, p. 21)

The steps to the cycle are:

- Step 1: Plan—Plan the test or observation, including a plan for collecting data,
- Step 2: Do—Try out the test on a small scale,
- Step 3: Study—Set aside time to analyze the data and study the results, and
- Step 4: Act—Refine the change, based on what was learned from the test.

The major finding of the PDSA throughout the 2017-2018 residency year was the ability to create a structure that benefited the growth of the residents within their method courses. This resulted in a major action to be taken by the partnership. The result was modification of the coursework day and structure. Coursework was moved from Saturdays at CSU Bakersfield to Fridays at a

BCSD school site, alleviating long drives for residents to the college campus and the purchase of parking passes, while immersing the residents in a school setting. Ultimately, we realized that it was more beneficial to support the emotional well-being of the staff, residents, and coordinators than to have the residents substitute teach on Fridays and attend method courses on Saturdays. We came to understand that up to six days of working, going to school and maintaining all other factors for a year-long residency was not sustainable. The 2018–2019 PDSA cycle results yielded two structural implications that will be addressed moving into the 2019–2020 school year: the phaseout of the middle school placement, and single subject authorization. Our data shows that less than 10 percent of residents who chose to earn a single subject authorization went on to complete the requirements to earn a primary credential. The residency was awarded a single subject expansion grant to create two tracks and will pursue candidates who have a passion for math, science, and bilingual education.

Mentor development is vital to the sustainability of trailblazing the teacher preparation pathway. Excitingly, the pursuit of developing mentors is a journey that will produce day one classroom teachers who are ready for the workforce. The PDSA cycle will guide structural modifications as well as lead the continuous improvement cycle. Into the "adult stage" of development.

ANALYZING PROGRAMMATIC GAPS

Practice makes perfect—or so they say. What if the practice is done incorrectly? Consider the homework sent home with students each day. Will the students' learning increase if the content or skill was not learned correctly or completely? Assuming your answer is "no," we are on the same page.

Let's shift gears and think about the learning trajectory and practice a teacher candidate goes through while in a teacher preparation program. Aligning a teacher candidate's clinical practice and learned theory through coursework is a delicate balancing act. In order for learning and progress to occur for the candidate, the preparation program must prioritize a distinct and well-planned alignment of content and skills to be learned, and when and how they are practiced, monitored, and assessed. In order to gauge where a program is in regard to alignment of theory and practice, carrying out a gap analysis is vital. The gap analysis should include gathering of a wide scope of general information pertaining to the teacher preparation program theory, or coursework, and the clinical practice experience.

As a starting point for the gap analysis, our team determined where the residents fell on the continuum of skills the program had adopted (a set of core practices established). At this point in the process, we did not! Therefore, we began to consider what content and skills the program deems a priority or requirement for candidates while in residency and when exiting the program. While brainstorming and compiling this list, we looked closely at each theory or methods course throughout the program. Also, we examined our program's standards for teachers, candidate dispositions, and the assessment tools used to monitor a candidate's progress. We conducted a course-by-course crosswalk of what overarching concepts or skills are taught and whether they are introduced, practiced, or mastered.

The core leadership team met frequently to determine and commit to maintaining an agreed-upon set of prioritized skills for our program. These prioritized skills live at the heart of the KUTR learning experience, whether it be in coursework or in the clinical practice classroom. Resident teachers need this clear list of goals and expectations as they navigate the choppy waters of teacher preparation.

This programmatic specific list of prioritized skills is the perfect segue into the next key detail in this gap analysis process, the phase-in schedule or gradual release of the teacher candidate. With the list of prioritized skills, we determined when the candidate will learn theory, content, or skills in coursework. With this information, we created a backward mapping or timeline of when a candidate should be released to practice the skills in the clinical experience setting. This scope and sequencing tool is the perfect resource to anchor the teacher candidates' and mentor teachers' professional development. This document serves as a guide that provides a clear outline of when skills should be introduced, practiced, and mastered in coursework and clinical practice.

A RECAP

Let us review what we have gathered thus far: the program's course-by-course crosswalk of concepts, the list of program-specific prioritized skills, and the phase-in schedule. With this information gathered, the time has come! Yes, it is time to analyze the gaps! (Warning: All programs have gaps—even the awesome ones.) The analysis process will consist of a comparison of what prioritized skills are addressed at what point in the program's coursework and clinical practice, and whether or not there is alignment.

After completing the analysis described above, we established the short- and long-term goals the program will commit to and pursue. When making next steps, goals, or decisions, we brought as many "players" to the table as possible. The gathering of the course instructors, a mentor and resident panel, district stakeholders, and other program staff allowed us to make a plan with measurable goals and "due dates" that will encourage accountability.

With the next steps in place, the team revised coursework program plans and syllabi to reflect accurate or more program-appropriate pacing of theory taught in coursework and skill. We adjusted the phase-in schedule, revamped professional development program, and repaired misconceptions. Bottom line—we communicated like crazy! We also continued to ensure that all programmatic shareholders were aware of and understood the prioritized skills and phase-in process and how they anchored the desired trajectory of teacher candidate learning. We must all realize that a teacher candidate's progress and learning are directly correlated with the program's alignment of theory taught in coursework and clinical practice—or sadly, lack thereof.

Conducting this audit of programmatic structures was a vital component of our success. We are not talking about success as in the outside perception of the program, but rather the success of the teacher candidates in the program. We not only want to "get them through" the teacher preparation program, we want to create agents of change who will successfully remain in the profession because they want to serve children and positively shape minds. Let us all charge ourselves with fostering this kind of teacher preparation program because the students in our communities deserve it.

THE VALUE OF CLARITY: ROLES AND RESPONSIBILITIES

The manager calls a timeout. It's the bottom on the ninth, two outs, and the star player walks the plate in the biggest game of their life. The preparation and coaching before this moment can either make or break the entire season. Professional athletes spend countless hours perfecting their craft. This metaphor is parallel to the KUTR approach taken in the preparation of resident and mentor teachers.

We begin with clarifying the roles and responsibilities of the individuals leading the organization. Understanding who does what, and when they are expected to do it, can be a game changer! If a clear set of roles and responsibilities are not defined for each player "in the game" of teacher preparation, there is a strong likelihood that programmatic structures will begin to break down. Tensions from lack of clarity will arise and the culture of the organization could potentially take a serious hit.

The Leadership Team

So let us consider who is on the residency team. The leadership team for the program plays a key role in the success of programmatic outcomes and must serve to provide consistent structural support. They set the tone for the program and ensure that the program is not only running smoothly, but effectively. Each leadership team member must realize their role in the program and understand what responsibilities and integrity they must uphold. A leadership team that is dedicated to the development and success of the resident teachers will results in PK-12 students receiving the quality education they deserve. This team should consist of members from both sides of the partnership, inclusive of coordinators, faculty, and the top-tiered management in the organizations.

The Mentors

As KUTR has progressed through several years of recruitment and cohort structural changes, there has been ongoing learning. Although the goal is to reach and recruit a wide, equitable pool of mentors and residents, the program has to hold fast to the ethical and professional expectations surrounding the program.

As the players assume their roles and responsibilities, there has to be a clear game plan. The game plan will consist of strategic moves and well-thought-out timing. In a teacher residency program, this consists of the clear alignment between theory and practice—or coursework and clinical practice. The resident and mentor co-teaching pairs must have access and training around the gradual release of responsibility process and expectations that are set forth for the learning trajectory.

From our program experience, if a resident is observed or evaluated on a skill that has yet to be introduced and practiced in coursework, the outcome often times tends to be less than proficient. It is important to create a dual system approach to coursework, one that introduces theory and provides opportunities for practice, specifically focusing on the microteaching method. Once these opportunities have been afforded, the resident can begin to transfer the learning and practice of skills into the classroom. An initial mentor and resident pairs training, as well as ongoing monthly training with individual coaching the pairs helps to facilitate the transition from coursework to clinical practice. Therefore, mentors receive professional development of how to model and incorporate skills and strategies pertaining to the gradual release of their classroom. This pattern of learning and practice should continually flow throughout the residency experience, similar to the PDSA cycle previously mentioned.

A residency program must also consider the fact that mentors are not all created equally. Consider this as a blessing, not a curse. Having a team of diverse mentor teachers can be a great gift! Consider ways to build capacity in the mentor teachers, leverage the skills of each, and create opportunities for collaborative learning.

Monthly Professional Development

How often do you attend a meeting or training that seems like a broken record—the kind with little to no new learning and unclear expectations? The proverbial head nod is most likely occurring at this moment. This kind of thing can easily happen when an organization does not prioritize the value of time and clarity. Bringing clarity solidifies consistency along with autonomy and the ability to trust that each faction of the partnership is operating at the optimal performance level.

A mentor teacher is one of the resident's greatest and most prominent educators. The amount of time the mentor and resident spend together is significant, making the need for clarity around which practices to leverage during what time, that much more important. Professional development is intentionally scheduled throughout the year. The process begins with a two-day "Pairs Training," where the resident and mentor are trained in co-teaching strategies, programmatic structures, and expectations. Once the school year begins, the residents and mentor teachers attend monthly meetings in which they receive training and support surrounding prioritized skills, the phase-in process, and dissemination of programmatic data on a cyclical basis. The monthly meetings are co-facilitated by the district and university coordinators in an effort to maintain consistent communication and a shared vision.

Progress Monitoring

With the strategic implementation of the program's Phase-In Schedule and scaffolded prioritized skills, there is a clear learning trajectory set forth for the resident teacher. The skills along this continuum are gradually released in the clinical classroom so that the resident's learning progress can be analyzed along a concise continuum.

We place a high priority on the data collected regarding resident learning, as this set of data serves as the pulse or temperature check for the alignment of coursework and clinical practice throughout the program. When data reflects a need, the resident and mentor monthly meetings must integrate strategies to address the data trends.

In an effort to effectively collect data, it is vital that a residency program commits to a rubric for observing and providing support to master teaching practices that align with the program's prioritized skill. Mentor and resident teachers should be provided with clear, professional expectations and development around each component of the rubric.

To strengthen calibration and feedback, any observer or evaluator of the resident's progress must have a strong understanding of the "look-fors" and "listen-fors" that correlate with the adopted evaluative rubric. These other evaluators may consist of any individuals represented in the partnership. In turn, this creates a clear and consistent feedback structure to support the residents on their individualized learning sequence.

In order to gather valuable, accurate data, all evaluators must be calibrated. Creating consistent opportunities for evaluators to practice scoring and providing feedback on teaching using scenarios or video samples formulates the process. This process and understanding is also valuable for the resident teacher, so they have a clear set of expectations for their planning, teaching practices, as well as a set of resources for self-evaluation, reflection, and goal setting.

You may ask yourself, is there such a thing as too much feedback? In our program, we do not think so, however, we do believe that ineffective, biased, or inaccurate feedback is dangerous. When you think about feedback to the resident, consider quality and frequency. The scoring and feedback that a resident receives from the mentor teacher or other evaluators is the cornerstone of the learning trajectory. Maintaining these expectations will support the alignment between the clinical and coursework experience.

Depending on the accuracy, consistency, and use of language, feedback can either progress the resident's learning, or impede it. Evaluations and feedback on a resident's practice should be fact-based and free from biases or opinions. Feedback should include accurate scoring and most importantly, evidence to support the criteria selected. Observation frequency is important when discussing accurate feedback. When the frequency of feedback is inconsistent, data has proven that mentor and resident relationships break down. Consistent, accurate feedback allows for open, ongoing conversations around progress monitoring and growth. Setting observation protocols and an occurrence schedule may support the facilitation of analyzing data and goal setting between mentor and resident.

WRAPPING THINGS UP

After glancing into the programmatic structures surrounding the KUTR, please reflect on the central question, *"How important is the teacher candidate clinical experience?"* When answering this poignant question, consider the implementation process for your individual context.

Unique contexts create the importance of establishing a partnership with a clearly defined mission and vision that drive the work of the program. This consists of more than taking time, wordsmithing, and slapping the program's mission and vision on everything that represents the program. Ensuring that the mission and vision steer all decision-making processes for programmatic improvements is a delicate balancing act in which the partnership must commit. Maintaining the essence of the program is the responsibility of all stakeholders working toward implementation of the change. Caution—the work will be immense but focus on the foundation of strong relationships and clear communication. Continually revisit and define the overall committal by the partnership's organizations, while outlining the roles and responsibilities often.

Keep in mind, there were instances when KUTR worked in a state of building the plane and flying it at the same time. Although this strategy is not ideal, maintaining a growth mindset and continuously being dedicated to improvement will keep the plane in motion, even while reconstruction takes place. Structural components and placing importance on operational design of the program is just as important as the relationship of the partnership. Invite others into the collaborative processes and always value their time. Natural shifting of positions along with protocols and procedures will occur. Just make sure that the shifts are pivots and not hard left or right turns. This may create unwanted or unforeseen stressors throughout the organization.

Tips from the KUTR Team

As evolution of the KUTR continues to progress, sharing best practices across organizations is a key contributor to our programmatic structure. Therefore, we continue to pay it forward with the following tips, gathered throughout our growth process:

- Maintain consistent and transparent communication between partners.
- Ensure that the program provides a gradual release of responsibility that has a clear learning trajectory of when skills are introduced, practiced, and mastered.
- Provide ongoing professional development for the mentor teacher, supporting them in accessing effective strategies that align with the program's prioritized skills, as well as in coaching techniques.
- Analyze data often in order to continuously improve programmatic structures.
- Define roles and responsibilities.
- Stay open to suggestions from all stakeholders.
- Remember the importance of the work and for whom we are doing it.

Above all, continually reflect, remain flexible, and remember, celebrate often.

BIBLIOGRAPHY

"ACT Academy, Quality, Service Improvement and Redesign Tools: Plan, Do, Study, Act (PDSA) cycles and the model for improvement." *NHS Improvement online.* Accessed January 14, 2019. https://improvement.nhs.uk/documents/2142/plan-do-study-act.pdf.

Kern Urban Teacher Residency. http://www.kernurbanteacherresidency.org/.

Moen, D. Ronald & Clifford L. Norman. "Circling Back: Clearing up myths about the Deming cycle and seeing how it keeps evolving." *Quality Progress*, November 2010.

Swift, Johnathan. (2008). *Thoughts on Various Subjects.* Adelaide: The University of Adelaide Library.

Chapter 7

An Examination of the Teaching and Learning Structures at the Dudley Street Neighborhood Charter School

Lilly Siu, Marcie Osinsky, and Lynne Godfrey

INTRODUCTION

It's 8:15 a.m. on a rainy Friday morning at the Dudley Street Neighborhood School (DSNCS) in Roxbury, Massachusetts. Inside, children's voices begin to fill the stairwells. In the learning lab, a second grade teacher and her resident have been meeting the past hour to read through drafts of student stories and talk through the writing lesson for the day. The teacher, a graduate of the Boston Teacher Residency (BTR), has been mentoring the resident throughout the year, and the resident is now taking the lead on the writing unit on *how-to* stories. In looking at the students' *how-to* stories, they are having a laugh about the last page of Nyisha's story, "How to Feed a Baby," in which she has written, "Insert spoon in baby's mouth and repeat until baby is full." The teacher and resident are particularly delighted to witness Nyisha's pride in her hard-earned, newly gained knowledge as a big sister and as a writer of her own experiences.

This small mentoring moment illustrates the daily work at BTR and the shared investment and ownership of student engagement, learning, and growth. BTR instilled in the graduate a deep commitment to her professional growth, ongoing collaboration with colleagues, and the development and well-being of her students. As a BTR graduate, she knows that learning to teach and teaching to learn are ongoing endeavors, and she models that learning stance with her resident as they collaborate on writing lessons for their students.

We, the staff at BTR, also engage in continual learning. We began preparing teachers for the Boston Public Schools (BPS) by asking, "How do we prepare excellent teachers for the Boston Public Schools?" Over the past sixteen years, we have articulated our definition of excellence, identified our teacher education practices, developed core program structures for adult learning across coursework and field work, and increased the impact that teacher preparation can have on the learning and engagement of students in the classrooms of Boston.

Currently, our elementary residency program operates within the Dudley Street Neighborhood Charter School (DSNCS). DSNCS is one of two teaching academies within the BPS system run by Boston Plan for Excellence (BPE), a nonprofit organization. At DSNCS, we aim to bring ambitious instruction to K-5 students and rigorous preparation to novice teachers. Our teaching academy immerses residents, who are aspiring teachers, into the daily work of teaching through BTR. At DSNCS, teams of individuals with differing expertise and experience levels—classroom teachers, special populations teachers, residents, and instructional coaches—work collaboratively to plan and implement instruction to address the range of learning needs of all students. In the teaching teams, we use a common set of data-driven practices to work effectively and coherently toward stated teaching and learning goals.

Teaching is complex work. While we do not simplify teaching, we illuminate the complexity of the work and make transparent the judgments, decision-making, and knowledge building embedded in the teaching practice. As we investigate our practice as educators, and the impact of our practices on student learning, we make our judgments and reasoning public so that all constituents—teachers, coaches, residents, and administrators—can learn and grow together. As learners, we respect the learning process and the cognitive struggle required for deep understanding of new material.

FEATURES OF A TEACHING ACADEMY

At the heart of our work in the teaching academy is the belief that all students are sense-makers. We also believe in the intellectual lives of teachers, who need to develop their knowledge of content, students, and pedagogy by engaging in and examining the work of teaching together. Planning and preparation, rehearsing and anticipating student engagement, enacting lessons, reflecting on lessons, and analyzing the learning data from the lessons to inform ongoing teaching are all key aspects of good teaching. The following aspects of our teaching academy foster these concepts, as noted in the Boston Plan for Excellence (n.d.):

- There is a coherent system of ambitious instruction that consistently engages all students in rigorous content.

- Teachers, coaches, and administrators use data to improve instruction and intervention.
- Staffing structures are flexible and student grouping ensures that students are matched with the instruction that is needed for their learning.
- Residents serve as part of a team of adults who take collective responsibility for student outcomes.
- Instruction is managed by a team of educators rather than a sole classroom teacher.
- Educators nurture constructive partnerships with families and communities.

We are guided by the common set of principles of instruction and instructional goals for resident and teacher learning, articulated below.

Principles of Instruction

1. The measure of good teaching is student learning.
2. Teachers know students as individuals and as learners.
3. Teachers treat all students as sense-makers.
4. Teachers must design instruction for all students to do complex thinking and work.
5. High cognitive demand teaching requires knowledge of content and understanding of how students interact with that content, knowledge of how students learn, and setting clear instructional goals.

Instructional Goals

1. Teach lessons with high cognitive demand (Van de Walle, Karp & Bay-Williams, 2012) that maintain a consistent focus on student reasoning and enable students to understand big ideas in academic content areas.
2. Assess students' understanding every day with ambitious learning goals in mind to inform instructional decisions and plan lessons and units of instruction.
3. Build a productive learning community where every student matters and participates.
4. Develop professional and collaborative relationships with colleagues and families in service of student engagement and learning.
    (Dudley Street Neighborhood Charter School, n.d.)

In this chapter, we will explore the history and evolution of our residency program and the transition to the teaching academy model. We will describe and illustrate the structures we have implemented in the teaching academies and reflect on how adult learning can have positive impact on student learning. These structures include Professional Development (PD), Common Planning Times (CPT), child study, Strategic Planning for Academic Achievement (SPA) days, coaching, resident coursework, and resident and collaborating teacher (CT) dialogue. Finally, we show the evolution of our own questions over the most recent years as we continue to develop as a community of educators who problem solve and aim to develop an expertise for teaching and learning.

EVOLUTION OF THE PROGRAM

According to Linda Darling-Hammond (1997),

> Bureaucratic solutions to problems of practice always fail because effective teaching is not routine, students are not passive, and questions of practice are not simple, predictable or standardized. Consequently, instructional decisions cannot be formulated on high, then packaged and handed down to teachers. (67)

The BPE began partnering with BPS in 1984 to develop and support initiatives to ensure access to high-quality instruction for all students. In 2003, the Boston Teacher Residency was launched in partnership with BPS. Although BTR was designed to operate completely within the BPS system, the program was firmly under the umbrella of BPE and its executive director, Ellen Guiney. A young entrepreneurial mathematics teacher, Jesse Solomon, was recruited to collaborate with Ellen and then superintendent, Thomas Payzant, to create a teacher preparation program that would work closely with BPS to develop and retain qualified teachers for high-needs areas in the BPS. BTR made a commitment to prepare a diverse group of residents for hard-to-fill positions including science, math, and special education. The program was guided by the question: *What does it take to recruit, prepare, and retain excellent teachers for the Boston Public Schools?*

In the early years of our BTR programming, we adapted to the district's hiring needs, as well as trends in the district's curricular initiatives. With each iteration and strategic shift, the core values of careful reflection of practice, collaborative conversations about content, and pursuit of student and teacher understanding have prevailed.

BTR has a strong track record of achievement in identifying, recruiting, preparing, and sustaining effective teachers in the areas of greatest need for the BPS. In the early years of the program, BTR residents were placed in fourteen schools across the district based on the interest of principals. In later years, we refined the model and placed residents in cohorts in a total of six to eight elementary and secondary schools. This deepened the partnerships between the schools and the residency program and allowed the residents to have an even more immersive whole-school experience. With fewer school partnerships, we were also better situated to explore a question that emerged from our work with graduates: *How do we ensure that the residency experiences with our partner schools provide rigorous teaching experiences for our residents, such that they are reliably able to transfer their knowledge and skills to a new setting as 1st year teachers?*

As a result of analyzing the results of the success of our new teachers, including the challenges, our program made another significant shift to place an instructional focus on the induction program. BTR developed an induction program as a significant part of the training and retention strategy. As we learned more about graduates' teaching skills, we recognized that much of what we were expecting them to transfer was not apparent in their own classrooms. BTR graduates appeared to be teaching for compliance and recitation of procedural and factual answers, rather than for rigor and understanding. In spite of BTR's explicit efforts to develop coursework and experiences around cultivating the desire and abilities of students to be critical thinkers, lifelong learners, and active participants in a democratic society, these concepts were not transferring into the first year of their teaching. We saw a need to address the disconnect from residency to induction.

Based on feedback from graduates and our own observations, BTR responded by hiring content coaches to support the induction program. These coaches were content specific and had the classroom experience and knowledge to provide feedback in both content domain and grade level. This team of committed educators was determined to figure out this very question: *How do we teach the kind of teaching that brings out the curiosity, creativity, and joy in children while ensuring strong learning outcomes?*

As we continued to refine the induction program, conduct focus groups, examine and analyze data, we learned more about the experiences of the graduates and the outcomes for their students. In 2012, the BTR team, both residency and induction programs, began a multiyear collaboration with Magdalene Lampert (2001), professor of Educational Studies, School of Education, University of Michigan, to investigate how our collective learning could improve the quality and impact of experiences across the program, from recruitment to induction. In collaboration with Lampert, we developed a set of principles, instructional goals, and teaching rubrics for ambitious teaching and rigorous instruction. These principles, instructional goals, and rubrics guide our work to this day.

WHY TEACHING ACADEMIES?

Working with six partner schools in BPS afforded opportunities for BTR residents to experience and learn alongside veteran teachers. However, as we collected data and reflected on the residency experiences, we saw that the residents' experiences enacting our principles and practices varied across the schools. In order to provide more consistent contexts and a shared understanding of the principles and instructional practices, BPE began a five-year process to design and operate teaching academies that would serve as places of ambitious learning for all learners: residents, teachers, coaches and, most importantly, children. In these teaching academies, residents, graduates, coaches, and students experience a learning community that embodies the principles of ambitious, high-quality teaching and learning. Teaching academies have structures embedded in the school to allow residents the space and opportunity to enact practices in the classroom, rehearse these practices with peers, reflect and receive in-the-moment feedback from their collaborating teachers and their coaches.

In 2014, eleven years after the program began, BTR moved away from a partner schools model to open BPE-operated teaching academies. In its current iteration, BPE runs two teaching academies: the Dudley Street Neighborhood Charter School (DSNCS), a PreK-5 in-district charter school; and the Dearborn Stem Academy (DSA), Grades 6-12. Together, these two schools create a PreK-12 pathway in the Dudley neighborhood of Roxbury, Massachusetts.

In the teaching academy, BTR coaches teach resident courses and coach residents in their classroom setting, holding the residents accountable for both their own and their students' learning. In this way, residents receive practical learning, hands-on experience in alignment with our principles and instructional goals, all in service of improving student engagement and learning in classrooms. BTR uses data to measure outcomes for students, effectiveness of residents, and instructional practices in order to determine next steps for instruction. In addition to data from standardized tests, BTR collects other data such as climate surveys from families, students, and staff; feedback from outside evaluators; and graduation and placement rates. For the purposes of this chapter, we examine the BPE teaching academy's structures and systems at DSNCS based on our experiences of developing and implementing structures for teaching and learning aligned with our principles and instructional goals.

DUDLEY STREET NEIGHBORHOOD CHARTER SCHOOL

DSNCS is committed to providing day-to-day experiences of school life where student understanding, growth, and the joy of learning are at the heart of every decision. Our learning in the residency thus far has led us to this question: *What does it take to build, sustain, and improve student learning and teacher learning (from novice to experienced educator) in a teaching academy model?*

We regularly discuss this question through the lens of our principles and instructional goals. Walking into any classroom in the school, one will most likely see a resident and collaborating teacher (CT) working together to ensure all students are engaged purposefully. The CT has years of experience engaging her students, and the resident is just beginning to learn how best to engage students. It is in the act of unpacking these moments of teaching that the principles of the teaching academy come alive and the resident learns the rationale behind effective teaching moves. In the scenario below, the resident and CT are reflecting on what it means to treat students as sense-makers. The resident concretizes the concept of sense-making for herself and distinguishes it from task and behavior-oriented direction on which she had previously focused.

It is quiet time in the third-grade classroom and students are about to transition to independent reading. The CT has instructed students at each table to get their books, go back to their seats, and begin reading. She comments that their stamina for reading has increased since the first day of school. Referring to the chart on the wall, she notes that the independent reading goal is twenty minutes. The CT quietly tells her resident to circulate for the next three minutes and check in with students on the right side of the room as they read. The CT begins to do the same on the left side of the room. The residency director shadows the resident as she looks over the shoulders of her students.

"Adonis, please open your book and pay attention. Start reading so you are reading the whole 20 minutes."

"Claire, you are not supposed to be writing right now. Please put your papers away and get focused on your reading."

The residency director motions to the resident to follow her CT instead of circulating through a different side of the room. The director poses the question, "What do you notice about what [the CT] is saying?" The resident observes as the CT interacts with two students.

"Crystal, you were so sad after you read yesterday that Adelynn might have to give away the dog. Tell me, how do you think Adelynn is feeling in this next chapter?"

Angel is playing with something in his desk, his book is on top of his desk but not yet open. The CT says, "Angel, you were telling me yesterday that the people in New York City were shocked about the giant peach and the Cloud men were going to do something. What do you think they will do today?"

The resident reflects on what she has observed in her CT. "She is asking questions about what the students are reading to get them involved in the book. She knows something about what they have read and that seems to help them to get right into reading, I didn't realize I should do that ... I was just telling the students what to do."

At the DSNCS teaching academy, the goal of classroom level teaching team is to work together to best meet the learning goals for students in the classroom. The CT works to ensure her students are engaged in meaningful learning, to support the development of the resident in her classroom, and to continue her own development as an educator. The BTR resident has primarily taken on the goal of learning to teach, but is expected to positively impact student learning, not simply practice with students. There is an inherent tension in this work: a novice needs to be able to make mistakes and learn from those mistakes, and yet, the elementary students' academic and social growth must have all adults working strategically in service of students' learning and improvement.

At DSNCS, supporting all adults to work strategically means structuring the ways teachers and residents work, such as how they learn the skills to teach what students need to learn and how they reflect on the student learning data to inform planning and instruction. Below are the structures we have developed to address this essential, collaborative work (see table 7.1):

School-Wide Professional Development

Professional development at DSNCS are weekly sessions planned and implemented by the elementary team consisting of the director, the literacy coach, and the math coach. The professional development program involves three five-week cycles of inquiry into the teachers' practice over the course of the school year. BTR principles inform this work, ground the professional learning in practice, and guide teachers as they develop authentic questions about their practice. Experienced teachers learn alongside their residents. Residents bring a curiosity about student learning while experienced teachers bring their knowledge and experience to predict, plan for, and reflect on the learning experiences in their classrooms. In the following scenario, we highlight the role of data to inform teaching practices.

It's a Wednesday afternoon at DSNCS. The teachers and residents are all gathered in the learning lab for professional development. This is the fourth professional development session in a five-session cycle organized around questions posed in service of student meaning-making. In the first week, teachers are presented a framework about the different ways that students make sense of their content. They have been asked to plan a lesson with clear objectives and questions and video themselves. This week, they have been paired up (cross grade or discipline) in order to observe each other in their classrooms. They have been asked to write low inference notes, especially noting the questions

An Examination of Teaching and Learning Structures   139

Table 7.1 DSNCS Teaching Academy Structure

Teaching Academy (TA) Structure	Description	Who Meets?	How Often?
Professional Development (PD)	School-wide teacher learning and improvement	All teaching staff and residents	Once a week 100 minutes
Common Planning Time (CPT)	Analysis of student academic data to inform instruction	Grade-level teams with residents. Coach or administrator facilitates	Once per week 90 minutes
Child Study Meetings	Using knowledge of students' social emotional strengths and needs to inform and support instruction	Grade-level teams with family engagement director and appropriate student support	Once per quarter 180 minutes
Strategic Planning for Academic Achievement (SPA) days	Examining individual academic progress	Grade-level teams. Coach or administrator facilitates	Once per quarter 180 minutes
Intensive Coaching	Individual teacher learning and improvement	Coach and teacher	3–5-week cycle 5 hours/week
Coursework for Residents	Resident learning of theory, pedagogy and practices in education	Coach or instructor and residents	Full time in summer 1.5 days a week through year
Resident-CT Time	Meetings to discuss and improve resident and student learning	Collaborating teacher and resident pairs or grade-level teams	Once per week for 45 minutes and daily in the moments of teaching

posed and student responses vis-à-vis their objectives. After a brief presentation of the framework which examines the types of responses students might make—on target, partial, confused, or completely off topic—the group breaks into pairs to reflect on their teaching. A veteran second-grade teacher and a first-year teacher are paired together to engage in an analysis of the veteran's teaching. As they examine a transcript of a recent guided reading that the veteran teacher has given, they code student responses and then discuss how the teacher responds to ensure that many students are engaged.

Transcript Excerpt

Teacher: "Ok readers, open up your folder to your list of reading strategies. Last week we learned about new strategies that readers can use when we are reading.

Look at the list of strategies we discussed and point to one of the new strategies. Point to one strategy we learned about."
Student 4: "Stop and re-read."
Teacher: "When you are confused, you stop and re-read. What is another strategy?"
Student 2: "Think, so far I know ... I wonder."
Teacher: "Yes, we stop and think when we are reading. What is another strategy? There are two more on our list."
Student 4: "I already know ... now I know."
Teacher: "Yes, when you are reading you make connections. One more we haven't read. Look here. Everyone, point to this one and say, read it twice."
Students: "Read it twice."
Teacher: "Why read it twice?"
Student 2: "So we can learn about the book."
Teacher: "Everyone point to read it twice. Why read it twice?"
    Pause. Silence.
Teacher: "What do we learn the first time we read it?"
Student 1: "The words."
Teacher: "We learn to read the words. Then when we read it a second time what do we learn?"
Student 3: "Words."
Teacher: "That is what Student 1 said, read the next part. G back to our list. What does it say?"
Student 3: "We understand the meaning of the story."
Teacher: "Yes, remember, when we read it the second time, we read to make sure we understand the meaning of the story."

"Ugh" the veteran teacher moans, "Drill and kill." She has noticed that her first line of questions is quite close ended and they yield predictable and limited responses. While most of the student responses are in fact on target, she realizes that the target responses have been read off an anchor chart and do not adequately reflect student thinking. She goes on to notice other places where she is able to push students to explain their responses. When it is time to share, the veteran teacher reflects two personal take-aways: (1) She has underestimated the amount of meaning making that can come in a discussion even if the book is simple. (2) She realizes she needs to experiment with the nature of her questions, perhaps becoming more conversational with the students so they have a clear idea WHY they are doing things rather than offering rote responses that have been drilled in their minds.

The professional development cycles ask teachers to step out of their classrooms, slow moments down from a lesson, and then think about how best to apply what works in the next lesson. The metacognitive opportunities instill in the teachers a sense of agency over their work. They are not simply doing as asked—from the administration, the state, the common core—but are examining their own practice to determine how to improve. In the above example, the veteran teacher examines her own data to arrive at a new understanding of what it means to ask questions. Only then can she make adjustments to her instruction that are meaningful to her and her students.

Common Planning Time

Common planning times (CPT) at the school, two ninety-minute blocks a week, allow coaches to meet with grade level teams at the teaching academy. These meetings focus on examining data and planning immediate next steps, related to the BTR instructional goal of data-driven planning. In the scenario that follows, the fourth-grade team works through the data toward next steps for instruction.

The fourth-grade team, which includes the literacy content teacher, the math content teacher, the learning specialist teachers for both special education and English language learning, and the BTR residents, and the ELA coach are examining data from the literacy notebooks.

The students have been asked to rewrite a section of *Small Steps* (Kehret, 1996) from another person's perspective. During the CPT, the group first agrees on the guiding questions for scoring this particular assignment: Are students able to write from another point of view? Is there a balance of grief and celebration in the tone? Do students include details from the text? Are students using proper writing conventions? The group then scores the pieces on a shared document and openly discusses the material in order to norm scoring. When all paragraphs are scored, the group takes time to note patterns among the responses, highlighting strengths first. In this instance, the group notes that the area that generated the highest average score were the students' abilities to switch perspectives and use the "I" pronoun in their writing. The group also notices that students are able to recall many details and are showing their motivation to be creative, using text-to-self connections. In addition, some students have written an outline before composing their piece.

While there were many notable strengths, there were also noted areas of challenge, including inconsistent *tone* throughout some of the writing as well as students' limited understanding of their stories' trajectories that they were writing about a joyful event amidst a rather tragic context. In a small amount of time, the team has gathered a great amount of information about the fourth graders and then move to consider possible next steps that will enable students to move forward in instruction. The group concludes that there is a need to teach the concept of *tone* more explicitly and also to check for understanding in whatever concept is taught during other times of the day, such as interactive read aloud or in an exit ticket. The English Language Arts CT assumes the former responsibility, and the math CT, the special populations teachers, and the resident assume the latter. The group also agrees that the students would benefit from peer critique and peer editing, as they are showing great motivation and progress in their work. The entire team thus fulfills the goals of the CPT to use data to plan for and improve instruction, as well as utilizing all the adults in the room in a productive way.

Child Study

At DSNCS, meeting the needs of the whole child includes addressing their social and emotional health and well-being. The director of student and family support is the facilitator of child study, a component of student support where grade-level teams (teachers, residents, and other school staff as needed) meet to brainstorm strategies for students in need of additional social emotional help. In efforts to meet our achievement plan goals, grade-level teams review student data and assess student profiles once a month to determine appropriate interventions for continued student growth. Through this evaluative process, the teams examine students' presentation through the prisms of their physical, social-emotional, behavioral, and cognitive domains as they manifest in the school environment. Mining through these data points allows the team to distill some of the lagging skills that a student could use some scaffolding, modeling, and social emotional learning instruction to foster improved functioning within the areas of social relationships which will influence academic performance. Residents and teachers join the director of student and family support to share their insights and questions about their students which often leads to the examination of their beliefs about student behavior and communication. The discussion will demand deeper analysis of these beliefs to inform new ways of responding to students by engaging with students' strengths, as opposed to reacting to student behaviors or misbehaviors.

Strategic Planning for Academic Achievement (SPA) Days

At the first September staff meeting of the school year, the principal speaks of the importance of personalized learning, reinforcing the expectation that each teacher should know and plan instruction for the unique learning needs and interests of her students. With that expectation in mind, the SPA meetings were designed. SPA meetings occur once per quarter during which grade-level team teachers, residents, and special populations teachers meet to discuss the academic progress of each student. The primary purpose of SPA meetings is to review the cumulative data for each child and plan for each student's continued learning. Different adults are assigned to track individual student progress until the next meeting. As a team, they ensure that each adult has an eye on all aspects of the child's learning: progress, gaps, and goals.

The chart below shows an excerpt of the data tracker used at DSNCS which captures all the assessment data to date; for example, STEP Reading data, pre- and post-writing assessments, end of unit math assessments, for review at the SPA meeting (see figure 7.1).

The chart includes the name of the teacher, resident, or special populations teacher who is assigned to monitor the learning and growth of a particular student. After reviewing the data for each child, the teams determine plausible next steps of instruction. Much of the differentiated instruction occurs during the intervention block, where the team divides up the class and works with small groups or individual students. In the fall, the residents are assigned to work with students who are on or above grade level, so that the most experienced teacher will teach students currently identified with the greatest learning needs. When residents gain stronger skills and knowledge for teaching specific content, they work with students who need support to reach grade-level standards. As the year progresses, residents also develop stronger knowledge of their students and how to use specific data to share the stories of their students' growth and learning. As a result, the residents contribute more meaningfully to the conversation in the second half of the year.

Coaching

In a teaching academy, all who enter—students, teachers, residents—arrive as learners. Content coaches thus play an integral role in maintaining the learning stance with adults as they work to advance student achievement. The content coaches teach the content courses and coach both the CT's and residents in the classroom, meeting for full coaching cycles that involve several components:

1. *Planning.* At a planning meeting, the resident, collaborating teacher and the content coach meet ahead of the lesson to review the lesson plan. They may work together to anticipate student engagement, their enthusiasm or their confusions. In addition, residents might rehearse their lessons for timing, clarity, or proper sequencing.
2. *Lesson.* During the lesson enactment, coaches will take low inference notes and coach into lessons as necessary, modeling teaching moves or probing further of students.
3. *Debrief.* After a lesson, the resident and CT will meet with the coach to review the lesson and examine data. The group first notes successful moments in the lesson as well as discuss areas that presented a challenge.

SPA Tracker	ELL/IEP	September Sight Words (List 1) K	December Sight Words (List 1) K	March Sight Words (List 1) K	September Baseline STEP	December Cycle 1 STEP	March Cycle 2 STEP	STEP	STEP Instructional Goal December	STEP Instructional Goal March
Leah	LLI	100%	100%	100%	3	4	5	5		
		70%	100%	100%	2	4	4	6	Accuracy/ Rate/ Comprehension	Oral and Silent Comprehension
Lucy	ELD 3	53%	85%	100%						
	LLI				2	3	3	4	Accuracy/ Rate/ Fluency/ Comprehension	Accuracy/ Comprehension (all areas)
Jenae	LLI	8%	20%	70%	Pre-Read		2	2	Accuracy	Accuracy/ Comprehension (Critical Thinking)
Leah		93%	100%	100%	4	4	4	6	Comprehension (Critical Thinking)	Oral and Silent Comprehension
Jenae	IEP	58%	80%	100%	2	3	3	3	Fluency/ Rate/ Accuracy	Comprehension (critical thinking)
Leah		53%	93%	98%	2	2	3	5	Accuracy/ Rate	Accuracy/ Reading Rate/ Fluency/ Comprehension
Lucy	IEP	100%	100%	100%	2	2	4	5	Comprehension (Factual/ Critical Thinking/ Inferential)	Oral and Silent Comprehension (Critical Thinking)
Leah		98%	100%	98%	2	2	4	5	Comprehension (Inferential/ Critical Thinking)	Oral Comprehension (Critical Thinking)
Leah		100%	100%	100%	6	6	6	7	Silent Comprehension (Inferential)	Comprehension (all areas)
Lucy	ELD 4	100%	100%	100%	2	2	5	7	Fluency/ Comprehension (all areas)	Fluency/ Comprehension(Inferential)
Jenae	LLI	33%	60%	80%	1	2	2	2	Accuracy	Comprehension (critical thinking)

Figure 7.1 Excerpt of DSNCS Student Data Tracker.

From the meeting, all agree on clear next steps and this information is entered into coaching logs. These meetings support the ongoing conversations between the CT and the resident about teaching and learning.

For the residents, a regularly used tool to prepare them for teaching is a rehearsal. The rehearsal can focus on anything from precise language in the launch to the use of probing questions for deeper discussion and sense-making, or naming talk moves to enhance intentionality in the lesson. The rehearsal thereby affords the residents an opportunity to try out a lesson before the actual enactment in order to anticipate possible barriers to student learning. A successful rehearsal can deepen many aspects of the residents' teaching, including their presence, their pace or concision, but mostly, their efficacy as an instructional leader in the classroom.

Within the school, in the spirit of a teaching academy, coaches facilitate both resident and student learning in creative and intentional ways. The integration of student learning and resident learning facilitated by the coach is best exemplified in the following description of one instructional activity: guided reading, a core instructional activity that residents learn in their course for literacy instruction and lead a group in their classroom beginning late fall. The scenario reflects the layered and complex learning that teaching academies can enable for all those involved.

The residents and the literacy coach have named the group of first graders *The Minions*. They are early literacy learners in a first-grade class with a first-year teacher. The teacher does not have a full-time resident in her classroom; hence, this is an opportunity for the residents as a group to have impact on student learning in this first-year teacher's class.

In the literacy class, the residents have learned about the parts and purposes of guided reading through readings, lecture, a comparison to interactive read aloud, videos, and discussion. They have then examined the SPA data, including a cumulation of STEP testing, classroom integral testing, student work samples, Fundations data, and anecdotal observation of the students assigned to us. From there, they have developed a trajectory of learning that they agree makes most sense for this group. The trajectory considers what specific literacy skills these students need in order to advance their reading skills. Each resident signs up for one day to teach the group over the next few weeks. At most lessons, the literacy coach is also present to oversee the residents' abilities to teach lessons with fidelity.

Today, a fifth-grade resident is teaching a nonfiction book about carrots to four children. She wants the students to focus on tapping out words they don't know. "Good readers tap out words. We will continue today." "How do you know it's non-fiction?" "Because it's real ... not a story about carrots." She then transitions into silent reading time, when she confers with individual students. "Quietly read independently and make sure you're tapping them out and pointing and using the pictures." As the resident confers with the students, the coach listens and takes notes on the readers' reading as well as the resident teaching. She reminds the resident to acknowledge something the first reader does well and provide a next step for them to remember as they read. When the conferring is done, the group has a brief discussion about what they have learned about carrots. Then the resident walks the group back to their class, and she briefly debriefs with the coach. Together they review notes from the session on student reading, and she notes who is able to tap out, that is (student), tapped out but couldn't put it together. She also notes that she will need something to keep the student focused. The coach provides feedback on the quality of the teaching itself and determines next steps if necessary. In this case, the resident will focus on developing more in-the-moment suggestions for students by reviewing literature that discusses the skillset for children at this reading level. Later that afternoon, the resident will enter her data into a shared document that the cohort keeps to track the students' progress. She has read the previous notes from other residents leading up to her lesson to make sure there is alignment. Her notes will guide the next resident for tomorrow's lesson. In this way, an entire group of residents has cohesion in working with a group of students while only taking fifteen to twenty minutes of their time once every four weeks.

Coaches also take opportunities to enact intensive coaching cycles with different teachers. Over a period of six to eight weeks, coaches work with a specific teacher on specific elements of their practice or program. It may involve regular planning and observation sessions of up to five hours in a week, or it may involve a full day of long-term planning and regular follow-up coaching visits to follow through with implementation with fidelity. In turn, residents participate in these meetings where teachers open up their teaching practice and their students' learning for investigation and model continual learning professionally.

COURSEWORK FOR RESIDENTS

Before the residents get to this skill level, they participate as students themselves in their methods coursework. On hot July days in Boston, the new residents arrive with enthusiasm and optimism about learning to teach and also embark on a largely transformational personal process in an intense year. Residents are initiated into the work with an exploration of the Dudley Street Neighborhood of Roxbury to begin to understand the context and history of the community they will serve. In addition to content courses in math and literacy, residents take courses in human development, building productive learning communities, inclusive educational practices, and language, power, and democracy. In each summer course, residents are engaged in learning experiences to examine and develop their knowledge of the content and context, their beliefs and values about learning, and their beginning understanding of the pedagogies used to support their learning. They are introduced to their new roles as educators and continual learners through rigorous reflection and collaboration among the cohort. In combination, the courses form a philosophical foundation upon which to base pedagogy and provide a practical preparation for serving the entire year in the BPS.

In the week-long literacy course, for example, there are three separate layers of learning that residents are tasked to engage and analyze—their own relationship with literacy, the philosophical underpinnings of what it means to be literate in society, and also practical preparation in anticipation of the early responsibilities in their classrooms. One aspect of the course asks residents to create literacy life maps, including drawings that highlight points in their lives that were significant in terms of literacy. Through examining their history and relationships with reading, writing, speaking, and listening, and naming texts that changed their whole perception of reading or themselves, residents recall the warm memory of reading with their grandmothers, or the shame of being put into the "low" reading groups. These memories develop a personal lens through which residents use to plan and execute lessons that are authentic and meaningful to them and their students.

In addition, residents read different positions on the definition of literacy and debate its essence, eventually arriving at their own definitions, for example, *Literacy is the evolving cultural process of learning how to obtain, interpret, and communicate information through diverse mediums for the purpose of engaging with the world* (Cohort 16, July 2018).

Finally, they have learned how to administer a running record (Clay, 2000) and they have learned the parts and purposes of an interactive read aloud (Fountas & Pinnell, 2006). Their week culminates with a visit to a nearby summer school to enact their lessons, returning to class to report on the literate life of the student they have worked with. In the fall, they will be well equipped to administer benchmark assessments and teach interactive read-alouds of their favorite books. The authenticity of these experiences provides the necessary preparation for the residents to be contributing members to their classrooms from day one.

For residents, early teaching experiences rely heavily on summer course content. The content courses continue into the school year one evening and the entire Friday of every week. Otherwise, from Day 1 to Day 181, residents' coursework is woven into the fabric of the school in multiple ways.

An operating principle of the teaching academy is how best to leverage all the adults in the building to maximize student outcomes.

RESIDENT AND COLLABORATING TEACHER (CT) MEETING

In BTR, there are a set of teaching practices that residents learn to enact, aligned with our principles and instructional goals. Collaborating teachers and coaches model, rehearse, and discuss these practices with residents so they can reflect on how the practices impact the learning of students in a variety of content and contexts. While many programs, including our own, have structured-time for resident and mentor to meet regularly, the shift to training residents in one school required our program to be flexible in how we used our time; with the addition of opportunities for conversations in the moments of teaching.

At BTR, we believe that at the heart of mentoring a novice teacher is supporting them to develop the judgments needed in the moments of teaching, to decide which practices will be most effective with students. Teachers are primarily focused on their students and experienced teachers often don't realize the knowledge and skill they use in each of their decisions and teaching moves. To that end, collaborating teachers have been focused on the question of how to make one's own thinking and teaching decisions transparent for residents to learn from. It is not enough to put the two adults in the classroom; we must create opportunities for the novice to learn from the experienced teacher both in the moments of teaching and throughout the day. Our goal at our teaching academy has been to cultivate the habit and space for these kinds of exchanges to further resident agency for effective teaching. These conversations happen during resident and CT meeting time, collaborating teacher PD, and as demonstrated below, during conversations in the moments of teaching.

Third-grade students are working on solving three-digit addition problems and the resident has assigned them to first solve the problem, and then go work in partners to share strategies. Partners are tasked with thinking of how they will explain their reasoning to each other. Students move to different areas of the room with their partners. The plan for CT and resident is to circulate, to make sure students are focused on the problem solving and sharing of their ideas and solutions. The pair circulates in different directions. The residency director facilitates a conversation between the CT and resident, effectively coaching the CT to coach the resident. The residency director first asks the CT to make transparent her actions as she circulates.

CT: "I am listening in to the pairs to hear if they have solved the problem, if they are stuck on a strategy or if each can share his/her reasoning and listen to the other. If they are stuck, I ask a question/make a comment to move them forward and then I step out to see what they do with each other."

The residency director then asks if the CT has noticed anything in the resident's actions. The CT mentions that she notices that the resident has checked in with three groups and that the resident is still with the group with which she started. Together, they observe the interaction between the resident and the student pair to who she attends. The resident has the student's pencil in her hand and is reviewing the work the student did to solve the problem with the pair. The CT coaches the resident.

CT: "So, when you are circulating, your role is to listen in and insert yourself where necessary to keep the pairs sharing their thinking so they can understand each other's math thinking. What did you notice with this pair when you first came over?"
Resident: "Georgio was having a hard time sharing his thinking, he was a bit confused and Akil was not listening because it was taking a while."
CT: "What is something you could do to support Georgio to share his thinking and hold Akil accountable to helping him, so that you do not take over the talking and become the one who is trying to share Georgio's thinking during the partner time?"
Resident: "I am not sure. I guess I could have asked Georgio to share the actual work he did on the paper so Akil could see the process he used and help him find the words to share how and why he used the strategy he did to solve the problem. Like what we do as a whole group; we always look at the actual work and talk through the decisions and steps for solving it."
CT: "Yes, then tell them you will be back in two minutes to see if they have done this and go to another group to check in. That way you are setting them up for a next step and checking to see if that actually helped them, without hovering over them. Now, let's go over to the next group and see what they are doing together and figure out a next step if necessary. We have ten more minutes. After that we can break up and see where all students are, discuss who you want to have share their strategy with the whole group and why, before you bring the group back together."

In these short and purposeful conversations, during moments of instruction, residents and CTs analyze very specific teaching moves that will support maintaining the cognitive demand for students during independent work; a challenging task for a novice teacher. These kinds of adult conferring, in the moments of teaching, are built into the daily structures at DSNCS to support residents to keep investigating how specific teaching decisions impact student engagement in sense-making.

THE NEXT DECADE

We believe that we have developed an important model of teacher training by intentionally building teams of teachers and residents who enact practice and teach ambitiously, and use data to investigate the impact of their teaching and teaching decisions. As such, a year-long residency training can have an immediate positive impact on student achievement within our school while we prepare teachers who are up to the challenge in their first year at another school. We believe that we have made significant progress in our pursuits to answer the question: *What does it take to build, sustain, and improve student learning and teacher learning (from novice to experienced educator) in a teaching academy model?* At the same time, we recognize that this is a continual evolution of ideas; hence we have identified areas that we believe, once addressed, will make our program stronger.

While we have worked to develop clarity about each structure of the school and have made gains in their consistency and depth, we continue to strive to ensure these structures do not occur in isolation, but are instead well-aligned, so as to be efficient and effective in moving the teaching and learning forward. We believe, for example, that SPA days are more impactful in conjunction with child study. We therefore schedule SPA days and child study on consecutive weeks in the school year calendar. Because SPA days focus on academics and child study days focus on social and emotional issues, such coordination allows for a whole-child approach to intervention.

Another example of efforts to improve coordination lies in the trajectory of learning in the resident courses. The course instructors ensure that residents are introduced to topics, and well versed in them, with readings, modeling, or opportunities to practice, well ahead of PD sessions on similar topics. For example, in advance of a PD session on questioning, residents are introduced (in their courses or course readings) to types and functions of questions to elicit meaning. They then analyze a transcript of a lesson and discuss the efficacy of the line of questioning within it and then have opportunity to plan and enact one-on-one interviews with students in order to elicit understanding. They view their videotaped lesson and analyze the efficacy of their own teaching and that of a colleague. When residents are prepared in this way, they can engage and contribute meaningfully to the PD session, and often bring new questions or ideas into the conversation.

A third example lies in our efforts to coordinate common planning times to support content coaching. During a CPT, we seek to examine data that comes directly from a coaching session. This allows us to focus on prioritizing outcomes while eliminating a need for a separate coaching cycle. In this way, teachers, residents, and coaches can examine the data and debrief the lesson concurrently, as well as plan for logical next steps. This coordination makes efficient the praxis of adult learning within the school.

At this moment in the evolution of our programming, we also recognize that our focus has been on strengthening grade-level teams of collaborating teachers and residents by purposefully structuring how they teach in each classroom to meet the needs of their students. We are eager to revisit our cross-grade structures to ensure that the curricular and teaching practices we have strengthened at each grade level are aligned and purposeful across the grades to ensure students and residents have a consistent and aligned learning experience across the school.

Finally, as we work with our graduates, we gain insight into their preparation for the landscape of BPS and their abilities to articulate and use the knowledge and skills they gained in the residency year. Graduates who are steeped in the *why* or the reasoning behind their teaching decisions, and who investigate teaching practice and their students as an ingrained habit, continue to grow and develop more adaptive forms of expertise. We want residents to learn effective practice and to be able to make meaningful judgments about when, how, and for whom these practices will be effective. This enables BTR residents to go into any BPS school and transfer to the new contexts all the learning from BTR that reflects our principles and instructional goals. To this end, we have begun to focus more explicitly on resident and CT conversations in which CT's are not simply transferring knowledge, but engaging in reasoning about teaching decisions and judgments. Doing so reflects a paradigm shift for most teachers who are focused on the *doing* of teaching, not the sharing of their reasoning behind their teaching decisions to support the development of the novice teacher. By slowing down and providing conversation scaffolds and protocols within the context of the structures we have created, we can better support habits of teachers to communicate intentionally about the decisions they make and why.

BIBLIOGRAPHY

Boston Teacher Residency. "Boston Teacher Residency: Teaching Academies." *Boston Plan for Excellence*. https://www.bpe.org/boston-teacher-residency/about/teaching-academies/.

Clay, Marie. *Running Records*. New Zealand: Pearson Education, 2000.

Dana, John Cotton. "John Cotton Dana/Quotes: Quotable Quote." *Good Reads*. https://www.goodreads.com/author/quotes/1334164.John_Cotton_Dana.

Darling-Hammond, Linda. *The Right to Learn: A Blueprint for Creating Schools that Work*. San Francisco: Jossey-Bass, 1997.

Dudley Street Neighborhood Charter School. "Academics". *Boston Plan for Excellence*. https://www.bpe.org/dudley-street-neighborhood-charter-school/about/approach/.

Feiman-Nemser, Sharon. *Teachers as Learners*. Cambridge: Harvard Education Press, 2012.

Fountas, Irene and Gay Su Pinnell. *Teaching for Comprehending and Fluency: Thinking, Talking and Writing about Reading, K-8*. Portsmouth: Heinemann, 2006.

Freire, Paolo. *Pedagogy of the Oppressed*, 30th Anniversary Ed. New York: Bloomsbury, 1968.

Kehret, Peg. *Small Steps: The Year I Got Polio*. Chicago: Albert Whitman & Company, 1996.

Lampert, Magdalene. *Teaching Problems and the Problems of Teaching*. New Haven: Yale University, 2001.

Chapter 8

Evaluating and Continuously Improving Program Quality in the Teacher Residency

Marisa Harford and Rachelle Verdier

NEW VISIONS FOR PUBLIC SCHOOLS URBAN TEACHER RESIDENCY

Teacher Residency partnerships present opportunities for deeper feedback loops between schools of education, districts, and K-12 schools to continuously improve the quality of preparation of new teachers. What systems, structures, processes, and tools are most effective for tracking data about meaningful metrics and outcomes, analyzing that information to make decisions about the program elements, and developing a shared understanding of the impact of the program? In this chapter, we share over ten years of experience using protocols informed by inquiry and continuous improvement, core data collection and analysis systems, and parallel learning processes to prepare all stakeholders, from residents to program leadership, to use data to inform decision-making.

GERALDINA: A COMPOSITE CASE STUDY

It is a warm day at the end of March. Geraldina, a ninth grader, stares out her classroom window as her group members discuss how to interpret a graph showing the relationship between the population of deer and wolves in a national park. The novice teacher resident assigned to their class, Ms. Fresh, stops by their group and prompts them with some guiding questions. "Geraldina," she says, "What did you notice about the graph? What happens when the deer population goes up?" "I dunno," Geraldina responds, and shrugs. Ms. Fresh moves on: "What about you, Bertrand?"

Later that afternoon, Ms. Fresh and her mentor, Mr. Wise, are reviewing the students' exit tickets together. Ms. Fresh furrows her brow. "Mr. Wise, Geraldina didn't even try to answer the questions! She is so unmotivated. What are we going to do with her?" Mr. Wise pauses, then asks Ms. Fresh, "What have you been noticing about her work in class? What do you think might be behind her challenge with this unit?" Mr. Wise opens up Geraldina's folder of classwork and guides Ms. Fresh through a discussion of what they know about Geraldina's foundational skills, her assets and challenges, and common misconceptions in this particular unit. They also look up her IEP to inform their conversation. Later that day, Mr. Wise asks, "Ms. Fresh, do you want to use Geraldina as one of your focus students in your inquiry project on interpreting charts and graphs? I think we just scratched the surface of how to support her."

The next week, Mr. Wise attends a quarterly mentor professional development (PD) session where he shares his ongoing analysis of Ms. Fresh's progress and his mentoring strategies with a group of peers and a program coach. "Ms. Fresh is really struggling to use assessment information to differentiate," he notes. "She attributes students' difficulties to motivation, when I think it's mostly that they lack fundamental skills—for example, one student didn't know how to plot points on a graph, and Ms. Fresh was expecting her to interpret the relationships on the graph. I'm not sure how to equip her with both the strategies and the mindset to consider what might be challenging for these students." Other mentors chime in, "My resident has that issue too!" and they point to the data in the shared program tracker where they can view residents' monthly formative assessments on *The Framework for Teaching* (Danielson, 2013). The framework is used throughout New York City to evaluate and provide feedback to teachers and is used by the residency program to monitor resident progress and to communicate residents' strengths and areas for growth. The mentors notice that residents' scores on component 3d, Using Assessment in Instruction, are mostly in the "Developing" range. In searching the comments stored in the tracker, they notice a common trend around residents not collecting and reviewing student work to inform their next steps. The mentors in the peer group provide suggestions and strategies for Mr. Wise to try when he returns to school the next day. They each leave with a plan for next steps, and several begin a practice of analyzing student work twice per week with their residents, using a Looking at Student Work protocol provided by the program coach.

At the end of the mentor PD day, the program coach, Ms. Sage, debriefs with the coaches who facilitated other groups, and compares notes. The coaches notice that many mentors shared challenges related to residents' ability to assess and diagnose skill gaps in their students, and then to address those gaps through differentiation. They open up the data tracker again and note that the trend around Danielson component 3d applies across the entire cohort; only a few residents are performing well in that area, even though being rated Effective on 3d is an end-of-year benchmark for successfully completing the program. Using the tracker, the coaches also identify a few outlier residents who are using assessment well, and then review their resident-mentor coaching logs to see what those successful pairs are doing. They take note of a few promising practices from these outliers to share with the mentors whose next step plans included work around assessment.

One coach also suggests looking at the residents' midyear self-assessments to identify how many set personal goals in the area of assessment. It turns out that many did, but in the intervening time between January and March, several coaches had not revisited those goals to assess progress and refocus resident and mentor energy on them as needed; those coaches plan to do just that in their next visit. They discuss how to model and reinforce the process of revisiting goals so that the mentors can continually check in around long-term goals rather than simply reacting to each day's lesson. Then, the coaches turn their attention to planning for the next resident seminar. "We already have a full agenda! How can we incorporate more work on assessment into our April seminar? What needs to be deprioritized? How can we fit it in?" The coach group grapples with revising the plan to address using assessment in instruction during the session, and eventually settles on an opening activity that asks each resident to bring an example of student work that surprised them and gave them an actionable insight and discuss how they followed up.

At the monthly program management team meeting, the program director, Ms. Keen, meets with faculty who teach the residents' coursework. As they review resident progress trends together, she highlights that residents are a bit behind the curve in the area of using assessment in instruction and asks the professors to reflect on what they've noticed. Professor Validity, who teaches Assessment, is a bit taken aback at first. "They all did very well on their end of semester project," he notes.

"I think they understand the core concepts that you taught them," clarifies Ms. Keen. "We just know from experience that sometimes making the leap to integrate those principles into daily instruction is hard work. Are there any touchstone processes or frameworks you shared with them that we could be reinforcing?"

"As a matter of fact, there are. I stressed the use of medial checks for understanding using *Embedded Formative Assessment*" (Wiliam, 2011) says Professor Validity.

"Oh! That's a great set of strategies, but I don't think our coaches are aware that the residents were exposed to Wiliam's work, and I think our mentors may not be familiar with it. Professor Strategy, since you teach the Methods course this semester, do you use Dylan Wiliam?"

"No, but I could revisit it during my class in two weeks—we have a section on assessment planned for that day," Professor Strategy volunteers.

"Great! We'll include it in our next coaching meeting and figure out whether or not mentors need a refresher on that approach," concludes Ms. Keen, happy to have found a shared strategy to promote. She makes a note to herself to ask the external evaluators, the Appraisal Group, to add a question about assessment strategies to both the midyear and end-of-year resident and mentor surveys.

The warm weather continues, spring break passes, and all of a sudden, it's June! Ms. Fresh is about to unveil her summative student achievement during her end of year Defense of Learning presentation. "The student I'm most proud of is Geraldina—this is her work from May right here. As you can see, she started off not even knowing how to plot points on the graph. Thanks to our small-group work and a few carefully-chosen scaffolds aligned to her IEP, she got 80 percent of the questions about interpreting graphs correct on this mock final exam! I was so happy—and she was so happy to have met our goal. She still needs help with more complex relationships between variables, but I know that she doesn't shut down now when she sees a graph; she has methods for making sense of it. In addition, I have better strategies to use next year when I encounter other students who have struggles similar to Geraldina's." Mr. Wise looks on, and beams.

In August, Ms. Keen and the rest of the program leadership are gathered in a conference room to hear about the results of the midyear and end-of-year program surveys from the Appraisal Group. They project a graph showing resident and mentor self-reported sense of efficacy around many different instructional areas. Ms. Keen notices that the score for assessment was fairly low around midyear and increased by June. "Now that's progress," she says, satisfied.

GETTING BETTER ALL THE TIME: CORE PRINCIPLES FOR PROGRAM ASSESSMENT AND IMPROVEMENT

Teacher Residency partnerships present opportunities for deeper feedback loops between colleges of education, districts, and K-12 schools to continuously improve the quality of preparation of new teachers and ensure better and more equitable outcomes for all students. If we are dedicated to a vision of education where all students, especially those who have been historically marginalized and under-served by our school systems, are able to achieve their goals and aspirations, we must be committed to frequent, disciplined examination and revision of our practices that is grounded in learning, experiences, and data generated by stakeholders. Over the past ten years, New

Visions for Public Schools has developed and iterated on systems, structures, processes, and tools for tracking data about meaningful metrics and outcomes, analyzing that information to make decisions about the program elements, and developing a shared understanding of the impact of the program. These approaches have allowed us to achieve strong retention and student achievement impacts, as measured by our external evaluators. In this chapter, we share our approach, processes, and lessons learned in the realm of formative program assessment and summative evaluation.

Throughout our experience, we have utilized four core principles to guide our work around program assessment and improvement: inquiry, continuous improvement, data analysis, and parallel learning processes. Inquiry and continuous improvement are the learning and decision-making frameworks that provide a disciplined process for our collaborative reflection. The development of systems for the collection and regular analysis of meaningful data by stakeholders is a prerequisite for using inquiry and continuous improvement methodologies. Finally, we have designed the program to incorporate structures that engage all of us, from residents to program leadership, in using data to drive decision-making within our respective spheres of influence and simultaneously improving our abilities to use those processes. Stakeholders at all levels of the program use and develop skills in parallel decision-making practices. After providing general context, we delve more deeply into each of these core principles below, providing background and case studies related to each stakeholder group.

CONTEXT: NEW VISIONS FOR PUBLIC SCHOOLS AND THE URBAN TEACHER RESIDENCY

For nearly thirty years, New Visions for Public Schools, a nonprofit education support organization, has provided innovative solutions to the myriad challenges public high schools in New York City face. As the lead nonprofit partner to a large and diverse group of public schools in the nation's largest school district, New Visions works to strengthen schools through multiple channels, including promoting ambitious, rigorous instruction; student-centered learning environments; parent and community involvement; professional capacity of school staff; and effective leadership, with a focus on systems development and data-driven decision-making.

Since 2009, New Visions has worked in partnership with Hunter College and Queens College at the City University of New York (CUNY) and the NYC Department of Education with the goal of improving student outcomes in high-need New York City schools and increasing the retention of effective teachers, both novice and experienced, through the creation of successful residency programs. Through multiple iterations, New Visions-affiliated Urban Teacher Residency programs have focused on the preparation of highly qualified, diverse teachers in high-need content areas, such as Special Education and STEM, and the development of school capacity to support novice teachers. We believe that teachers whose skill set includes reflection, collaboration, and inquiry are better equipped to meet the needs of diverse students and to positively impact their school communities.

Through partnerships with the Department of Education, individual schools, and institutions of higher education, we promote systemic improvements to teacher preparation and development structures and build capacity in teacher educators and leaders.

The key elements of our program model include:

- A rigorous admissions process for residents, alongside strategic recruitment partnerships and a strong value proposition to increase the yield of diverse, highly qualified candidates.
- Full-year residency, where residents are integrated into the staff of their host school, engage in a gradual release of responsibility for instruction, and receive frequent observation, feedback, and support.
- One-on-one pairing with a rigorously selected mentor who is engaged in initial and ongoing professional development and receives frequent support from program staff or school-based coaches.
- Alignment of graduate coursework and clinical experiences to prepare residents to teach for equity; make collaborative, data-driven instructional decisions; and develop reflective practice, in addition to the core capacities of planning, instruction, assessment, content knowledge, and pedagogical content knowledge.
- Host school leadership commitment to resident and mentor support and development to build effective systems for induction for novices and professional growth opportunities for experienced teachers.
- Authentic, performance-based assessments of residents and mentors which are aligned to district standards and expectations of teacher practice and promote K-12 student learning in resident and mentor classrooms.
- Strategic partnerships committed to continuous reflection and adaptation, including collaborative analysis of data around resident, mentor, program, and K-12 student outcomes and progress to reflect and revise all program elements on a regular basis.

Residency Outcomes

Since 2008–2009, New Visions affiliated residency programs have prepared around 300 highly qualified teachers in high-need content areas, such as

Special Education and STEM. Our graduates have had a positive impact on student outcomes and defied trends in teacher retention: 82 percent of our program graduates have taught for at least four years in high-need NYC DOE schools, and students taught by teachers trained in the program outperform the students of non-UTR-prepared peers on key standardized exams and course grades (Rockman et al., 2018). Our emphasis on the recruitment and retention of diverse candidates has allowed us to prepare 50–60 percent candidates of color in each cohort during the past few years. We believe that our shared commitment to reflection and revision, while simultaneously helping all stakeholders to build habits of mind for effective decision-making, has been a major factor in achieving these outcomes.

THE CORE PRINCIPLES: INQUIRY, CONTINUOUS IMPROVEMENT, DATA SYSTEMS, AND PARALLEL LEARNING PROCESSES

Theoretical Grounding: Inquiry and Continuous Improvement

Two related but distinct constructs have informed our approach to reflection, analysis, and revision of our program at all levels: inquiry and continuous improvement. The main thread connecting the two is a focus on collaborative, evidence-based decision-making that centers on how stakeholders are progressing toward goals and includes all stakeholders in making meaning within their spheres of influence.

Inquiry

At the heart of the "teacher as researcher" or inquiry approach to educator development is the view of teachers as decision-makers who need to learn habits of mind and ways of acting on the data that are always being generated in the classroom (student responses, behaviors, etc.) in order to be effective. As Deborah Ball notes, in an average ninety seconds, teachers may make twenty or more decisions that are significant for their students' learning. She identifies these as "discretionary spaces," where teachers can either support their students' learning and well-being or derail the learning process (Ball, 2018). Teachers must utilize their knowledge about their content, context, and instructional plans while continually acting as researchers—learning about their students' thinking and what strategies are successful in facilitating their learning, a continuous process of acting, analysis, reflection, and revision. They must also learn to put student learning, rather than their teacher actions or self-perceived effectiveness, at the center of their development and decisions. Inquiry, or action research, provides a structure that allows teachers to practice applying these complex skills. Cochran-Smith and Lytle (1993) define teacher research as "systematic, intentional inquiry by teachers about their own school and classroom work." They claim that "only teachers themselves can integrate their assumptions and their interpretive frameworks and then decide on the actions that are appropriate for their local contexts."

How can we support novice teachers in acquiring these key "habits of mind" (Sagor, 2009), including reliance on assessment, implementing deliberate interventions, monitoring and revising those interventions, and reflecting on successes and challenges to generalize their learning? In our Urban Teacher Residency program, the answer has been teacher inquiry. At the inception of the Urban Teacher Residency, we selected a model of teacher inquiry aligned to the school-based collaborative inquiry work in use across the New York City Department of Education since 2008, which is based on an approach developed in partnership with New Visions for Public Schools' Scaffolded Apprenticeship Model (SAM) program. This inquiry approach is defined by the use of structured protocols; identification of criteria for success and a specific goal based on initial data-gathering; grounding in analysis of student work and evidence of student thinking (interviews, assessments) in order to understand the impact of teacher instructional strategies and track progress; implementation of iterative cycles to refine and develop the work; final reflection and incorporation of changes into practice; and collaboration or peer feedback. Both residents and mentors complete multiple projects during the year that require them to develop and apply inquiry skills and share their learning with peers; for residents, this is the capstone Defense of Learning project that is completed at midyear and at the end of the year. Mentors complete a less-intensive but no less-reflective process called the Jedi Project.

Inquiry fosters shifts in teacher focus from summative to formative assessment and from teaching activities to student learning, as seen in the research conducted by Talbert (2011) on inquiry models for school improvement in New York City. This occurs because inquiry requires teachers to justify their decisions through data and apply new strategies through content-specific professional development, just when they need them to help students reach a learning goal. Langer, Colton, and Goff (2003) found that powerful teacher learning occurs as teachers analyze their students' work to determine which teaching methods are most effective. This finding seems to be equally true for novice teachers, who may need additional support to reflect more on their students' learning and less on their own experiences. As documented by Tabachnick and Zeichner (1999),

> More quickly than is usually the case for prospective teachers, they [new teachers] shifted their focus away from themselves as teachers to their students as

learners. The process of doing action research, including as it does the gathering of data about student learning, encouraged this shift in focus.

Another important reason to focus on inquiry in teacher preparation is its potential to positively impact student learning outcomes through bridging the gap between research-based best practices learned in graduate coursework and daily classroom decision-making. In a study on teacher inquiry in professional development schools, Dana and Silva (2001) found that developing a collaborative inquiry stance simultaneously improves outcomes for students and preparation for novice teachers. Several studies have documented significant achievement gains for students when grade-level teams use a structured and consistent collaborative inquiry process (Griffiths, 2009; Saunders, Goldenberg, and Gallimore, 2009). In preparing our residents to engage in collaborative inquiry, we equip them for a career of making a difference in students' learning.

Continuous Improvement

The principles and practices of continuous (quality) improvement for education, as developed by Tony Bryk and his colleagues at the Carnegie Foundation for the Advancement of Teaching, also form a cornerstone of our approach to examining the effectiveness of the UTR program, testing out our theory of change, and making program adjustments in real time. The concept of continuous improvement emerged from William Edwards Deming's Plan-Do-Study-Act (PDSA) approach via the Institute for Healthcare Improvement (IHI). New Visions UTR participated in the Carnegie Foundation's Building a Teaching Effectiveness Network (BTEN) networked improvement community in 2012–2013 (LeMahieu, 2017), and many of their approaches to program improvement (e.g., ninety-day projects, PDSA cycles) inform how we structure our ongoing learning. As Bryk articulates, continuous improvement is a method of using a systems-focused approach to conduct "problem-specific and user-centered" research. It emphasizes the creation and use of clear metrics for improvement, sharing data across networks to identify both positive and counterproductive variation, and using a disciplined process to track the impact of changes. In continuous improvement, one starts with small tests of change prior to implementing any idea at scale (Bryk et al., 2015).

An example of our use of continuous improvement methodology is our work around various iterations of our resident-mentor coaching log. The coaching log is a crucial tool used by residents, mentors, and coaches to document the feedback and next steps that residents, mentors, and coaches discuss and act upon in order to build the resident's practice. As a team, we knew that the structure, format, required fields, and other features of the log could have an educative aspect to them by impacting the focus of resident, mentor, and coach conversations. There were many different design considerations for these logs, from the format—word document, Google document, excel spreadsheet, Google form; open text boxes or drop-down lists—to the content and framing of the required fields. We hoped that an improved version of the log would lead to improved resident performance in the classroom through clearer tracking of specific, actionable next steps and follow-through. Before implementing a suite of dramatic changes all at once, we established metrics for tracking improvement, including the rate of log completion by residents and mentors and sampling for quality, piloted a new version with a subset of residents and mentors, solicited their feedback based on their use of the pilot version, and revised several times based on our trials and cycles of data collected, prior to rolling out a revised version with new features and options to all residents and mentors.

Building and Utilizing Data Systems to Track and Analyze Meaningful Metrics

A prerequisite for using inquiry-based and continuous improvement approaches is the ability to collect and analyze data that are meaningful for tracking program progress based on the program's theory of change. Once meaningful metrics are identified, then the program must build systems to collect the data and make it accessible to stakeholders in both comprehensive and easily digestible ways. We are fortunate that New Visions for Public Schools is a national leader in building systems to support meaningful data collection, tracking, and sense-making, so we were able to work with our Systems and Data Team to create specialized tools for capturing and reporting on our data. Our work with our program partners and evaluators in drafting our logic model and theory of change informed our articulation of the metrics we wanted to track, both for formative information and around program outputs and outcomes. Because alignment to district expectations is crucial, we started with the selected components of the Danielson Framework for Teaching (2013) used by the NYC DOE to evaluate all teachers, then added program-specific assessments around core components of resident practice captured in our Vision of Effective Teaching (lesson planning, professionalism, the defense of learning) and assessments of mentors and coaches. A series of performance-based assessments of resident practice formed a set of program "gateways" or benchmarks, which are calibrated for appropriate novice-level expectations. Graduate coursework and certification exams that assess content knowledge and understanding of pedagogical theory through written assessments also form part of our progress monitoring for candidates. To capture outcomes, we worked with our external evaluators and the NYC

DOE to create systems to gather and track ongoing retention information and K-12 student achievement data for the students of our program graduates and comparison teachers. Collecting data related to formative or interim measures and longer-term outcomes allowed our external evaluators to analyze the alignment between our formative measures and the program's impact—for example, examining whether or not higher resident scores on assessments of practice during the residency year correlated with stronger induction-year practice or retention for those individuals after they graduated.

Data Collection and Sharing Systems

A core tenet of our partnership is that all key stakeholders are engaged in assessment, both in generating progress monitoring data and analyzing and acting on it at an appropriate level: mentors, teacher educators from the college and program staff, school administration, and even residents, through self-assessment and assessment of their mentors and program staff supports. The program assessments are administered through a set of Google forms that stakeholders complete on a regular schedule. The schedule of assessments is shared at the beginning of the year, and stakeholders receive reminder emails frequently to encourage them to submit their data. They can access their forms directly via their email or the program website. Program coaches are also available to support any difficulties in completing the assessments, whether technical, interpersonal, or pedagogical, and we often set aside time in program professional development sessions and meetings for residents and mentors to complete their assessments to maximize our response rates.

Once the data are entered, they are displayed in a set of dashboards developed by our Systems and Data team using the data visualization system Tableau. Tableau software enables us to translate our raw data into dashboards and analysis tools. Through our Tableau dashboards, we can create a personalized data profile for each resident or mentor—including only their data—that can be securely accessed via a personal password, and also create dashboards for coaching and program-level staff and faculty that aggregate data across the program so we can see trends and patterns to analyze them for program improvement. The dashboards can be set up to "slice and dice" the data to allow us to compare across administrations of assessments to examine growth over time, look at alignment between scores of different stakeholders (such as coach versus mentor ratings of the same resident), and break down the data according to demographics such as content areas, host schools, new mentors versus returning mentors, and so on. Our Tableau dashboards are set to check for and update data on a daily basis, so residents, mentors, and coaches can see their data in nearly real time.

While the Tableau data are available twenty-four hours a day, accessible from any computer, we have found that it is crucial to provide structured times when residents, mentors, coaches, and program staff or faculty are required to log in, view their data, reflect on it, and create action plans. Without building in some required checkpoints, the progress-monitoring data becomes just another competing voice in the flood of information that confronts us all each day. Coaches use the Tableau data in conversations with residents and mentors; opportunities to analyze the data and discuss next steps based on it are incorporated into mentor professional development sessions and resident seminars. In addition, the program staff and faculty analyze at least some slice of the data during each leadership check in and create midyear and end-of-year summaries to inform major program changes and adjustments for each semester or cohort (see figures 8.1 and 8.2).

A Note on a Data Collection Challenge: Increasing Response Rates

Ensuring 100 percent response rates is a constant struggle; besides initial clarity around the schedule of assessments, frequent reminders in the weekly email, and sharing overall response rates to motivate completion, we

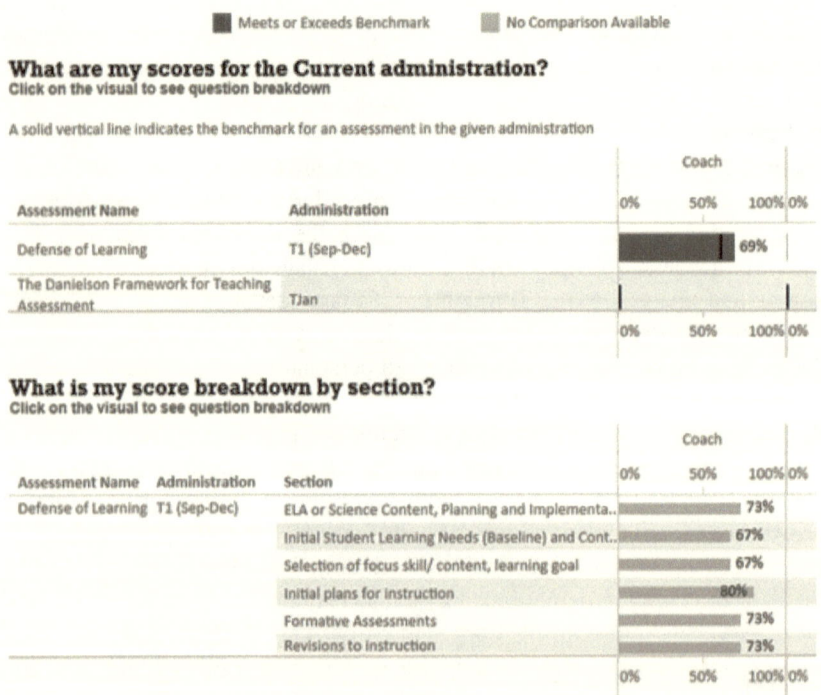

Figure 8.1 Sample Individual Resident Profile for One Assessment.

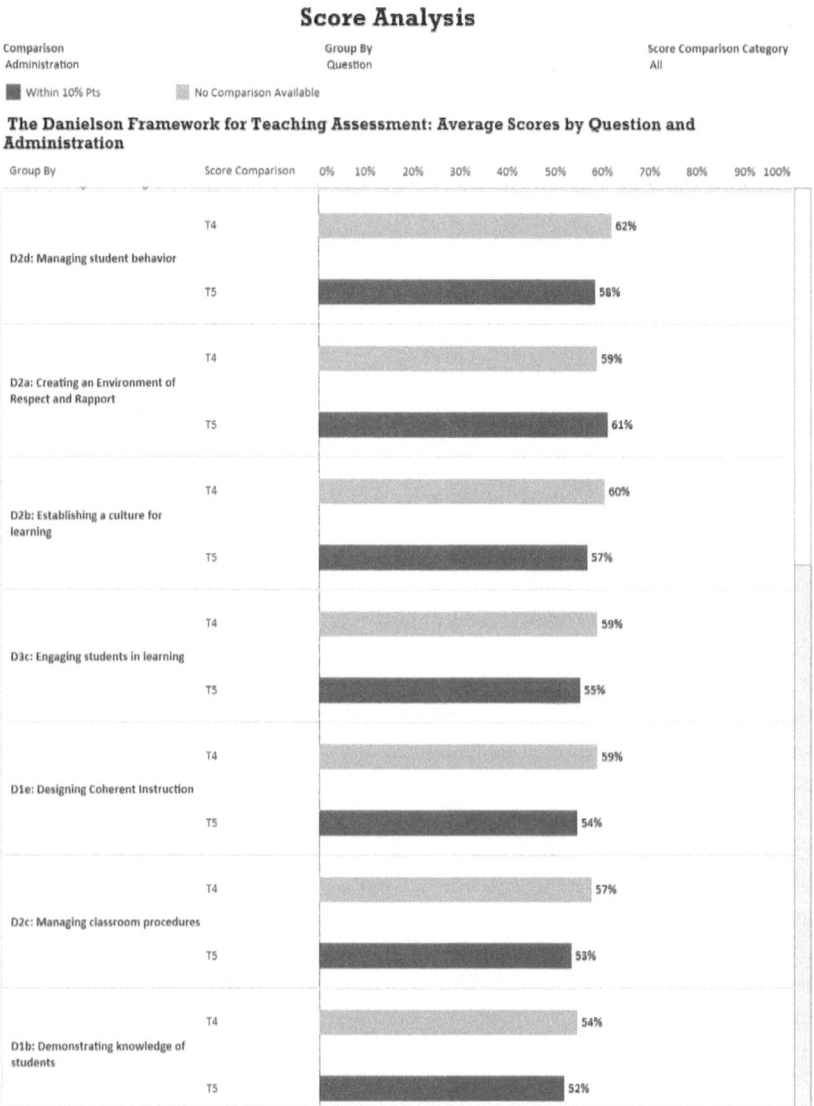

Figure 8.2 Sample of Score Analysis Comparing Average School Administrator Danielson Framework Assessment of Residents to Mentor Assessment by Rubric Component.

emphasize the authentic use of the data to support coaching conversations and resident growth. Coaches open up the feedback on our Tableau dashboards during their coaching debriefs or check-ins to engage residents and mentors in looking at the data and discussing how they are reflecting on it and using it to set goals and design a road map for improvement. Mentors also review aggregate data across the cohort together during mentor PD sessions, which helps mentors feel accountable to their peers for submitting their feedback. When mentors and residents feel the data is purposeful and will be analyzed and used for reflection, they are much more likely to actually complete the forms. We are also very conscious of the need to balance mentor and coach workload with the need to collect enough formative data to have actionable "just-in-time" information about a range of resident and mentor practices. Our mentors, especially, are busy professionals and often struggle to find time to complete their assessments. After years of experimenting with different assessment schedules, we have generally concluded that we should only ask mentors to record one major assessment per month if it requires an observation and debrief and the documentation of rubric scores, comments and feedback.

Structures for Data Analysis across Stakeholders

Our data collection systems generate information that is relevant to all stakeholders and help us to organize the data for analysis. However, without regular structures for collaborative examination of the data and meaning-making, all of our data collection would have no impact on our program. In addition, protocols around how the data are used in feedback and coaching conversations are crucial. Our program handbooks and mentor resources provide frameworks and key questions or agendas for resident-mentor meetings that are modeled, practiced, and discussed in mentor professional development and by the program coaches throughout the year. If the rubrics are completed, but never discussed, reflected upon, or analyzed in a productive way that leads to next steps, then the whole endeavor is pointless! Providing clear, normed models for how to have those sometimes difficult feedback conversations, and returning to practice them throughout the year, is essential to using the data in a meaningful way. The table below summarizes and illustrates how different stakeholder groups analyze and act on data generated through our systems (see table 8.1).

Each of these sets of data analysis processes has its own set of protocols and structures that has developed over time. In the case studies, we delve into some of the data analysis processes we feel may be most unique to our Urban Teacher Residency.

Parallel Learning Structures

We are guided by the conviction that parallel learning processes for novice teachers, mentor teachers, coaches, and program leadership, such as those described in the Geraldina vignette, are crucial for "just-in-time" formative input for the program. Using the same processes to make decisions, whether

Evaluating and Continuously Improving Program Quality   167

Table 8.1 Gathering and Using Data in UTR

Stakeholders	Types of Data Analyzed	Settings for Data Analysis	Application for Program Improvement
Residents, Mentors, and Coaches	Student work and assessment results captured by residents and mentors in their classes	• Twice-weekly sacred meetings and other conversations with mentor • Monthly coaching debriefs with coaches • Monthly resident seminar as part of the Defense of Learning inquiry project	• Used to guide resident's instructional strategies and development of teaching practice • Capstone Defense of Learning assessment (residents must demonstrate impact on student learning and use of assessment to inform instruction)
Residents	Resident's own scores and comments on performance-based assessments captured in our process-monitoring system (assessors: mentors, coaches, and administrators) • Lesson and unit design • Danielson observations • Defense of Learning • Professionalism Resident self-assessment and goal-setting	• Twice-weekly sacred meetings and other conversations with mentor • Monthly coaching debriefs with coaches • Monthly resident seminars • Accessed through the Resident Profile in the process-monitoring system	• Used to guide resident's instructional strategies and development of teaching practice • Support the resident in building capacity for self-reflection and improvement
Mentors	• Their resident's scores and comments on performance-based assessments (see above) • Mentor Competencies rubric • Cohort-wide trends and patterns in performance-based assessments	• Monthly coaching debriefs with coaches • Monthly mentor seminars • Quarterly mentor professional development sessions • Accessed through the Resident Profile and various analysis views in the process-monitoring system	• Used to guide mentor's development of goals for resident improvement, monitoring of resident progress • Analysis of cohort trends and patterns informs recommendations for program revisions • Guide mentor's self-assessment and personal development goals

(Continued)

Table 8.1 Gathering and Using Data in UTR (Continued)

Stakeholders	Types of Data Analyzed	Settings for Data Analysis	Application for Program Improvement
Coaches	• Individual resident scores and comments on performance-based assessments (see above) • Cohort-wide trends and patterns in performance-based assessments • Response rates for assessments • Mentor and coach competencies rubrics • Mentor feedback on seminar sessions • Resident academic progress in coursework	• Monthly coach team meetings • Mentor and coach professional development • Accessed through the Resident Profile and various analysis views in the process-monitoring system	• Inform coaching of individual resident-mentor pairs • Inform design of school team and resident seminars • Inform design of mentor PD • Inform check-ins with school administrators • In cases where a struggling resident is on an intervention plan, used to monitor the intervention plan • Guide coach's self-assessment and personal development goals
Program Leadership Team	• Cohort-wide trends and patterns in performance-based assessments, including mentor and coach competencies • Resident academic progress in coursework • Admissions and recruitment data • Retention data • Induction coaching data • External evaluation reports, including survey and focus group data, student outcomes data, etc.	• Monthly leadership team/planning meetings • Monthly Teacher Certification team meetings • Periodic meetings with broader groups of stakeholders • External evaluation presentations	Inform choices related to program design such as: • Course sequences and other coursework-related program elements • Design of resident and mentor seminars • Design of coach professional development • Mentor and coach selection • Host school selection • Recruitment and admission process strategies and targets • Induction coaching approach

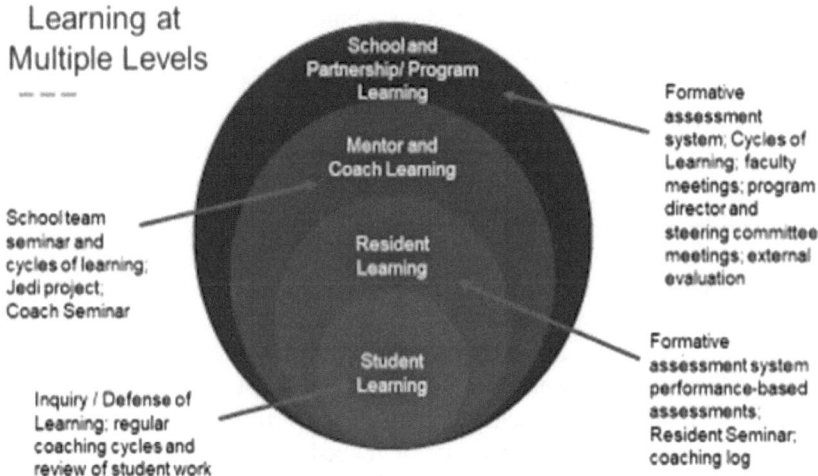

Figure 8.3 Learning Structures for All Stakeholders.

our focus is K-12 student learners or our program coaches and faculty, improves internal coherence, provides models for residents and mentors, and affirms our commitment to growth and learning. Consistently utilizing and reflecting on a disciplined approach to decision-making also builds all stakeholders' skills in making choices based on trends and patterns in outcomes, rather than merely anecdotal information or intuitions that may or may not be reflective of more generalizable data. Effective teaching is complex, focused on learning outcomes for students, and based on cycles of assessment and reflection, and our leadership's use of these practices honors that complexity and focus. The graphic in figure 8.3 illustrates how different levels of learning inform each other in the program.

CASE STUDIES: PRACTICES AND LESSONS LEARNED

In the case studies below, we progress through each stakeholder group—residents, mentors, coaches, and program leadership—and take a deep dive into each of the core principles in application to that group. We also discuss challenges and specific examples of program systems we've changed over time due to our continuous improvement work.

Resident Inquiry: The Defense of Learning

During the residency year, UTR residents engage in iterative cycles of teacher inquiry that culminate each semester in a "Defense of Learning" presentation. Monthly seminar sessions—built around structured protocols for task analysis, examination of student work, and revising instructional strategies—guide residents through each phase of the inquiry process and provide opportunities for them to receive feedback on their thinking and analysis from peers and seminar facilitators. In addition to peer and coach feedback in seminar, mentors support residents in the daily use of the inquiry process and applying the insights gleaned through more formal inquiry in their teaching.

The Defense of Learning serves as the culminating assessment in the resident seminar and engages residents in explaining and demonstrating the link between theory and practice through implementing theory-based interventions and analyzing their efficacy with a specific set of students, in a specific context, with specific instructional goals. The overall purpose is to engage candidates in an intentional practice of reflection that includes observation and critique of one's own teaching practice as well as the ability to respond effectively to feedback from others and collaborate with colleagues. At the end of the semester, residents present their Defense of Learning to an audience that includes clinical supervisors, mentors, teacher colleagues, their peers in the cohort, and school administrators as a way of demonstrating their ability to positively impact student learning and well-being. Residents are asked to "defend" the learning that they facilitated for students over the course of the semester using the inquiry cycle. These experiences also help to prepare candidates to meet the edTPA (Education Teacher Performance Assessment) Certification requirements. The formal inquiry process is structured as follows:

1. Use a diagnostic/baseline assessment to select a focus skill or content goal and describe students' initial understanding of the focus skill or content;
2. Establish a learning goal(s) for students and an initial instructional plan;
3. Implement the instructional plan;
4. Assess and analyze student learning through formative assessment, using specific protocols for looking at student work;
5. Revise instructional strategies based on the analysis, and implement the revised strategies;
6. Complete at least three cycles of steps three through five;
7. Administer a summative assessment to capture evidence of student progress since the baseline;
8. Reflect on implications of the assessment results and the inquiry cycle;
9. Present the inquiry process to mentor, program coach, administrators, and peers, using student work and data as evidence (see figure 8.4).

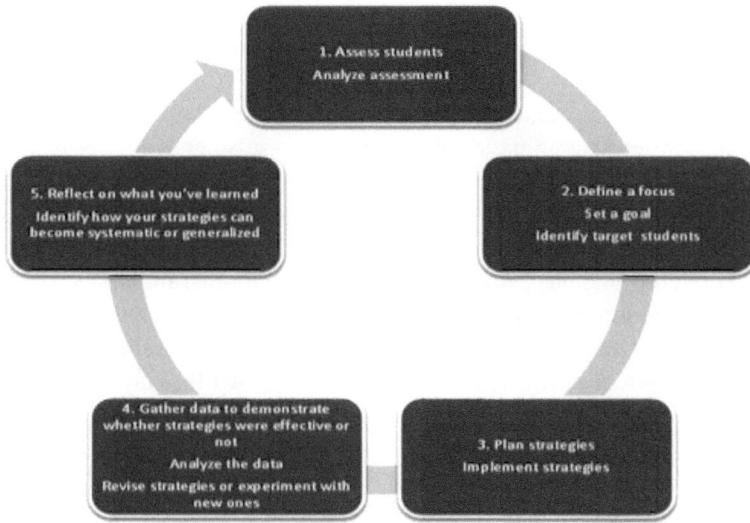

Figure 8.4 The UTR Teacher Inquiry Cycle.

Resident Defense of Learning Case Study

Residents participate in many learning spaces which expose them to multiple theories, resources and strategies: their coursework, coaching conversations with program staff, feedback from mentors and school administrators, inquiry work, school professional development, and co-planning conversations. One of the challenges the program experiences is supporting residents with aligning their day-to-day teaching practice, the inputs from these multiple learning spaces, and student learning goals targeted in their inquiry process which culminates in the Defense of Learning. Residents struggle to identify the most significant instructional strategies, develop a sense of efficacy about their teaching, and build their own teacher decision-making skills. The example below demonstrates how the resident initially struggled to identify instructional strategies that produced student learning. Through the iterative cycles of the inquiry process, the resident ultimately implemented a strategy developed at the school and was able to identify that in this context, with these students, this strategy had the most impact on student learning. This case study exemplifies a pattern that we see frequently: only after completing several inquiry cycles do residents become aware of the power of making teaching decisions more intentionally.

Resident L, in secondary English Language Arts, discovered through their baseline assessment and work from previous units in the year that 80% of the students in their focus class needed more support in making inferences. This led the resident to identify inferencing as the focus skill. With the support of their mentor, they proposed differentiated learning goals for subgroups in the class: for example, "By December, group one will be able to make inferences with 100% accuracy and identify effective textual evidence 50% of the time." After examining student work and assessments, the resident was able to further refine the subskills to include identifying effective evidence, analyzing evidence and connecting it back to inferences with 80 percent accuracy. In iterative cycles, the resident tested out instructional strategies such as an inference-making game, teacher-facilitated discussion with scaffolded questions, and graphic organizers to scaffold and organize student thinking, all in service of helping the students improve on the focus skill. However, the students had not demonstrated the desired growth after the end of two cycles, partially because the resident had not honed in on and addressed the students' foundational reading comprehension struggles, which prevented them from making effective inferences.

After each strategy was deployed, the resident assessed its impact and reflected on student progress, describing gains and areas for continued growth: "Students are able to identify evidence, make inferences and begin to explain ideas more thoroughly, but still struggled with reading comprehension." In response to this reflection, the resident decided to introduce a new strategy, "QMIAL," an in-school developed reading comprehension strategy that helps students remember the following steps: read the questions first, identify the main idea of each paragraph in the passage, answer the questions, and look back in the passage for clues. After two additional cycles of data collection, analysis, strategy refinement and revision, the students in the focus class were able to show that their scores on inferencing questions had doubled. The resident shared a wide variety of take-aways from the inquiry process, including that in the future they would incorporate visual aids and graphic organizers in lessons to make skills accessible, introduce QMIAL earlier in the year, research better ways to scaffold questions that are difficult for students to grasp, teach students to create their own questions to ask each other using Costa's Three Levels of Questioning (Costa and Kallick, 2008), and to continue to practice backward planning when building scaffolds. In this case study, we can see how engaging in inquiry cycles enables residents to bridge theory and practice and build habits of mind around using data to inform their decision-making and continually tailor their instruction to students' needs. Furthermore, the resident was able to identify next steps to continue meeting their students' needs.

Mentor Professional Learning and Inquiry

Mentor professional learning is designed to build mentor capacity in data analysis, inquiry, and instructional coaching as a teacher leader. There are three major learning spaces mentors engage in: the mentor seminar, quarterly mentor professional development, and the three-way coaching meeting. The mentor seminar is a monthly small group meeting facilitated by one of the program coaches, while quarterly professional development is structured for engagement with the whole mentor cohort together. Mentors prepare for the mentor seminar and quarterly mentor professional development by submitting resident data, reading relevant texts, and reflecting on their own mentoring practice. During the professional development, mentors meet in groups in order to discuss the most recent administration of resident and mentor performance data on program assessment tools as well as problems of practice and coaching strategies. Mentors engage in various structured protocols that allow them to solve problems of practice together and build rapport across the cohort. These learning opportunities are also utilized to discuss and analyze the mentor competencies in order to deepen the mentors' understanding of each component on the mentor performance assessment tool. Mentor whole-group sessions include three main components:

A. Aligning expectations for effective instruction in a focus area and identifying coaching strategies for that area of instruction. Based on whole-cohort assessment data, the program staff identifies a focus area of instruction where all residents are struggling or need additional assistance. This is usually also an area where there may be a discrepancy between different mentors' understanding of effective practice or the mentors' and coaches' understandings of best practices. The group reviews best practices related to this area together and norms around expectations. For example, one year many residents were struggling early on with writing specific, measurable objectives aligned to their lesson activities, as seen in our assessment data, and coaches and mentors were assessing their residents differently on this component. During the session, we discussed the criteria for effective objectives, explored examples together, and asked mentors to share their ideas and examples to build shared understanding. Then, we brainstormed strategies for coaching residents to improve in this area, making sure to elicit subject-specific examples.

B. Peer problem-solving. Mentors have the opportunity to identify areas of concern or challenge in their mentoring practice and self-select into small groups to problem-solve around these challenges, getting advice and hearing successful strategies from peer mentors. For example, one mentor identified that her resident was having difficulty pacing the lesson and integrating opportunities for formative assessments, so she presented this question to the other mentors and they shared how they had developed their residents' capacity for pacing and implementing quick formative assessments during lessons.

C. Goal-Setting. Mentors review their resident's assessment data up to this point and reflect on the resident's progress and areas for growth. Based on activities A and B, as well as on their reflection on their own resident, they set mentoring goals for their residents and describe their next steps. The program coaches then follow up on these goals with each mentor.

D. Jedi Project. Mentors, similar to residents, engage in inquiry by completing the Jedi Project. The Jedi Project, affectionately named from the Star Wars universe to recall the mentors' role as guides and gurus, asks mentors to investigate their own practices in order to show impact on resident development. Through this inquiry process, mentors gather evidence and show how their specific coaching strategies supported their resident in demonstrating growth. Mentors compile lesson plans, coaching logs, or even video as evidence to show their work over time. This process culminates in a brief presentation to a group of peers in the quarterly mentor meeting; mentors receive feedback and suggestions for next steps from their group. The mentors were reluctant to engage in this at first, but over time, it has become an essential part of our mentor professional learning and developing our mentor community.

Mentor Jedi Project Case Study

Mentors provide support to residents across all areas of their teaching practice and are often targeting multiple goals at once. Just as the Defense of Learning asks residents to focus on a key instructional goal in order to reflect deeply on their decision-making and demonstrate impact on students, the Jedi Project encourages mentors to hone in on one specific, high-priority learning target for their resident, engage in inquiry cycles related to their mentoring, and demonstrate impact on their resident's practice. The process of selecting a goal, planning and executing support, and reflecting using artifacts and other data allows mentors to assess the effectiveness of their coaching practice. Sharing their learnings allows the mentors to showcase their work and receive feedback, which benefits the whole cohort. In the following transcript of a Jedi Project presentation, a Special Education mentor describes her semester-long coaching, using artifacts to show progress.

> B [the resident] is working with two different co-teachers. One thing that I thought that B should be working on was co-teaching. He was not including any co-teaching models in his lesson plans; they were just doing team teaching for an entire period. [The mentor shows the group one of the resident's lesson plans.] After that first observation, B and I sat down and we started to talk about how he could use different models [of co-teaching] ... I invited him into a couple of different classrooms ... so that he could see the different ways that I use

co-teaching with my co-teachers. During our debrief, we talked about the different kinds of models and when you would choose to use each of those models.

Then I went back [to observe the resident] to see him again in a different class. [Mentor shows second lesson plan.] And you'll see he used "one teach and one assist" and he also used "alternate teaching." So now he's actually starting to put these items into the lesson plan. However, when I was in the class, they didn't actually happen. So it was great that he started here, he's got them written out, he's been thoughtful, but he doesn't know how to implement them. So I thought that the best way for him to do this would be to sit down and talk about how he could rearrange his lesson and pace his lesson better to make sure that he's including multiple strategies and he's actually acting them out, which can be hard to ... [for example] getting the students to move into a group in the lesson. So really taking the time to not only plan it, but to pay attention to the lesson plan as you're actually teaching the lesson.

I went back for a third observation. And that is your final paper here. [Mentor shows third lesson plan.] And now he has included all of the teaching models ... And while I was in the class, he did implement the strategies and this is by far his best lesson. So we celebrated the fact that he actually used the teaching strategies. It works best with his students. He did have other groups going around the room which we need to ... restructure, [for example] how do you get those directions out if you're not standing with them. But the students that he pulled into his alternate group, it was perfect ... he had them in their space, answering questions and asking them appropriate questions.

I noticed ... we're not getting through the whole lesson now that he is using the different strategies. It's wonderful that he's now using the different strategies, he's making good decisions about how to put students in groups, but it's taking a little bit longer. Now we have to work on how we adjust the lessons so we can still use multiple models and get through to the end point of the lesson. And if we don't, how are we going to restructure tomorrow's lesson to ensure that the students reach the point that you wanted them to reach at the end of the day yesterday?

As evident in this transcript, the mentor was able to use observation and lesson plan data to reflect on the effectiveness of her mentoring and revise her strategies in order to help the resident meet student needs. She ends her Jedi Project presentation with her next area of focus, demonstrating that she has internalized this process of setting a goal, working toward it, assessing progress, adjusting strategies, and defining a next step or new goal based on the outcomes.

These examples demonstrate how program structures help residents and mentors keep student learning at the center of their decision-making processes. Another, urgent question for the program leadership is how we, who are located farthest away from K-12 students, maintain that focus and hold ourselves accountable for using real data about resident progress through the program to improve program quality over time. It is easy to let political issues, anecdotal information, and inertia prevent us from being disciplined and honest with ourselves about what most needs attention and revision, but we know that it is impossible to accomplish the goals of our residency program without that focus. Below, we share some of our program's methods.

Coach Learning: Connecting Resident and Mentor Practice to Broader Program Improvement

In the residency, coaches play a crucial role in helping residents to bridge theory and practice, supporting resident-mentor pairs to ensure that residents become effective teachers, guiding the resident's inquiry practice, and liaising between the host school and the program. At least monthly, coaches observe and debrief with each resident-mentor pair, providing feedback using program assessment tools. Resident and mentor professional development seminars are facilitated by coaches, and coaches also serve as the first point of contact for residents, mentors, and school administrators for problem-solving and support.

To support their own learning and effectiveness, coaches meet together in a professional learning community once per month, as well as participating in initial coach training and the ongoing mentor development sessions. During the monthly coaching team meetings, coaches have the opportunity to share accomplishments, growth, and areas of concern and to engage in collaborative problem-solving around problems of practice. The team as a whole always examines a particular "slice" of resident or mentor performance data together to understand how their resident-mentor pairs are doing in relationship to the cohort and surface trends and patterns that can inform coaching for particular schools or content areas, or that will suggest revisions for the resident or mentor seminar content (see Appendix C). Coaches also norm together around the program assessment tools to build a shared understanding of effective teaching practice and expectations for resident performance. As a final component, coaches use the coaching rubric to self-assess around their own practice as coaches and set goals for improvement.

Coaching Case Study One: Norming Use of Assessment Tools for Data Collection

Norming is a central challenge any time a diverse group of stakeholders utilizes the same tool. While sometimes we think about norming as a process that is accomplished once and for all initially prior to implementing a tool, within the context of a residency program, norming is an ongoing, authentic part of building shared ideas about effective teacher practice and developing coherence. In an ideal world, our mentors, coaches, school administrators, residents, and program faculty would all assess the same observation in the exact same way. The reality is that with a constantly changing context and cast of new residents, mentors, faculty, and staff, we need to continuously attend to norming and alignment. However, conversations around norming provide an excellent way in to meaningful discussions of our ideas about best practices and expectations for our residents that, if done well, build all of our capacity to use low-inference evidence connected to our rubrics to support our assessments.

We build opportunities for norming exercises into the initial and ongoing mentor and coach professional development. During ongoing professional development, we often use the data to highlight areas of misalignment between stakeholder groups, which allows us to build a shared understanding of strong teacher practice. In one example, we noticed that mentors' ratings of residents on Danielson Framework component 3c, Engaging Students in Learning, were consistently higher than program coaches' ratings on that component, both on average and for individual residents. We highlighted that data during the professional development session and used a sample video of teacher practice, asking mentors and coaches to rate the sample on component 3c. In the norming discussion afterward, mentors and coaches shared their concrete evidence for their ratings, and coaches surfaced that many mentors defined Engaging Students in Learning as affective engagement—on-task, compliant behavior. However, coaches were looking for evidence of students' intellectual engagement, aligned to the lesson objectives. After consulting the actual rubric criteria, mentors identified that they were missing some components in their definition of engagement. In this instance, coaches needed to address mentors' concerns about the rigor of the rubric and what was realistic for novice teachers, which they did. The group then proceeded to a discussion of what evidence of intellectual engagement looks like, especially in the classroom of a novice teacher, how it is different from compliance, and what kinds of goals and coaching strategies they could use to support residents struggling in this area.

Coaching Case Study Two: Using Continuous Improvement for Benchmark Development and Revision

The development and revision of our program benchmarks is another example of our use of continuous improvement processes. Data from assessments is regularly analyzed by the team of teacher educators and the leadership team to drive coaching for individual residents and resident-mentor pairs, and to guide revisions to coursework and program design for the cohort. Each year, we examine resident performance against the benchmarks and connect that performance to effectiveness and retention during the induction year. We examine questions such as:

- If residents met our benchmarks, did that signal that they were truly "day one ready" and would be successful as full-time first year teachers?
- If residents met benchmarks and still struggled during their induction year, in what areas did they struggle? Should we increase the program support and benchmark rigor in that area?
- Is the progression of benchmarks both realistic and rigorous? Was it possible for residents to miss benchmarks during the year but still be ready to be effective in the fall? If so, which ones?
- Does the emphasis in our program benchmarks align to any changes in DOE emphasis or initiatives for new teachers? Should we shift our expectations in any way based on external policy shifts?

Each year, we adjusted our benchmarks based on our data and analysis of these questions, moving from hypotheses about what constituted competent practice to benchmarks based on experience. In addition, our program evaluators were able to support us in analyzing whether meeting benchmarks during the residency year correlated with whether or not residents were successful during their induction year. They generated several useful findings for us, such as the importance of Danielson Domain Two (the Classroom Environment) scores in predicting a successful transition to full-time teaching. This informed our setting of more rigorous Danielson Domain Two benchmarks during the residency year and emphasizing a review of classroom environment-building skills during the summer induction workshops. In the benchmarks revision process, the coaches' expertise around novice and mentor teacher practice was honored and triangulated with quantitative analysis of outcomes to develop a realistic and rigorous set of expectations for all program graduates.

Program Leadership: Continuous Improvement of Program Systems and Structures

The program's leadership team meets regularly to analyze program-wide resident, mentor, course, and outputs data for trends and patterns; use data to review current status and track progress toward goals; monitor alignment and coherence in the program; and draft, revise, and confirm program policy decisions. During meetings, the program leadership uses a variety of approaches and protocols to analyze data, reflect on progress, problem-solve, and revise the program model when needed. In order to foster productive and disciplined discussions, program stakeholders need to be committed to transparency around data, understanding the reality of the implementation of a complex program such as UTR, examining assumptions, and being open to changing the program model. Our use of data to revise program elements addresses all aspects of the program, but almost always involves triangulating data from multiple sources, eliciting various perspectives on the outcomes, and agreeing on a pilot plan and a way to return to the decision to identify whether or not our change is effective. Some past examples include:

- our use of resident grades, professor feedback, and resident survey results to make an informed decision to remove a particularly time-intensive genetics course from the Biology Education sequence and replace it with a course that examined common high school Biology student misconceptions and how to address them in the classroom;
- our use of mentor feedback and resident performance on the Danielson Framework competencies related to classroom environment to surface the fact that residents were struggling to build effective relationships with students; this resulted in our design and facilitation of resident seminar sessions related to cultural competency and building relationships with students and to a session on coaching for equity with our mentors; and
- our use of feedback from residents, faculty, and host schools to identify that TESOL residents were not being scheduled effectively to allow them to have a variety of experiences in supporting students' English Language Learning in different settings, which resulted in new guidelines to host schools about how to program and support TESOL residents, and engagement of a TESOL professor in the mentor PD to better communicate expectations and discuss an aligned vision of effective TESOL teaching.

Building Trust

For program leadership, building the trust to share data and confront our own errors or weaknesses publicly is not easy, especially when stakeholders come from diverse institutions with different organizational cultures and expectations. In these types of settings, it is easy to revert to the norm of the "culture of nice" (MacDonald, 2011). Our team found that at the beginning of the partnership, we, as the lead partners, needed to model that openness first and make ourselves vulnerable by sharing data about the program activities we were most responsible for, before asking anyone else to share their own data.

We found that five key best practices helped us to maintain a productive approach to doing continuous improvement with our various teams: norming expectations, using clear and consistent data analysis protocols, sharing data ahead of meetings with context, celebrating successes, and keeping the conversations solutions-oriented. First, in any ongoing meeting series or team charged with decision-making, it is important to set group norms and clarify expectations, including identifying the overall purpose for the series of meetings, the types of decisions the group will make together, shared goals, and rules around data confidentiality and appropriate sharing. These norms and expectations should be a touchpoint when any conflicts or questions arise and should be revisited by the group periodically. Second, the use of consistent and clear protocols helps participants to ground their observations and inferences in evidence and know what to expect from the process.

A wealth of data analysis protocols can be found from many different sources and matched to the specific types of data sets and purpose for the analysis. Often, discussing our observations or noticings from the data in small, cross-organizational groups first before a whole-group discussion helped stakeholders to process their emotional responses and prioritize the most important points to explore as a whole group. We also found it helpful to share the data to be analyzed ahead of the meeting and ask the "owners" or generators of the data to provide context and background information to introduce their data so that they felt that the data were being represented fairly.

Even given norms and clear protocols, it is easy for data analysis discussions to focus exclusively on challenges, gaps, and problems. Celebrating successes and acknowledging "status quo" effectiveness is crucial for all stakeholders so they feel appreciated, and more importantly so that we can identify program elements to continue and highlight strengths to investigate and build on. Any protocol selected should include a significant amount of time identifying and exploring what's working, and the meeting facilitator should be committed to honoring that time. In addition, the protocols and meeting agendas should always be solutions-focused; it is frustrating for teams to raise many challenges and issues and then leave a meeting with the sense that they will not be addressed or remedied. Although the data may surface many problems that could or should be addressed, the team needs a process for prioritizing a realistic number of those challenges and then identifying immediate next steps to respond, even if those next steps primarily involve doing more research to learn more about the specifics of the challenge. While we definitely experienced—and still experience—challenging moments with program partners during data analysis, we found that our shared commitment to the overall program goals ultimately keeps us in the conversation together.

Program Leadership Case Study One: Revising Admissions Processes to Increase Equitable Outcomes

One of the most important aspects of a disciplined and solutions-oriented approach to using data is the opportunity to investigate, learn about, and address challenges that may be uncomfortable or difficult to confront without data or a process for inquiring and problem-solving. Our program seeks to recruit and prepare a high proportion of teachers of color in order to address the problem of teacher populations that are not representative of the student populations they serve, and to respond to the many recent studies that have shown the positive impact that teachers of color have on students of color. As part of our commitment to recruiting and retaining diverse candidates, our team wanted to study whether or not our admission processes might provide openings for unconscious bias to enter the assessment process, especially since we are committed to having mentors, school administrators, program staff, and faculty all take part in the admissions process. Our internal New Visions policy and research team conducted an analysis of our admissions process scoring, comments, and rubrics by candidate race and other demographic factors. Unfortunately, they concluded that the various stakeholders who were engaged in evaluating candidates did not always demonstrate norming and consistency in their use of the rubrics, and that some of the questions or prompts were too prone to an idiosyncratic or culturally dependent interpretation, which could open up the process to the influence of unconscious bias.

Using the information from that analysis, our team committed to revision of our assessment tools and norming processes so they could be executed more reliably and equitably by multiple stakeholders. We utilized a continuous improvement approach, first conducting research around implicit bias in recruitment and assessment and best practices from other teacher preparation programs and the field of human resources at large. Then, we revised our rubrics in alignment with our research and elicited feedback from various stakeholders on the revisions. We subsequently designed a process to norm and then pilot the use of those rubrics to score interviews. Each interview was scored by multiple normed stakeholders, and we examined interrater reliability at several points throughout the review process in order to assess whether or not our new tool and protocols were resulting in greater alignment between raters. Although we did not adjust the rubrics midstream during the admissions process, we did utilize the information from our study of the interrater reliability to inform and structure the norming process and content for school-based interviews. In addition, we surveyed raters and candidates afterward to learn about their perceptions of the process.

At the end of this inquiry, we had attained an improved level of interrater reliability and noted a marked increase in alignment between the revised rubric criteria and the evidence raters were using to justify their evaluations. Our resident cohort that year comprised over 60 percent individuals of color, and candidates reported that they felt supported throughout the interview process regardless of whether or not they were ultimately accepted. However, we identified several additional areas for future revisions to further examine the equity of our admissions processes and used those foci to pilot changes for the following year.

Program Leadership Case Study Two: Partnering with Program Evaluators to Maximize Learning from External Evaluation

External evaluation plays a role that is different from inquiry and continuous improvement, but just as crucial in providing a more comprehensive look across the program that examines outputs and outcomes, tests our broader theory of action, triangulates data from multiple qualitative and quantitative sources using validated tools, and provides an independent perspective.

Throughout the development of our program, we worked with Rockman et al. (REA), an independent research firm with extensive experience studying school reform efforts, on the project's external evaluation. From the outset, we recognized that understanding the impact of our program was crucial not only for our own learning and accountability to partners, stakeholders, and funders, but also for contributing to the national body of research around teacher residencies. The partners shared the conviction that in order to justify the significant investment of resources required for a successful residency program, we needed to demonstrate our graduates' increased effectiveness and retention. We also shared a commitment to using our interim or annual evaluation reports as formative feedback to help us make program improvements, especially the information gleaned from focus groups and surveys administered to residents and mentors, which provided us with input that could only have been elicited by an external entity.

Our key research questions included:

- What impacts do UTR graduates have on their students' learning outcomes, with separate analyses for students of residents, graduates, and mentors and for school-wide effects?
- What impact does the model have on teacher efficacy, effectiveness, satisfaction, and retention?
- How do UTR candidates compare to other teacher preparation candidates, based on candidate demographics, performance, degree completion, and NYC evaluation and certification metrics?
- What implementation elements are most closely linked to residents' and mentors' growth and effectiveness, and to improved student achievement?
- To what extent are essential program components implemented with fidelity?
- Are certain school conditions a better fit for implementation of the model?
- What characteristics predict mentor success? How does participation influence practice?
- What supports and structures at the host school and college are necessary for the effective implementation of the residency model?

In order to learn about the full range of program impacts and evaluate elements of our theory of change, Rockman designed a mixed-methods approach that allowed them to examine student, resident, mentor, and school-level outcomes, utilizing data that was part of the program's systems for resident and mentor tracking, available through New Visions' data-sharing agreement with the DOE, or generated through Rockman's activities, such as surveys and focus groups. They could then triangulate these quantitative and qualitative data sources to draw inferences about the program. Data collection activities included:

- Quasi-experimental comparison of Regents exam (high school standardized culminating exam) scores of and credits earned by students taught by resident-mentor pairs and residency graduates to those of students taught by other teachers (matched for comparison);
- Comparison of retention rates of residency graduates versus NYC averages;
- Analysis of resident program completion and certification rates;
- Resident performance on formative assessments against program benchmarks;
- Surveys of residents and mentors around efficacy, perceptions of resident readiness, and opinions about program supports; and
- Focus groups or interviews with residents, mentors, coaches, school leaders, and program faculty and staff around efficacy, perceptions of resident readiness, and opinions about program supports.

The program staff communicated frequently with Rockman, not only to coordinate evaluation activities and access to data, but also to share major program revisions so that Rockman could tweak the evaluation instruments to gather information about the impact of those changes. For example, when Rockman's focus groups and surveys surfaced evidence of lack of coherence between various program structures, we created a monthly "program syllabus" to outline a clear focus for resident and mentor work each month connected to each program structure, and to streamline communication about program expectations and access to resources. In the following year, after we implemented the program syllabus, we asked Rockman to include targeted questions during their focus groups about resident and mentor use of and opinions about the syllabus, and compared the data about coherence from the prior year to the following so that we could gauge whether or not our new strategy had addressed the issue effectively. Keeping Rockman informed about changes in program structures, strategies, or focus also helped them to make sense of and triangulate their data.

On an annual basis, Rockman issued an interim memo or report. To ensure that we were using the data for program improvement, we always scheduled a meeting with program leadership that included representatives from all partners to review the findings and discuss implications or next steps for the partnership. Often, because of our attention to gathering and using formative data, we were not surprised by the overall findings, but this summative annual look helped us to assess whether or not our interventions or revisions were successful, inform our decisions about any changes for the following year, develop a shared understanding across the partnership of the program's status, and build buy-in around revisions.

STAYING FOCUSED ON GERALDINA

Teacher residency programs are tremendously complex endeavors that involve partnerships between stakeholders that are themselves complicated. Building reliable systems that can be consistently yet flexibly applied is the only way to ensure a coherent program. However, programs must also respond to constant changes, both external and internal (such as changes in legislation and requirements for program accreditation, district policies, or staffing changes); meet the needs of a new cohort of novice teachers and mentors each year that presents its own strengths and areas for growth; and strive for constant improvement in a field where we are still a very long way from serving all of our students well. Throughout our ten years of residency work, we have constantly monitored program effectiveness and revised our processes and systems to improve our outcomes, so our partnership benefits from the expertise developed over time and through multiple iterations of strategic program changes.

At the heart of these layers of complexity, however, is one focus: our K-12 students. We build teacher residency programs in order to recruit, prepare, and support novice and experienced teachers who will increase student achievement and remain in education as lifelong learners and leaders. At the heart of a teacher's efficacy is his or her ability to make effective decisions based on reflection, collaboration, and inquiry. Without modeling a parallel process of data-driven inquiry, we cannot effectively support our residents and mentors in learning and applying these skills. Disciplining ourselves to engage in continuous improvement and inquiry with our partners, using authentic data about our outcomes and progress, allows us to confront issues of equity and begin to address the gaps we identify. As a community, we are not yet doing enough to provide Geraldina and her peers with the opportunities they deserve; in holding ourselves accountable to confronting our strengths, areas for growth, and to a continual process of revision and improvement, we are being honest with ourselves about how far we've come and how far we still have to go.

BIBLIOGRAPHY

Ball, Deborah Loewenberg. "Just Dreams and Imperatives: The Power of Teaching in the Struggle for Public Education." *Presidential Address at 2018 American Educational Research Association Annual Meeting*, New York, NY, April 15, 2018.

Bryk, Anthony, Louis Gomez, Alicia Grunow, and Paul LeMahieu. *Learning to Improve: How America's Schools Can Get Better at Getting Better*. Cambridge: Harvard Education Publishing Group.

Cochran-Smith, Marilyn, and Susan Lytle. *Inside/Outside: Teacher Research and Knowledge*. New York: Teachers College Press, 1993.

Dana, Nancy Fichtman, and Denise Silva. "Student Teachers as Researchers: Developing an Inquiry Stance Towards Teaching." In *Research on the Effects of Teacher Education on Teacher Performance: Teacher Education Yearbook IX*, edited by Julie D. Rainer and Edith M. Guyton, 94–104. Richmond Hill: ATE, 2001.

Langer, Georgea M., Amy B. Colton, and Loretta S. Goff. *Collaborative Analysis of Student Work: Improving Teaching and Learning*. Alexandria: ASCD, 2003.

LeMahieu, Paul G., Anthony S. Bryk, Alicia Grunow, and Louis M. Gomez. "Working to Improve: Seven Approaches to Improvement in Science Education." *Quality Assurance in Education* 25, no. 1 (2017): 2–4. doi:10.1108/QAE-12-2016-008.

Rockman, Saul, Kay Sloan, Alison Allen, Julie Blazevski, and Fatima Carson. "A Different, More Durable Model." *New Visions For Public Schools: Hunter College Urban Teacher Residency Project*, September 2018. http://rockman.com/docs/downloads/TQPXCombinedReport_10.23.18-1.pdf.

Sagor, Richard. "Collaborative Action Research and School Improvement: We Can't Have One Without the Other." *Journal of Curriculum and Instruction* 3, no. 1 (2009): 7–14.

Saunders, William M., Claude N. Goldenberg, and Ronald Gallimore. "Increasing Achievement by Focusing Grade-Level Teams on Improving Classroom Learning: A Prospective, Quasi-Experimental Study of Title 1 Schools." *American Educational Research Journal* 46, no. 4 (2009): 1006–1033.

Tabachnick B. Robert, and Kenneth M. Zeichner. "Idea and Action: Action Research and the Development of Conceptual Change Teaching of Science." *Science Education* 83, no. 3 (April 16, 1999): 309–322. https://onlinelibrary.wiley.com/doi/epdf/10.1002/%28SICI%291098-237X%28199905%2983%3A3%3C309%3A%3AAID-SCE3%3E3.0.CO%3B2-1.

Talbert, Joan E., M. Ken Cor, Pai-rou Chen, Lambrina Mileva Kless, and Milbrey McLaughlin. "Inquiry-based School Reform: Lessons from SAM in NYC." *Center for Research on the Context of Teaching at Stanford University*, January 2012. https://www.researchgate.net/publication/265490218_Inquiry-based_School_Reform_Lessons_from_SAM_in_NYC.

Chapter 9

Moving from Resident to Teacher-of-Record

Bill Kennedy and Rebecca Hendrickson

INTRODUCTION

Learning to be an effective teacher is a career-long process; the notion that a one-year residency is sufficient time to be fully prepared to lead a classroom is an unfair expectation to place on residency programs. Residency programs do provide teacher candidates with more time and experience in classrooms than alternative certification and traditional teacher education programs, which likely leads to a greater sense of efficacy for graduates of residency programs. However, there is a need to extend the learning that takes place in residencies, supporting graduates to apply that learning in their work when they are no longer learning alongside a mentor, but on their own leading classrooms of students.

This was a realization that the University of Chicago Urban Teacher Education Program (UChicago UTEP) faculty came to after observing the first cohort of graduates having uneven experiences in their initial years as teachers-of-record in Chicago Public Schools (CPS). Established in 2003, UChicago UTEP was one of the first residency programs in the United States, and the community of residencies that NCTR has since created did not yet exist. At the time, we had no clear roadmap for what support systems a graduate of our residency might need, but it was clear that some induction coaching would help even the strongest graduates make the transition from resident to teacher.

As the second cohort of graduates entered CPS classrooms, the program hired one of its initial mentor teachers to come out of her classroom to coach the newest UTEP graduates. Two years later, the program hired another experienced urban teacher (one of the authors of this chapter) to meet growing demands and extend the in-classroom coaching support into the second year as teacher-of-record. In 2010, UChicago UTEP extended the in-classroom coaching even further to include a third year of induction support, making UChicago UTEP a "five-year program." We believe that the three years of continued teacher education post-graduation is directly related to the success and retention of our teachers in the field.

UCHICAGO UTEP PROGRAM OVERVIEW

UChicago UTEP is a two-year master's degree in the Elementary and Middle Grades Program with Illinois Certification (either a first-to-sixth grade license, a fifth-to-eighth grade license, or both) over seven UChicago quarters, followed by three years of continuing teacher education for those who stay in Chicago. The program consists of the following:

The Foundations Year (Fall, Winter, Spring, Summer of Year 1)
The Residency Year (Fall, Winter, Spring of Year 2)
Three Continuing Teacher Education Years

The Foundations Year builds fundamental knowledge for effective teaching in an urban school through seminar-based coursework, diverse urban field experiences, and gradually increasing, highly supported clinical teaching in University of Chicago Charter School classrooms. At the center of the Foundations Year is the Foundations of Education Seminar, a day-long seminar course that covers Education Policy (with a focus on the Chicago context and a field experience rooted in Chicago Community-Based Organizations), Human/child development with a critical focus on identity and the impacts of trauma, and curriculum and pedagogy with a focus on critical pedagogy and guided field experiences in a variety of Chicago schools.

Interns in the Foundations Year also take content and methods courses in literacy, mathematics, science, social studies, and differentiation and engage in two major clinical experiences: math and literacy tutoring (September through February) and math and literacy micro-teaching in "Homebase" classrooms.

The Residency Year is an intensive three-quarter (one academic year) clinical experience that is complemented by methods coursework and a seminar in professional teaching. As in Foundations, the center of the Residency Year is the yearlong, day-long professional teaching seminar, which creates a space for residents to deepen and extend their learning about pedagogy across all content areas, strengthen their understanding of classroom community and management, and engage in collaborative problem solving, inquiry, and reflection.

Residents work four days a week alongside UTEP-selected mentor teachers, called Clinical Instructors, in two half-year placements in two different partner CPS. They observe, teach, and assess student learning using the instructional best practices learned in content-area and methods coursework. As the placement progresses, residents assume increasingly more complex teaching tasks and day-to-day responsibilities.

The classroom teaching experiences in the residency placements align very closely with the coursework taught by UTEP faculty that takes place one full day each week. The courses require residents to connect the theory directly to their clinical practice. The same UTEP course instructors then conduct informal and formal observations of the residents in their clinical settings to create a tighter fit between the academic and the clinical experiences.

UChicago UTEP is a five-year program for those who choose to teach in Chicago; graduates receive three years of support from UTEP Induction Coaches at no cost to the graduate. Through a combination of philanthropy and other funding, UChicago UTEP has a number of full-time induction coaches who extend the learning of those graduates working in CPS. The three Continuing Teacher Education years begin with intensive initial support, and gradually decrease.

First year teachers receive weekly individual, in-class induction coaching along with a monthly professional meeting with their cohort and UTEP induction faculty. Second year teachers receive biweekly individual, in-class induction coaching. Third year teachers receive monthly support. By intentionally connecting the postgraduate years with the pre-graduate years, UTEP is sending a message to its students from the moment that they enter the program that each experience they engage with will be part of a five-year process of growth and development.

Since 2003, UChicago UTEP has 316 graduates currently teaching in urban areas across the country, with 175 currently teaching in CPS, and is currently admitting its seventeenth cohort. Over the last eight years, more than 50 percent of UChicago UTEP graduates are teachers of color. Although CPS does not hire centrally, principals hire teachers directly at the school. UChicago UTEP has a 100 percent hire rate in CPS.

UCHICAGO UTEP CURRICULUM: BE THE CHANGE YOU WISH TO SEE

A particular dilemma that UChicago UTEP has grappled with since its inception is how to prepare teachers to simultaneously fit into and stay in their positions at CPS while also challenging and making positive changes in the system. The curriculum of UChicago UTEP, therefore, has always attempted to simultaneously equip candidates with the practical skills that they need to be hirable and effective within more traditional schools while at the same time engaging teacher candidates in understanding educational theory, drawn from the progressive education tradition and a critical lens on race and class.

This two-pronged mission drives our selection of mentor teachers for the residents. We only select mentors who can demonstrate abilities to both excel within the demands and approaches of the district and also demonstrate social justice, anti-racist approaches to teaching. Interested mentors must apply to our program, complete an application, and be observed and interviewed by our residency instructors before being matched with a resident. We also invite and welcome recommendations from principals who understand and share our vision of justice-oriented teaching. Given our programs' maturity, we've also recently been able to select our strongest graduates as mentors, as well; in the two most recent school years, 50 percent of our mentors have been UChicago UTEP graduates.

Teachers are subject to their own formal and informal socialization as they enter the profession (Lortie, 1977), and are often inducted into the field with or without a formal program. The most common iteration of informal induction—a veteran "buddy," or mentor down the hall—is unpredictable, reliant on goodwill, and likely informed by an apprenticeship, *do-as-I-do model* (Feiman-Nemser, 2001). Teacher induction programming has tended to focus on helping teachers adjust to their school context, stay in their jobs, and teach in ways that support the schools' curriculum standards (Wang, Odell, and Schwille, 2008). These more traditional, socializing approaches to induction can end up reinforcing status-quo norms and practices (Feiman-Nemser and Parker, 1993; Zeichner and Gore, 1989). For candidates prepared in more critical, justice-oriented programs, these experiences can send teachers "into a bunker mentality to protect themselves from the onslaught of institutional resistance" (Stovall and Duncan-Andrade, 2006, p. 213).

As a program, we realized that our induction work needed to include not only the strengthening and ongoing learning of foundational practices of classroom teaching—for example, routines and procedures, lesson and unit planning, student relationships, differentiating instruction, but also needed to include an explicit space for helping graduates mediate those mixed messages and navigate the socialization of the profession, what Kelchtermans and Ballet (2002) call *praxis shock*. Facilitating this broad set of experiences can be complex and requires a well-rounded coaching team who continue to push their own practice as they work with our graduates.

UCHICAGO UTEP'S COACHING MODEL

At UChicago UTEP, we believe coaches, just like teachers, need to be decision-makers, using their professional knowledge to assess and plan a course of action for their teachers. Drawing on common tools, shared values, and a coherent vision of effective teaching, coaches tailor their work to the needs of each teacher they service. In this way, our coaching philosophy and pedagogy mirrors the vision of teaching and learning that is at the heart of our program. Just as we expect teachers to put learners at the center of curriculum development and instruction, and we expect teachers to differentiate instruction to meet the needs of their learners, we expect coaches to tailor their coaching practices and focus to the needs of their individual teachers. Just as we expect teachers to use formative and summative standards-based assessment practices, we expect coaches to assess the progress of their teacher both formally and informally using a holistic lens and variety of tools. Just as we believe social and emotional learning and attention to the whole child are critical for supporting children's development, we believe coaches, too, must attend to all aspects of their teachers' well-being. And just as we expect teachers to bring a lens of equity and critical reflection to the systems in public education and to work actively toward equity, we expect coaches to support and push teachers to continue to view their work as justice-oriented, to examine and question their own bias, and to work in solidarity with the low-income communities of color that they serve.

As full-time employees of the program, UTEP's induction coaches are faculty instructors on a parallel level with the UTEP instructors in Foundations and Residency courses. In the program's vision of five years of teacher education, it is only the location of teacher education that has shifted in the Induction years, from the graduate classroom of the University of Chicago to the CPS classrooms of the graduates. This intentional philosophy and language alignment has come about recently as we move to help graduates realize that coaching work is not merely "support," but an expectation that graduates continue to learn and grow through coaching.

Qualifications for the role, therefore, include demonstrated success teaching both children and adults. All of UTEP's coaches are former experienced urban school teachers, most of whom taught for many years in CPS. We also expect coaches to have some prior background in teacher education, either through being professional leaders within their schools or through formal coaching or professional development positions. Though induction coaches often bring a particular age level or content area expertise, all induction coaches are qualified to coach as generalists across the first-to-eighth grade spectrum in which our graduates are certified to teach. Most importantly, UTEP coaches must demonstrate an alignment to the values and pedagogy at the heart of our program.

As a program, we provide coaches with initial, as well as ongoing, professional development both on coaching and teaching practices. The initial and primary forms of development come from being immersed in the UChicago UTEP program. Our monthly day-long staff professional development meetings are structured so that the induction team has time to learn with one another, following a collaboratively designed learning cycle that focuses on both adult learning and coaching practices, as well as student learning and classroom teaching practices. Additionally, these day-long staff professional development meetings are structured to provide opportunities to collaborate and learn across the program with the Foundations and Residency Instructor teams. Teams work across their domains to help push for coherence and alignment across the program and keep one another informed about what our teacher candidates are learning as they progress through five years.

The induction team also engages in outside-the-program learning in both adult/coach professional development as well as student/urban classroom teaching professional development. The New Teacher Center's coaching program has been integral to the initial formation of a coaching framework at UChicago UTEP, and recent high-leverage teaching practice workshops in coordination with NCTR and University of Michigan's Teaching Works have pushed our coaches to think about the classroom instruction of our graduates in new ways. Coaches also pursue self-directed professional development in a variety of topics each year.

As residents approach graduation and find employment in a district school, UTEP induction coaches begin a thoughtful matching process that takes a variety of factors into consideration, including school location, grade level, and identified coaching needs and coach strengths. This intentional matching process is consistent with the student-centered pedagogy of the program, and is also meant to create a successful, lasting partnership. Ideally, each graduate/coach match will last for the three years of continuing teacher education—a continuity that allows for deep, meaningful relationship-building between coach and teacher. Just as we believe strong relationships are critical between teacher and student in the urban classroom, we believe a trusting and deep relationship between coach and teacher is critical. Additionally, just as looping has been shown to be effective in urban classrooms (e.g., Irving, et al., 2008), our model allows the coach to scaffold and track the teacher's development over time.

Coaches work on building productive relationships with all UTEP teachers before official matches are made. During the residency year, coaches participate in and lead a variety of experiences for with the teachers in training, so graduate teachers have already had meaningful interactions with their coaches through residency programming. In their first official meeting, coach and teacher spend time getting to know one another more deeply, sharing their histories and experiences in education and beyond. Additionally, coach and teacher preview and set expectations for their coaching work.

As the school year begins, coaches schedule initial face-to-face meetings between coach, teacher, and the school principal to outline coaching services and build a productive relationship at the school sites. During this meeting, coaches provide principals with a written description of the coaching program and share contact information. We have found it critical that principals have

Table 9.1 UChicago UTEP Praxis Cycle for Coaching

Point on the Praxis Cycle	As Coaches and Teacher, Together, We
Backward, at the recent past	reflect on the decisions that the teacher made and suggest/imagine different decisions that could have been made.
At the present	use tools that track evidence. We share this evidence with our teachers and engage in collaborative analysis.
Ahead, to the short- and long-term future	constantly, collaboratively, set goals. We set formal goals at the start, middle, and end of each year.
At history, and how it connects to now	look back at what we've learned in Years 1 and 2 of UTEP, as well as what we know from our experiences and our lives, to connect what is going on in our classrooms to the theory and practices and policies that have shaped the urban school realities we hope to strengthen.
At our well-being	focus on caring for the teacher, and helping the teacher take care of themselves.
At the process	facilitate ongoing discussion about the partnership between UTEP graduate and UTEP faculty, so that it can maximize the time spent toward improving the teaching and learning.

knowledge of our coaching work—what it offers, but also what it doesn't. Commonly, after this initial meeting the coach and school leadership do not meet regularly. In certain cases, where either principal, teacher, or coach believe it needed or appropriate, there may be more frequent check-ins scheduled to share progress and discuss emerging issues to inform further coaching work. In these instances, the coach walks a fine line, working to protect and respect the confidentiality of the coaching relationship, while maintaining a collaborative stance with school leadership.

UChicago UTEP coaching is flexible and adaptive to the needs of the teacher. Our coaching materials lay out a praxis cycle for coaching which consists of teacher and coach looking, collaboratively (see Table 9.1).

This praxis cycle is brought alive through a blended coaching model (Bloom, et al., 2005) which allows UTEP coaches to tailor the coaching modality, from more facilitative to more instructional, to the teacher and the issues at hand. Coaches use a variety of pedagogical tools and activities in their coaching work including classroom observation, facilitated debrief, collaborative problem-solving, analysis of student work, curricular planning, and more.

LOOKING BACKWARD AT THE RECENT PAST

Classroom observation and debrief using a cognitive coaching model is the cornerstone of induction coaching at UChicago UTEP. This method of coaching is characterized by focused classroom observations followed by a structured reflective debrief. During the post-observation debrief sessions, teacher and coach work through a tiered series of reflective questions including:

- What were the learning goals for your lesson?
- What were your instructional/pedagogical goals for your lessons?
- Thinking about your goals, what went well? How do you know?
- Thinking about your goals, what did not go well? Where were the challenges and trouble spots?
- What would you do differently? How would you revise?
- What are next steps or future goals?
- What support do you need from me (the coach)?

The debrief is rooted first in teacher perception and open reflection. Then the coach works to ground the teacher in the data and observations collected during the observation.

UTEP graduates are well practiced and comfortable with this reflective process; as teacher candidates in the Foundations and Residency years, they engaged in reflection about their practice on a regular basis. As a result, induction coaches find that UTEP teachers exhibit a lot of comfort with and capacity for the critical reflection that is at the heart of cognitive coaching practice. They are often able to identify areas of strength in their practice as well as areas for growth. They are open to input from coaches but are also invested in creating solutions to their own dilemmas. UTEP-trained teachers don't tend to exhibit the behaviors that serve as typical barriers to critical reflection and coaching—defensiveness, unwillingness, or mistrust. In this way, real learning and improvement can begin.

LOOKING AT THE PRESENT

Coach and teacher designate an area of focus for classroom observations. The coach tracks data using one of several observational tools, choosing from both qualitative and quantitative tools. Examples of qualitative data collection include selective scripting of teacher and student discourse, mapping teacher movement throughout the classroom on a seating chart, or tracking student disruptions and teacher responses. Student work on a classroom task, exit ticket, or summative assessment also act as sources of data to ground the reflective debrief. Quantitative tools are also helpful to the coaching process. Coaches may use a seating chart to track on-task behavior over timed intervals. They may tally the number of student responses from a variety of subgroups by gender or race, for example. As we have developed the coaching model, coaches have been bringing increasing focus to student actions, tracking not just teacher moves and choices but, additionally, their impact. This data is used to prompt reflection, problem-solving, and goal setting during the debrief.

New teachers can tend to over-generalize, stating, for example, that all children were engaged or disengaged or everyone "got it" or no one "got it." The work of the coach is to help the teacher get more specific and focused: Which children were struggling? What were the specific times in the lesson where engagement was high or low? A teacher may feel they used a strategy repeatedly, like asking higher order questions or giving positive praise, when the coach only recorded minimal use of that strategy. The data the coach collects as well as the coach's perspective and experience are helpful to focus and balance the teacher's reflections.

Looking Ahead, to the Short- and Long-Term Future

Debriefing session often become planning sessions in which coach and teacher work collaboratively to plan for implementation of next steps. Additionally, coaches conduct stand-alone planning sessions with teachers to revise or develop curriculum (units, lessons, and/or assessments), classroom management structures and protocols, interventions (behavior or academic) for struggling students, and more. Induction coaches have a much broader repertoire of curricular resources, content knowledge, instructional tools and strategies, and professional networks than the novice teachers they are working with. Coaches may, therefore, take a more instructional approach when needed, providing professional development and resources around key content or content pedagogy during a coaching session.

Another facet of coaching work includes beginning, midyear, and end of year goal setting. Three times a year, coaches use a common tool adapted from the Danielson Framework for Teaching to facilitate a detailed discussion around areas of success and challenge for each teacher. The coach then helps the teacher drill down around an area of growth to set goals, make an action plan, and identify a new coaching focus for upcoming observations. Often during these sessions, teachers will share data and feedback from their formal evaluations conducted by the school principal.

These goal-setting sessions stand apart from specific classroom observations, which also include more discreet goal setting. Teachers look more holistically and consider their overall progress since their last goal-setting session, celebrating growth and success and identifying new opportunities for professional learning. An important aspect of these goal-setting sessions is reflection on the coaching relationship and coaching process itself. During these sessions, coaches solicit feedback from their teachers about what has worked and what they would like to see changed. In this way, teacher and coach also set goals for the coach's development and the coaching work ahead.

AT HISTORY, AND HOW IT CONNECTS TO NOW

UTEP's critically prepared teachers often leave the program with a steadfast commitment to equity, critical care, and liberating pedagogies, but quickly find themselves focused on putting out fires and dealing with a variety of different challenges in a day. Some lose sight of the human elements of the work—the lives of the children, families, and communities that teachers serve every day—when the procedural elements such as mandates and paperwork are so present. In addition, the socialization that teachers experience from their peers and administrators is real and powerful and can create dissonance for the UTEP teacher. Even the most committed teachers may struggle to align their critical beliefs and practices with the traditional approaches they encounter or are expected to enact at their school site.

Induction faculty are keenly aware of helping their new teachers identify and negotiate this praxis shock. UTEP coaches use a critical dialogue praxis cycle with five distinct phases, specifically:

1. Open Dialogue,
2. Naming and Validating Success,
3. Critical Sense-Making,
4. Stretching Critical Practice, and
5. Committing to the Attainable and Aspirational.

Strategizing about how to be change-agents while respecting and building relationships within the school building, identifying which battles to fight, and finding spaces for resistance are all aspects of UTEP coaching.

LOOKING AT OUR WELL-BEING

Social and emotional support and learning is another critical facet of induction coaching. In their first years, teachers can experience a range of difficult emotions including disillusionment, helplessness, frustration, and overwhelm (Moir and Gless, 2001). Our coaches play an important role in helping new teachers weather the storm both figuratively and literally especially as Chicago winters are long and brutal. Coaches are intentional in asking teachers about how they are doing overall and supporting them in working toward work-life balance. Coaches may assist teachers with time management, identifying where and when they will accomplish the various tasks they need to be successful. Or, they may just simply act as a sounding board and a source of reassurance.

In addition to the on-site individual coaching graduates receive, first year teachers also participate in a structure called FYI, First Year Induction. These monthly events are co-facilitated by a coach and teacher and hosted at the teacher's school site in the evening. The agenda and focus are set by the coach and teacher, but always includes gathering over a meal, a tour of the teacher's classroom, and problem-posing/problem-solving. These meetings give graduates an opportunity to reconnect with their cohort and their training, providing a needed sense of camaraderie and support. Discussing shared struggles and celebrating success during these sessions helps teachers fight the isolation and overwhelm they often experience. Teachers also get the chance to structure learning for one another at FYI. Topics are often varied, touching on all aspects of teaching. Topics identified by teachers this year include managing cooperating adults in the classroom, differentiation, and negotiating toxic masculinity.

We believe having three years to complete the transition from novice to established teacher with a coach who has known and supported the teacher is an important step to creating career teachers. The gradual release of responsibility over the three years of induction coaching is intentional, as our goal is not merely to stem the tide of attrition or to temporarily fill a classroom position in an underserved, hard-to-staff school, but rather to create systemic change through teacher development. So much of the learning in which graduates engage during the first year is about survival and beginning to ground the practices they learned in the residency into their own day-to-day practice as teachers-of-record. Often the focus for coaching is dictated by the most pressing issues at hand, and teachers can often be vague or unsure about what they want to focus on during coaching sessions. Coaching at this stage helps teachers navigate the new school culture, establish their teacher persona independent of their mentor, and handle crises.

At the conclusion of the first year of teaching, coach and teacher use an end-of-year reflection protocol to capture concrete suggestions for improvement, focusing on lessons learned over the year, to guide summer planning and the work of the coming school year. Year two provides a useful "do-over," a time to correct the mistakes of year one, implement predictable and thoughtful routines, and deepen and extend curriculum and instruction. By the third year of continuing teacher education, which is the fifth and final year of their experience at UTEP, teachers have navigated their initial challenges and are ready to innovate their planning and practices. We find at this stage teachers are more focused, directive, and specific in their coaching relationship; they have a greater sense of what they need and are better able to leverage the expertise of their coach. They become more focused on working to strengthen their practice in a specific area. They may try out theories or practices they encountered during the residency that seemed more aspirational in year one of classroom teaching by asking coaches to plan for, observe, and provide feedback as they do so. They also may engage their coach in seeking further opportunities for professional development or in writing a study or classroom grant. It is in their second and third years that teachers are ready to thrive, not just survive; the guidance of a trusted coach is critical at this stage.

CHALLENGES TO PROGRAM-BASED INDUCTION COACHING

One challenge we've encountered in the development of our coaching model is the graduates' occasional ambivalence or rejection of coaching. The coaching that UChicago UTEP provides is free and comes with no formal obligation; almost all graduates take full advantage of this opportunity for continuing teacher education, but not everyone is interested or open to it. Graduates sometimes have too many other coaches in their schools who hold evaluative power over them; other times the graduate does not see the value or agree with the approach the coach brings. Other times, the graduate may not want to be seen struggling; the type of honest, critical coaching in which we engage refuses to simply sugarcoat or gloss over the challenges of being a new teacher. On the rare occasion that this honest evaluative coaching occurs, this ambivalence or rejection can be challenging for coaches, as they continue to make themselves available to graduates and try to juggle full coaching loads. It can be particularly difficult to watch a novice teacher, who clearly still has room to grow, reject the opportunity to further refine their craft.

To address this, we have developed a set of formal expectations for both the coach and teacher that includes: an outline of the coaching process generally; descriptions of the variety of coaching activities offered; expectations around scheduling, participation, and mindset; and suggestions for how to prepare for coaching sessions. We ask graduates now to "opt-in" to the coaching, as a symbolic commitment to the work. We have found that having a more formal document shared uniformly across the program is helpful for teacher and coach alike and provides a general frame from which coach and teacher differentiate.

Another challenge has been the limitations that come with reliance on only one model of coaching, the in-classroom, one-on-one coaching. This central approach has proven to be successful for most graduates most of the time, but UTEP induction coaches have begun to experiment with an additional approach that has both drawn in reticent graduates and simultaneously enriched the experience of graduates already satisfied with in-classroom coaching. Called *collaboratives*, these meetings are organized and facilitated by coaches as off-site collaborative planning sessions for their cohort of teachers. Designating a regular day, time, and location, coaches invite the teachers on their caseload (as well as any colleagues they choose) to meet, share plans, engage in informal problem-solving, and more. This approach broadens the learning community beyond the one-on-one relationship with the coach and leverages peer learning, a familiar learning community for graduates of the program who were members of a cohort in the Foundations and Residency years. This collaborative model also allows the coaches to intentionally pair more experienced novices (e.g., those in their final year of induction coaching and third year of teaching) with graduates in their first year of teaching.

The challenge from a program perspective, however, is that these collaboratives often occur outside of the regular work week, which requires coaches to work outside of typical work hours and rely on teacher willingness to meet outside of the school building and the school day. It is a long-standing labor issue that teachers end up working outside of the hours for which they are paid, and a model like the collaboratives encourages teachers and coaches to add to an already demanding work schedule.

Funding is a challenge to this five-year model. UChicago UTEP's three years of continuing teacher education have always been free to UTEP graduates who choose to teach in CPSs, paid for through a combination of grant funding and tuition dollars from enrolled students. We are always looking for new sources of funding for this work, including forming a partnership with our local school district to share the cost of this investment in teacher development.

A related challenge to funding is the difficulty of quantifying the impact of coaching. We know from the feedback we receive from graduates, coaches, and school leaders that coaching has a significant impact on teacher development and performance in the field. In recent years, we have taken steps to collect more data about our graduates as teachers through principal evaluation data and student achievement data. Because we are not the district, however, we must rely on our graduates to elect to collect and share this information back with the program. Each year we ask teachers to evaluate the impact of coaching on their teaching as well as the assets and growth areas for their coach. This survey has helped us gain a more detailed qualitative picture of the impact of coaching but does not yet meet the call to demonstrate "measurable gains."

IMPACT OF COACHING

Despite these challenges, we argue that the three years of continuing teacher education at UChicago UTEP can be linked to a number of positive impacts. Our induction programming supports and enhances the retention of teachers, program recruitment, teacher satisfaction, program improvement, and district change.

Teacher attrition is a major challenge for all schools, but particularly for urban public school like the ones in Chicago, who can lose half of their teaching staff every five years (Allensworth et al., 2009). To compound the attrition problem, students of color in schools in low-income neighborhoods are more likely than students in other areas to have new and inexperienced teachers throughout their K-12 career (Wei, Darling-Hammond, and Adamson, 2010). UChicago UTEP's decision to build a two-year residency with gradually increasing responsibility was always designed to combat retention problems in urban schools, believing that longer and more deliberate preparation would lead teachers to be and feel effective, and, as a result, stay longer in urban schools. But as we experienced within our own program, deliberate preparation without induction support may not be enough to curb teacher attrition.

Since we implemented our three years of continuing teacher education/induction coaching, internal data shows that UChicago UTEP teachers stay at a much higher rate than they did prior to this program shift, and at a higher rate than typical teachers in urban systems. Data from the last eight years shows that 94 percent of UTEP teachers who entered CPS and worked with a UTEP induction coach have stayed in the classroom for three years and 90 percent for five years (with some years/cohorts at 100 percent across those time frames). There may be other reasons beyond the induction we provide that account for why our graduates stay in CPS, but it is noteworthy that UTEP graduates who leave Chicago to teach elsewhere after graduation (and, thus, never engage in the three years of continuing teacher education/induction) leave the classroom and the field at higher rates than those who stay in Chicago and work with a coach. A more robust empirical study is warranted, but we believe our internal retention data serves as powerful evidence of the impact of our approach as a five-year program.

Another data point for us, in terms of the effectiveness and impact of our three years of continuing education/induction program, comes from the graduates themselves. In a 2015 program evaluation conducted by the Chicago Consortium on School Research, more than 80 percent of graduates surveyed agreed or strongly agreed that their coaches had helped them to become effective teachers and met their needs as growing professionals. Fully 50 percent of graduates surveyed strongly agreed and another 45 percent agreed that they had a trusting relationship with their coach. In the most recent (2017–2018) internal anonymous survey, graduates expressed a similar level of satisfaction with working with their coach. They also note a variety of reasons the value coaching support, as captured below:

> Yes, the coaching and support was essential for my growth as a teacher. There were many times when I felt overwhelmed, my coach was able to break it down and help me work through each situation. I appreciated the in-depth planning with math because it helped me to think more concretely about the needs of my students.
> Coaching gave me exactly what I needed this year; help with management, resources for ELs and struggling readers/writers, and a lot of emotional support. (My coach) tailored her coaching to my context, shifting our focus as the issues in my classroom shifted.
> Yes. My coach has done an excellent job in telling me what worked, and what I need to work on. She never lets me forget the significance of this tough, but meaningful job.
> Yes, (my coach) has helped me grow as an educator. She has validated much of what I was thinking and helped me to work around the issues I was having. She gave me support when I felt like I wasn't doing a good job and pushed me to grow when I started to feel more comfortable about things.

These voices from the field capture the varied nature of our coaching work and its impact. Teachers experience coaching as a lifeline, a vehicle for professional development, and an anchor to shared values and purpose.

The impact of our three years of continuing teacher education has now become a major recruitment tool; in the last two years, coaching support is consistently named in the top two reasons (the other is our critical, justice-oriented mission) by nearly all teacher candidates for why they chose UTEP. The prospect of being a teacher has always been daunting, with low pay, low prestige as a profession, challenging work conditions. Choosing a program that promises to get to know you, prepare you, and then promises to work with you well beyond graduation is intended to reassure candidates who want to do this hard work but may not feel like they can do it alone.

We have made the argument that our induction program contributes to the improved retention of our graduates, impacting Chicago kids, families, and schools. But there is also a reciprocal benefit to the program, as well. Induction faculty are constantly enmeshed in the Foundations and Residency years of the program. They participate in interview teams during prospective student days; they are in attendance for major culminating events in the first two years of the program, getting to know the teacher candidates who they will one day work with. In the middle of the Residency Year (year two of five), the induction faculty lead residents on guided observations in the classrooms of the graduates on their caseload, exposing the residents to the work of early career teachers. Induction coaches also collaborate with Residency Year faculty to design and deliver a Transition to Teaching course throughout the Residency Year to prepare teachers for entering the field. Induction faculty know and understand all of the aspects of the program so that they can draw from the curriculum and practices and build on them as part of the continuing teacher education of UTEP graduates.

As the induction faculty immerse themselves in the first two years of UTEP to help extend and deepen the teacher education of UTEP graduates, they also play an important role in improving the quality of the first two years of the program. Working daily in the district alongside our graduates, coaches learn valuable information about the policies, best practices, and trends operating in the system. Through ongoing professional development practices embedded in UTEP's faculty meetings, induction faculty share and inform the preservice faculty about what teachers need to know about in the system. They also serve as assessors of the program, able to measure and reflect back what UTEP teachers come out knowing and not knowing, what they are able to do right away, and what they struggle with in their first few years. Traditional teacher education programs rarely have the benefit of knowing whether or not the teachers they license and certify are effective. With a teacher education program like UTEP, where the induction faculty are part of the larger teacher education faculty, there is a built-in program improvement mechanism that ensures that the program stays current and up-to-date.

UChicago UTEP has always been a small program; ten residents a year in the first few years, moving up to our maximum of twenty-five to thirty in recent years. With most entering a system with over 20,000 teachers, UChicago UTEP is not looking to saturate CPS. But gradually over time, we have increased our reach and impact in the district from the ground up. It is particularly through our induction coaches and the graduates they support that our partnerships with district schools have increased.

In 2017–2018, UChicago UTEP graduates and residents were working in 103 CPS schools, with our induction coaches working in forty-eight. Additionally, there were ten schools where UChicago UTEP had a novice teacher, a UTEP-trained mentor teacher, a resident in training, a residency instructor, and an induction coach. Helping to improve the practice in these partner schools is an example of one of the future impacts for our induction work in the district.

Another growing impact is the way that induction can extend a career path from teacher education into teacher leadership. Shortly after completing the three years of induction with UTEP, our graduates become eligible to become mentor teachers who can host residents. Just last year, 50 percent of our mentor teachers were graduates of UTEP. Some graduates who were once mentor teachers have moved on to other leadership roles, including school instructional coaches and school leaders. Others have gone on to work in the district itself. Still others have been adjuncts in our program, and three of our earliest graduates are now full-time employees at UChicago UTEP, including two of our four full-time induction coaches.

CONCLUSION

The needs of novice teachers—particularly those who work in marginalized, under-resourced urban schools—are more than a teacher education program can adequately provide, and arguably more than the strongest teacher residencies can provide, as well. Teacher education programs, and teacher residencies like UChicago UTEP, could have a much greater impact on educating and retaining teachers if they extend their teacher education beyond the residency and into the classrooms of their graduates. External, disconnected induction coaching may provide some support for graduates of residencies, but induction coaching that is connected to the residency program creates a coherent experience for novice teachers who moves from simulated and supported practice into the more challenging experience of being a teacher-of-record. Extending that induction coaching beyond the first year, as we've documented here with UChicago UTEP's three-year model helps teachers move from surviving to thriving as they work with trusted professional teacher educators.

BIBLIOGRAPHY

Allensworth, Elaine, Stephen Ponisciak, and Christopher Mazzeo. "The Schools Teachers Leave: Teacher Mobility in Chicago Public Schools." *University of Chicago Urban Education Institute: Consortium on Chicago School Research*, 2009. https://consortium.uchicago.edu/publications/schools-teachers-leave-teacher-mobility-chicago-public-schools.

Bloom, Gary, Claire Castagna, Ellen Moir, and Betsy Warren, eds. *Blended Coaching: Skills and Strategies to Support Principal Development*. Thousand Oaks: Corwin Press, 2005.

Freire, Paulo. *Pedagogy of the Oppressed*. Translated by MB Ramos. New York: Continuum, 2007.

Irving, Miles, LaShawnda Lindsay, Tyrone Tanner, and Donnell Underdue. "In the Loop: An Examination of the Effectiveness of Looping for African American Students." *The National Journal of Urban Education and Practice* 1, no. 4 (2008): 150–162.

Feiman-Nemser, Sharon and Michelle Parker. "Mentoring in Context: A Comparison of Two US Programs for Beginning Teachers." *International Journal of Educational Research* 19, no. 8 (1993): 699–718.

Feiman-Nemser, Sharon. "Helping Novices Learn to Teach: Lessons from an Exemplary Support Teacher." *Journal of Teacher Education* 52, no. 1 (2001): 17–30.

Kelchtermans, Geert and Katrijn Ballet. "The Micropolitics of Teacher Induction: A Narrative-Biographical Study on Teacher Socialisation." *Teaching and Teacher Education* 18, no. 1 (2002): 105–120.

Ladson-Billings, Gloria. "Toward a Theory of Culturally Relevant Pedagogy." *American Educational Research Journal* 32, no. 3 (1995): 465–491.

Lortie, Dan. *Schoolteacher: A Sociological Study*. Chicago: University of Chicago Press, 1977.

Matsko, Kavita Kapadia and Karen Hammerness. "Unpacking the "Urban" in Urban Teacher Education: Making a Case for Context-Specific Preparation." *Journal of Teacher Education* 65, no. 2 (2014): 128–144.

Moir, Ellen and Janet Gless. "Quality Induction: An Investment in Teachers." *Teacher Education Quarterly* 28, no. 1 (2001): 109.

Stovall, David and Jeff Duncan-Andrade. "Urban Teacher Development for Critical Social Justice Pedagogy." In *Metropedagogy: Power, Justice and the Urban Classroom*, edited by J. L. Kincheloe and K. Hayes, 209–221. New York: Sense Publisher, 2006.

Wang, Jian, Sandra J. Odell, and Sharon A. Schwille. "Effects of Teacher Induction on Beginning Teachers' Teaching: A Critical Review of the Literature." *Journal of Teacher Education* 59, no. 2 (2008): 132–152.

Wei, Ruth, Linda Darling-Hammond, and Frank Adamson. "Professional Development in the United States: Trends and Challenges. Phase II of a Three-Phase Study: Technical Report." *The Standford Center for Opportunity Policy in Education*, 2010. https://www.learningforward.org/docs/defaultsource/pdf/nsdcstudytechnicalreport2010.pdf.

Zeichner, Kenneth and Jennifer Gore. "Teacher Socialization." In *Handbook of Research on Teacher Education*, edited by W. R. Houston, 329–348. New York: Macmillan, 1989.

Chapter 10

Principal Involvement in Teacher Residencies

Danaya Lamker Franke, Shelley Neilsen Gatti, and Amy Steele

PRINCIPAL INVOLVEMENT IN TEACHER RESIDENCIES INTRODUCTION

There are significant and complex issues surrounding teacher shortages and the lack of diversity in the teaching workforce. Districts and teacher preparation programs cannot maintain the status quo without multiple adverse effects on students, families, and communities. Instead, they must work collaboratively to recruit, prepare, and support teachers, and especially teachers of color. The Saint Paul Public Schools Urban Teacher Residency (SUTR) exemplifies this type of partnership between the Saint Paul Public Schools (SPPS) and the University of St. Thomas (St. Thomas). The SUTR program aims to recruit, prepare, support, and retain effective teachers from underrepresented backgrounds for SPPS. Many stakeholders have been involved in the development, implementation, and evaluation of SUTR, and continue to be integral in the recruitment, preparation, and induction of new teachers. In this chapter, we provide an overview of SUTR, specifically describing how SUTR has intentionally involved, collaborated with, and partnered with SPPS principals to recruit, prepare, and support teachers.

SETTING THE STAGE FOR SUTR

Diversity within the Saint Paul Public Schools

SPPS serves the diverse community of Saint Paul, Minnesota, and its surrounding communities. The SPPS mission is to "inspire students to think critically, pursue their dreams, and change the world" (About St. Paul Schools https://www.spps.org/domain/1235). The district employs 5,557 staff who serve at 56 schools/programs across the district. The district's four-year comprehensive graduation rate is 76 percent. SPPS constitute the second largest and most diverse school district in Minnesota. Students speak more than 125 languages and dialects, with 34 percent of students identifying as English Language Learners. Students receiving special education services comprise 15 percent of the student population. Seventy percent of students are eligible for free or reduced-priced lunch. On average, eighty percent of educators in the teacher-bargaining contract are in a tenured position each school year. In SPPS, the teacher–student diversity gap is also significant: 79 percent of the students are of color, while only nineteen percent of its teachers are of color. Statewide, only four percent of Minnesota teachers are of color (MDE, 2017). There is a critical need to diversify teachers in SPPS and across the state. A nondiverse teaching corps is a consistent barrier to producing strong racially equitable education outcomes (Sanchez, 2015) and Minnesota has some of the largest achievement/opportunity gaps in the nation (Magan, 2018).

Our University Partner

The University of St. Thomas is Minnesota's largest private university, with 10,000 students from fifty states and sixty-three countries. The School of Education at St. Thomas prepares Minnesota's teachers and education leaders in forty licensure areas. All teaching licensure programs meet the most recent Minnesota licensure requirements and are approved by the Minnesota Professional Educator Licensing and Standards Board. Full admissions requirements include a 3.0 GPA and passing scores on the state-required NES Essential Skills exam. Students must maintain a B-average to continue in the program (University of St. Thomas, Minnesota School of Education, 2018).

The University of St. Thomas and SPPS have a long history of partnership dating back to 1948. SPPS and St. Thomas have collaborated to provide services to children with disabilities and their families, prepared teachers through coauthored state and federal grants, and participated in the first residency in Minnesota, Twin Cities Teacher Collaborative (TC2). The SUTR partnership launched in 2015 when the Bush Foundation (Saint Paul, MN) awarded SPPS a $150,000 planning grant to develop a nonconventional teacher preparation program. The award allowed SPPS to work with the National Center for Teacher Residencies (NCTR) to develop a program model based on the New Site Development Program, which builds a residency program consistent with NCTR's Standards for Effective Residencies. In September 2015, SPPS received a grant from the NCTR, a sub-award from the U.S. Department of Education's Supporting Effective Educators Development (SEED) program. NCTR facilitated the district's connection with St. Thomas to engage in a full year of program design starting in 2015. SUTR was launched in June 2016, with the first cohort of twenty-two residents.

OVERVIEW OF SUTR

SPPS aims to address teacher shortages, as well as recruit and hire effective and dedicated educators who mirror the SPPS student population. Principals at our partner schools are a key element to success of this program. SUTR is one way this goal becomes a reality. The role of the principal will be explained in further detail later in the chapter.

SUTR provides a yearlong graduate-level teacher residency program in which residents earn masters' degrees and teaching licenses in fifteen months. Recruitment begins with non-licensed education professionals in SPPS, expanding to community members who are dedicated to educating SPPS students and who have bachelors' degrees. Based on SPPS's hiring needs for the past three cohorts, SUTR has prepared residents for elementary education (K-6 license) and Academic Behavior Strategist (ABS; K-12) licenses, which is a cross-categorical special education license in Minnesota.

Residents begin coursework in June and attend class for six hours per day, four days per week. They finish their first term in mid-August. Residents are matched with mentor teachers to provide a yearlong co-teaching partnership that fosters development of effective teaching practices for residents and improves learning outcomes for students. SUTR mentors are tenured teachers who possess a strong belief in the SPPS racial and gender equity policies and have demonstrated effective teaching as measured by the SPPS Standards of Effective Teaching rubric. Once the school year starts, residents take coursework on Mondays and teach alongside their mentor teacher Tuesday through Friday. Residents complete license-required coursework by the end of June of their second summer and complete the additional requirements for a Master of Arts in July and August. Throughout the program, the residents are both employees of the district and students at the university. During the academic year, residents earn a stipend of approximately $22,000 along with single medical and dental benefits. The residents pay tuition to St. Thomas and are eligible to apply for university scholarships, state scholarships, and federal loans.

For SUTR, St. Thomas and SPPS share responsibility and partner at all levels of planning, recruitment, course delivery, induction, evaluation, and support of SUTR teacher candidates. Partners also work with local and national committees and coalitions, such as the Saint Paul Federation of Educations (local teacher union), Coalition to Increase Teachers of Color and Native American Teachers, Saint Paul Foundation, Bigelow Foundation, and Minnesota Department of Education, to collaborate on strategies for teacher preparation and education reform. Within SPPS, the SUTR program is housed in the Office of Human Resources and the executive director provides oversight. Additionally, many offices and departments also consult with SUTR, such as the Equity Department, Office of Specialized Services (special education), Human Resources, and the Office of Teaching and Learning.

ADDRESSING A NEED IN SPPS AND THE STATE

As stated previously, SPPS and St. Thomas partnered on other teacher preparation projects before launching SUTR. Before SUTR, the Twin Cities Teacher Collaborative (TC2) provided the first residency path in Minnesota. This was a multi-district and multi-university partnership for residency in secondary science and math. When TC2 ended, SPPS administration saw a need and an opportunity to build on the work of TC2 and develop their own district-run teacher residency in the high-needs license area of special education, as well as diversify their elementary teachers by gender, race, and language.

The residency model was a perfect fit for St. Thomas's "all for the common good" mission statement. This model allows participants to advance the common good, remove barriers for underrepresented groups to become effective teachers in their own communities of Saint Paul, and to learn together to develop, implement, and evaluate SUTR. The SUTR model addresses common barriers that affect teacher candidates: cost, time commitment, and racial isolation. SUTR reduces the overall credits required for a license, decreases tuition, provides scholarships, offers the program at an accelerated rate, and uses a cohort model. Furthermore, residency programs have been shown to attract more diverse teacher candidates and develop more effective teachers, many of whom stay longer in the teaching field.

COLLABORATION WITH NCTR

NCTR was instrumental in the development and launch of SUTR and continues to play an integral role in the evaluation and continuous improvement of the program. When SPPS began planning a residency model, the design team reached out to NCTR for support. SPPS subsequently received a subcontract from NCTR to be in the first cohort of NCTR's SEED grant. As part of this project, SUTR staff received ongoing professional development and consultation during the planning year. This professional development included multiple visits to NCTR and two site visits from NCTR staff to SUTR. The focus of the professional development and consultation allowed staff and faculty to learn from NCTR and other residencies about partnership responsibilities, strategies for recruitment, mentor teacher selection and training, and curriculum design and implementation. As a result, SUTR developed many procedures and processes that staff continue to build off and improve each year. SUTR graduated from New Site Development into the network in May 2017. As part of the network, SUTR staff benefit from visiting other residencies (three to date) and participating in the annual symposium. In addition to the professional development, SUTR has benefited from NCTR research and evaluation team. SUTR receives midyear and end-of-the-year data summaries from residents, mentor teachers, and principals. With consultation from NCTR, SUTR staff analyze this data and use it to make continuous improvements in the program. The NCTR network has been an invaluable source of expertise, problem-solving, support, and friendships.

SUTR OUTCOMES

SUTR launched the first cohort during the 2016–2017 school year with twenty-two teaching candidates participating in the residency. SPPS hired all residents as teachers the following school year. Since then, SUTR has prepared a cohort of teachers each year with recruitment taking place for the most recent cohort for the 2019–2020 school year (see table 10.1).

Stakeholders

The residency model affords the opportunity to customize the program to the SPPS context, while meeting state licensure requirements. From the beginning of SUTR, the design team intentionally involved a variety of stakeholders in the development and implementation of the residency program. The most important stakeholders have been the students and families of SPPS. As stated previously, the goal of SUTR is to recruit and prepare effective teachers for SPPS that mirror the student population. Secondly, SUTR is accountable to the communities of Saint Paul and SPPS. Since the launch of SUTR, staff, residents, and graduates have presented to the school board, testified at the state legislature, been featured on the local news and newspaper, and participated on university advisory boards. District administration has been involved to help make programmatic decisions and provide professional development for the residents. SUTR staff have involved mentor teachers and graduates to provide feedback and suggestions on ways to improve the program. Finally, principals have played a very important role in designing and providing feedback on program components, recruiting residents and

Table 10.1 SUTR Demographic Data

	SUTR Demographic Data			
	2016–2017 Cohort 1	2017–2018 Cohort 2	2018–2019 Cohort 3	2019–2020 Cohort 4
Number of Residents	22	31	29	13
Licensure Area	8 Elementary	12 Elementary	12 Elementary	13 Elementary
	14 SPED	19 SPED	17 SPED	10 SPED
Number of Schools Hosting Residents	8	10	11	11
Attended SPPS as a K-12 student (%)	55	30	31	30
Persons of Color (%)	60	60	66	65
Gender (%)	50 Male	30 Male	52 Male	50 Male
	50 Female	70 Female	48 Female	50 Female
Multilingual (%)	20	34	21	30
SPPS Hire Rate (%)	100	86	96	In Progress
Number of Schools who Hired Residents	14	16	17	In Progress

mentors, providing mentor teacher coaching, and mentoring the residents. The remainder of this chapter will describe the ways that principals have been involved in SUTR.

Principal as Stakeholder

One of the most influential, powerful, and important stakeholders is the building principal. In the initial planning year, the design team realized administrators' perspectives and participation was critical to the success of the program. The team mapped out the principal role in SUTR, while being sensitive to the many demands and commitments of the building principal. SUTR staff already had connections with several administrators across the district and tapped their expertise and experience through informal conversations, collaborations, and participation at design team meetings. SUTR staff updated administrators at all stages of development and implementation of their feedback was incorporated in the model. Staff made a strong effort to be timely and consistent and continual in all of their communications with building leaders. After the first SUTR event, which introduced all residents to mentors and building principals, one of SPPS's veteran administration commented, "This is the best planned, communicated, and well laid out initiative I have seen in years."

In addition to including the principal perspective in the program, the design team intentionally included administrator voice in residency curriculum and instruction. At the beginning of cohort one, St. Thomas hosted an instructor retreat for all summer course instructors. This initiated the launch of quarterly instructor retreats. During these retreats, SUTR staff invited building administrators to share their perspective, allowing staff to learn together about ways to improve the program and more closely align course work to clinical experience. When a building administrator was not available to attend the entire session, accommodations were made to get their voices in the room via electronic meetings, such as Zoom, or by gathering data via surveys. This connection provided the bridge between coursework objectives and assignments, between application and priorities in SPPS.

Another way we included principal perspectives in curriculum and instruction was to invite SPPS administrators to teach or to co-teach a course with a St. Thomas instructor. With the help of foundation funding, we were able to provide full pay instead of splitting the course payment. This resulted in co-teaching up to five courses, and some district administrators went on to independently teach the course. This type of collaboration between the district and the university allowed residents to be able to learn from seasoned instructors, as well as from experienced district-level administrators and principals, while keeping the district context front and center.

Principal Role in Recruitment and Selection of Residents

Principals are an important partner in recruiting for SUTR. Principals promote SUTR in their buildings and make connections with families and community members. Principals post SUTR recruitment announcements in their buildings, forward SUTR emails to prospective candidates, post information on social media, and so on. Principals also have conversations with support staff and community members who show interest in being teachers, suggesting SUTR as a potential career path. Principals serve as initial connections to SUTR and then assist individuals in learning more about the program.

As a part of our application process, SUTR candidates are asked to provide two written references and at least one of those letters needs to be written by a current principal or supervisor. While reviewing applications and reading references, a principal's advocacy on behalf of a candidate is highly regarded. Principals offer a wealth of knowledge and provide a critical lens for those candidates most disposed to teaching. In their recommendations of paraprofessionals and other support staff, principals have seen the candidates function within the school and work with students. This is an invaluable perspective as an individual is being chosen for a residency program.

SUTR uses a rigorous interview and selection process. Residents participate in multiple sessions encompassing a traditional interview, participating in a group discussion focused on educational equity, and sharing their racial autobiography. Interview days require collaboration between the university and district, including principals. Approximately twenty SUTR stakeholders participate in the interview process and use rubrics to provide feedback on each candidate's disposition and potential to be an effective teacher for SPPS students. The district hosts the interview day with SUTR coordinators, program staff, and university personnel making final selections. The district extends an offer contingent on acceptance to the university.

In the interview design phase, it is essential to include district administrators, principals, and assistant principals in each of the selection sessions (interview, discussion, and racial autobiography). This proves to be very beneficial because principals become familiar with the rigorous process of SUTR resident selection. Principals partake in the work and hence are more willing to trust the team to pick high-quality candidates. Similarly, it is beneficial to the rest of the interview team to hear what principals and assistant principals really want in teachers for their buildings. Melissa Kalkinowski, a principal in a school that has hosted candidates for several years, commented, "SUTR recruits and selects high quality candidates that have had a deep commitment to our schools."

After being a part of the interview and selection phase, principals are ready to recruit additional staff who are a good fit for our residency program. Often, principals also consider particular candidates for positions in their buildings for the following year. In a district the size of SPPS, our administrators all know each other and often lean on each other for references. When our administrators are heavily involved in all aspects of residency work, they are more likely to talk positively to their colleagues about candidates they refer in the hiring process and beyond. Principals involved in the interview and selection portion report that it is absolutely worth their investment in a residency model. Elementary principal Laura Saatzer summarizes it well: "SUTR is directly addressing the needs of the district."

Principal Connection to Mentor Teachers

Principals play an essential role within SUTR related to mentor teacher selection and support. Residents are matched with mentor teachers to provide a yearlong co-teaching partnership. Principals look for mentor teachers who have robust experiences in the classroom and are equity leaders within their schools and communities. Principals seek to select mentor teachers who have a passion for education and adult learning and who want to give back to the education profession. Mentor teachers need to be able to dedicate time, energy, and resources to make the SUTR residency experience a yearlong learning journey. SPPS principals report that they look for teachers who are reflective and have a willingness to be transparent about their practices, actions, and educational moves with students and families.

Because principals know the teachers in their buildings, the conversations with SUTR staff and the selection team is vital in the process of narrowing down the pool of mentor teachers available for a specific school year. The process of mentor teacher selection starts with a conversation with the principal and other members of the administrative team about details in the program. Principals are asked to recommend enough staff who fit the required expectations, who are willing to open their classroom and teaching practices to a novice teacher, and to create a cluster site at their building of three to five residents. Principals recommend staff who are skilled in both instruction and mentorship. Administrators report that they seek mentor teachers who have strong practices and also know that this opportunity will allow them to continue to grow as reflective practitioners while enhancing their own teaching skills.

The next step for the SUTR coordinator is to meet with all recommended teachers to determine their fit for this role and ask them to complete the interest inventory. Based on this data, the principal and SUTR coordinator determine which teachers will make solid mentors. Specific mentor-resident matches are then made and shared with principals.

Once the match between the SUTR resident and the mentor teacher is determined, the role of the principal continues to be crucial. Principals support and provide feedback to mentor teachers throughout the clinical year.

While supports have proven to be helpful to the mentor and resident, SPPS principals report that they would like to be more intentional in working with mentors. Time is a factor that principals reference as a hindrance to providing feedback. In the future, SUTR would like to provide guidance and resources for principals to be more active in observing and providing feedback to mentor teachers, specifically related to their role as a mentor. One idea that SPPS principals indicate that they would like to incorporate more regularly is conducting joint observations with mentor teachers. Principals could observe a post-conference between the mentors and residents to later provide feedback to the mentors on how successfully they are providing feedback and coaching the residents.

In the experience of SUTR, there are few instances in which a mentor teacher and resident experience challenges. A solid partnership with the principal is essential in navigating these situations. SUTR coordinators and the principal convene to gather information and debrief the situation. They are continually in contact about next steps and progress in response to the challenge. If in fact, there is a situation where the resident-mentor pairing needs to be changed, the SUTR coordinator communicates the need immediately with the principal. Depending on the level of involvement and complexity of the challenge, principals participate with the SUTR team to make joint decisions whenever possible. If the principal is unable to partake in the process firsthand, the SUTR coordinators continually communicate what is happening and the progress that is made. Due to strong relationships created prior to the situation and clear communication, most principals are pleased to be kept in the loop during these situations and support the team's decision in the change of placement. Before a movement is made to a different school, the newly involved principal decides if she supports a match at her site.

Principals view the SUTR mentoring experience as a teacher leadership opportunity. It is a way for teachers to expand their personal growth and development while also contributing positively to the school culture. For schools that host residents for multiple years, the principal also plays a role in determining if an educator will continue in the role of an SUTR mentor. One of the key factors that SPPS principals look for when recommending mentors to the next cohort is whether or not the mentors demonstrated a willingness to learn along the SUTR journey. During the winter check-in between principals and the SUTR team, the discussions begin about considerations for mentors continuing their work for the following year. Factors discussed include willingness and ability to make their teaching explicit, willingness and ability to provide targeted and continuous feedback in the areas of strengths and growth, and ability to co-teach for the entire year. Being a SUTR mentor is a huge professional growth opportunity that principals recognize, but they also acknowledge that there are times when a mentor teacher needs to take a break and focus on a different area of their professional development. Ninety percent of SUTR mentors are selected to return to the work. Mentors who either decide to opt out or are not asked back generally did not fully understand the commitment to the intense residency work, had a difficult time being able to articulate their practice on a regular basis, or conduct evidence-based feedback sessions and conversations focused on areas for needed growth. Principals recognize when a mentor teacher needs a break; they acknowledge that being an effective SUTR mentor is a lot of work. SPPS principals support mentor teachers when they decline to mentor the next cohort, and honor mentors' other involvements and commitments.

Principals in the Clinical Year with Residents

During the SUTR residency, principal involvement is a central component. Principals welcome residents and treat them like other staff members working in the school. They connect and build relationships with residents and want to support residents to become career educators. They induct residents to becoming active members of the staff and thus believe it is their responsibility to support their growth and connection with other colleagues in a collaborative way. These connections include instructional, behavioral, and cultural practices specific to their school, such as co-teaching, professional learning communities, positive behavior intervention systems, and so on. To welcome residents, SUTR hosts onboarding sessions with all school administrators at cluster sites. Sessions are offered electronically and face-to-face to make it accessible to all principals and their busy schedules. During the session, an overview of the program and expectations for each site are reviewed. Time is provided for our returning sites to share what has worked for them and what they will do differently in the coming year to be more helpful to their mentors and their residents. At the beginning of the mentor selection process, SUTR provides principals with a site and mentor expectation document, an onboarding session with other administrators from the district, and a handbook for reference. While onboarding SUTR cluster sites into the expectations of the program, SUTR principals are asked to

- participate in SUTR onboarding prior to start of school,
- conduct fall and spring walkthroughs with post-observation conversation,
- coach and support mentor teachers,
- participate in check-ins three times a year with the SUTR team,
- participate in SUTR interviews in February and March, and
- conduct mock interviews with residents in January and February.

SUTR continues to review and evaluate what additional tools and practices need to be developed to better support our principals.

Residents also participate in school-level professional development at the cluster site, during opening week in August before students start and throughout the school year. In their roles as instructors and leaders for residents, principals greatly impact the growth and development of novice teachers. Principals may invite residents to participate in committees so they have a voice in the school. Principals recognize that SUTR residents can empower staff and add richness to the office culture.

Once the school year starts and residents are co-teaching lessons, principals observe and provide feedback similar to their regular teaching staff. This takes extra effort on behalf of the principal, as they incorporate walk-throughs, observations, and feedback to residents into their instructional leadership duties. Principals aim to make time and space for checking-in and providing feedback to residents and mentors. They want to take advantage of every opportunity to connect with and provide feedback during the residents' educational journey. SPPS principals report that some of the feedback happens more informally, such as during hallway conversations. However, many principals conduct at least one full-length formal observation of the resident during the winter months, when residents are leading the most lessons through the gradual release model. Principals relay that time can be a barrier to regular resident observations.

When pressed for time, principals know that SUTR has other support systems in place, such as mentor teachers, university supervisors, and SUTR team staff that support the residents throughout the year. Because of this, sometimes principal observations of and feedback to SUTR residents take on a lesser priority compared to principal interactions with licensed teachers on staff. Principals know this is not lessening their importance to SUTR but has more to do with time constraints and the balance of other duties in the building. SPPS principals explain that they need to be mindful of their time to make sure observations of and feedback to SUTR residents and mentors does not get postponed or cancelled. Principals also report that when there is a situation where more assistance is needed, they feel extremely well supported by the structure of the residency model and SUTR staff to step in if necessary.

Principals also assist residents in preparing for their first year as the teacher of record. For example, principals conduct mock interviews with residents. In SPPS, teacher candidates start the interview process with pool interviews at the district level. Once accepted into the pool, candidates then interview with school-based selection teams. Principals practice interview questions with residents to help them articulate their strengths and experiences in an interview setting. Principals also often serve as references for residents. This is an important networking connection, especially as not all schools that host residents will have openings for the residents' preferred grade levels or special education areas. In addition, building principals often sit in on the pool interviews. Since teaching positions exist across SPPS, support and principal recommendations from the residency year is crucial.

Principals also provide unique perspectives and guidance when there are challenges to the development of residents. In the past, residents have occasionally needed to exit the program for personal or professional reasons. Given the continual communication cycle, clear expectations, and readiness to intervene in a timely and supportive manner, principals are appreciative of SUTR and the decisions that need to be made around existing residents during the clinical year. Principals acknowledge that the interview and selection process is rigorous, but only real teaching experiences during a residency can reveal who may or may not be ready for such a career. Principals agree that it is better to work through exiting the program during a residency, rather than wait until the individual has earned his or her teaching credentials and is the teacher of record.

Principals Transitioning from the Clinical Year to the First Year of Teaching

In the spring, residents are involved in the interview and selection process at SPPS to be hired as the teacher of record. During this time, principals have strong feelings about who they want to hire and who they want to recommend to their colleagues. One of our committed and experienced principals, Dr. Mike McCollor, stated, "I am looking for goodness of fit when I interview folks. I want more career teachers, someone who will stay in the school and district. SUTR helps fill that need." During this phase of hiring, the SUTR residents follow the same procedures as all applicants to SPPS. Fortunately, the experiences they have had with principals in the residency year, such as observations and feedback cycles, mock interviews, and a full year of experience in one school, prepare residents for what lies ahead.

In late winter, SUTR invites a panel of principals into seminar class to discuss, from their viewpoint, the expectations for first year teachers. This experience has proven to be helpful to residents as they often have already met or will shortly be interviewing with this same administrator, and the panel gives them great insight as to what administrators in our district will be expecting from them in their first years. The message tends to be similar to what they have learned in their coursework, yet coming from a potential supervisor, a principal, it seems to have a different level of impact with residents.

The hiring of SUTR graduates has brought much excitement to SPPS. Given a pool of candidates who have completed the residency program, principals have had to compete against each other to claim the resident they want to hire. Frequently, one graduate is being recruited by multiple schools. Principals report that they feel like the candidates are interviewing the school as much as the school is interviewing the candidates. Principals take advantage of this situation by being intentional and open about what supports they have in place for newly hired teachers. It is encouraging to see principals recognize the importance of providing differentiated supports for new teachers from the very beginning of the hiring process. Principals share that SUTR graduates are assets to their schools. SUTR graduates are able to build relationships with students and communicate with families. They are culturally competent and have a passion for the communities within and around Saint Paul. Given all of these factors, principals believe SUTR graduates enter into their first year of teaching with a strong foundation and are more prepared than most first-year teachers. For these reasons, SPPS principals are extremely interested in hiring SUTR graduates.

Another interesting aspect emerging from the deep-rooted partnership between SUTR and principals is the ability for school administrators to understand a fuller picture of the SUTR graduates they are looking to hire. Principals are able to reach out to colleagues who host residents and seek perspectives on the SUTR graduates' abilities to be successful teachers in SPPS. In addition, some principals send teams (administrators and/or teachers) to observe the candidate in action, teaching before the end of the residency, in order to make fully informed decisions. On the other side, some residents ask to meet the team they may possibly be working with at the interviewing school. This in-depth opportunity to really get to know the job will ideally lead to greater teacher retention.

Principals and Induction

Once residents become SUTR graduates and are hired as teachers of record, the principal is involved in induction and support. Principals aim to provide an effective transition into an education career in SPPS. They want to support SUTR teachers with instruction and professional practices in order to increase professional success and ensure all students have a premier education. Principals start by welcoming first-year teachers and initiating them into the school's culture, systems, and structures. This is differentiated based on whether the teachers had their SUTR residencies in their school or a different location. SPPS principals take on the responsibility of connecting new teachers with colleagues to support instructional practices, behavior systems, and collaboration structures such as professional learning communities. LaNisha Paddock, middle school principal and adjunct instructor for SUTR, reports that she is always evaluating the induction process and the potential needs of new teachers in SPPS.

In the first year, principals match SUTR teachers with mentors who will best provide individualized and differentiated support and assist in meeting teachers' professional growth goals. Mentoring activities include but are not limited to observations with feedback, job shadowing, review of student work and data, and discussions around professional development goals. Oftentimes, when SUTR graduates are hired by the same schools in which they had their residencies, their SUTR mentors also takes on the role of their first-year teacher mentors.

During the second year of teaching principals partner with Peer Assistance and Review (PAR) educators who coach, collaborate, and consult probationary teachers. Participation in the PAR program has been a part of the teacher bargaining contract in SPPS since the 2009 labor agreement. The purpose of the PAR program is to support the professional growth of teachers. The primary role of the PAR educators is to enhance and habituate self-directed learning through regular observation and feedback cycles throughout the school year. During this year, principals conduct joint observations with the PAR educators for the formal observation process. Principals value this partnership and find it beneficial to the continued growth and development of SUTR graduates.

Throughout the three-year probationary period in SPPS, principals must conduct at least three formal observation and feedback cycles each year. During the residency year, SUTR residents are observed and given feedback on an evaluation tool that is a condensed version of the SPPS Standards of Effective Teaching. This leads to a smooth transition for principals in conducting observations of SUTR graduates. Principals report that, due to the feedback structure and familiarity of the SPPS evaluation structure, they are able to offer more effective feedback when supporting SUTR graduates. This continues to aid the growth and development of beginning teachers.

Due to a recent additional grant from Teacher Quality Partnership Program (TQP), SUTR hired two additional staff members as specialists (one in elementary education and one in special education) who focus their work on mentor development and specific one-on-one tiered induction support for SUTR graduates. Principals report a general area of growth for SUTR is support in due process within the first few years of teaching for special education teachers. Principals are overwhelmingly excited to learn that when they hire a SUTR graduate they can utilize additional supports provided by SUTR specialists if the need arises. Given the time constraints for principals, this added support is widely welcomed and used effectively. One principal reached out for supplemental support for an SUTR graduate and relayed, "Although this teacher is doing fine, the added support will only accelerate her growth and development."

All of the work with principals described above would not occur without consistent communication and collaboration among SUTR staff, creating ties among administration and across university personnel. The collaboration starts with SUTR staff communicating with SPPS administration to identify district principals and sites ready to take on residency work. Following the site selection, SUTR staff visit with and observe buildings examining school climate, collaboration, and teacher efficacy. Once a site is selected, SUTR staff engage in regular communication with building admin as well as mentor teachers. This includes all principals participating in a specially designed orientation for principals and then ongoing check-ins throughout the year. Additionally, university staff regularly communicate with the building administration each time they are conducting observations of the residents. This includes stopping in, leaving brief notes, and emailing to apprise the principals of the observations and next steps for the residents and, if applicable, the mentor teachers.

Finally, principals play an important role when a resident is struggling. They coach the mentor teacher to then provide feedback and coaching for the resident. Some principals have even joined feedback meetings to support the mentor teacher. They help the mentor teachers problem-solve and determine when additional supports need to be mobilized. Finally, they can help a mentor teacher unpack some of the various equity issues that may arise when the mentor and the resident are different races and/or cultures. Principals have experience and expertise managing staff issues and are invaluable in helping to problem-solve when challenges arise, especially professional issues.

Leadership Connections

We would be remiss not to mention the role of other district leaders in this chapter. We have shared the instrumental role principals have in SUTR. Similarly, there are several other district leaders who play invaluable roles in our residency work and partnerships with principals. From the earliest planning stages and implementation of SUTR, we knew it was important to have commitments and supports from leaders in the Equity Department; Office of Specialized Services (special education); Office of Teaching and Learning, Leadership Development; and Human Resources. Each department is invited to participate in steering committee meetings, sharing their perspectives in SUTR design, and provide references when questions arise. Several principals, leaders from the above-mentioned departments, and an assistant superintendent are adjunct faculty for SUTR courses and/or speak to the residents during seminars.

To show the depth of our commitment to truly understanding the impact of this program, the director of Human Resources, Laurin Cathey, makes it his personal mission and practice to meet with each SUTR resident twice a year to gain their perspectives on the program. He meets with them in the fall in his office in our district administrative building. In the spring, he sees them in their residency sites. This experience has allowed him to gain perspectives on the program both in areas of strengths and areas of growth, as well as allow the resident to have their perspectives heard and acted upon. Based on conversations with residents and connections with principals, several program improvements have been created and implemented. A SUTR graduate recently spoke at a gathering of superintendents across Minnesota and shared that she will always remember the impact of those meetings, stating she felt heard and supported, and hence very much a valued member of SPPS. This practice is proven to be so impactful that the Human Resource director has now shared this practice with his leadership team. They are also partaking in these individual meetings to gain perspectives and offer support to our new teachers.

TAKEAWAYS AND SUMMARY

When asked about the impact of SUTR across SPPS and in our schools, leaders and principals alike share that SUTR fills a need. By recruiting, preparing, and retaining highly qualified diverse teachers for our students, implications for the principals of teacher residency schools are massive. It is clear that residency cannot be successful without active principal involvement and commitments. Through our work with SUTR, we recommend the following:

- Involving principals in the initial planning of the residency program,
- Determining ongoing feedback loops for gathering principal perspective for residency program analysis and adjustments,
- Utilizing principals to recruit candidates and effective mentor teachers,
- Including principals as active participants in interviews and selection of candidates,
- Consulting with principals on site selection,
- Onboarding principals early and clearly,
- Supporting principals in understanding what to expect and how to support a resident and first-year teacher, and
- Collaborating with principals to support and coach mentor teachers.

More information about SUTR can be found at www.spps.org/SUTR.

BIBLIOGRAPHY

Burns, Kevin. "About Saint Paul Public Schools." *Saint Paul Public Schools*, 2019. https://www.spps.org/domain/1235.
Cassellius, Brenda, Hue Nguyen, and Nels Onstad. "Report of Teacher Supply and Demand in Minnesota's Public Schools." *Minnesota Department of Education*, 2017. https://education.mn.gov/MDE/about/rule/leg/rpt/rep17.

Lancaster, Simeon. "Admission and Aid." *University of St. Thomas, Minnesota School of Education*, 2019. https://education.stthomas.edu/admissionsandaid/.

Magan, C. "MN Students Near Top on National Test. Breaking Results Down by Race Tells Another Story." *Pioneer Press* (St. Paul, MN), April 10, 2018.

Sanchez, Jennifer. "Increasing Teacher of Color and American Indian Teachers – Minnesota Teachers of Color: Modernizing our Teacher Workforce." *Minnesota Education Equity Partnership (MnEEP) Policy Brief*, 2015. https://mneep.org/wp-content/uploads/2017/11/Teacher-Diversity_FinalRev.pdf.

Chapter 11

Scale and Sustainability of Residency Programs

Carrianne Scheib, Christine Brennan Davis, and the National Center for Teacher Residencies

INTRODUCTION

Up to 50 percent of teachers leave high-need schools within three years (Allensworth, Ponisciak, & Mazzeo 2009) and replacing a teacher who leaves costs the district upward of $20,000 ("What's the Cost," 2017). Research indicates that residency-prepared teachers stay longer, are more effective, and are more diverse than teachers prepared through other pathways (LiBetti & Trinidad 2018; Guha, Hyder & Darling-Hammond 2016). The significant benefits residencies provide in improving teaching quality and reducing teacher turnover offer real cost savings to partner school districts. Unfortunately, many residency programs, to date, have received little or no funding from partner school districts, even as they generate cost-savings. Not only does over-reliance on philanthropy and fixed grants lead to financial insecurity for many residency programs, it also creates barriers to scale that prevent programs from growing to better meet the needs of students and communities in the districts they serve.

With over a decade of experience in developing, launching, supporting, and accelerating the impact of teacher residency programs, the National Center for Teacher Residencies (NCTR) is now poised to advance the residency movement by enhancing the financial sustainability of residencies across the country. NCTR is currently providing consulting to both new programs as well as existing programs, which require distinct supports and approaches. A ten-year-old program has a much different foundation, relationship with the district, and research base than a program just being built. Additionally, programs across the country experience a variety of partnership opportunities and challenges. Some have limited partnerships with their districts based upon how they designed, while others are actually designed by the district itself. Some residencies partner with Charter Management Organizations (CMOs), while others are solely district-serving or based in neighborhood public schools. These contexts and relationships impact the residency's financial model. NCTR customizes its support to advance residencies in a variety of contexts and growth trajectories. NCTR recognizes that to advance the residency movement will require an increased focus on supporting partner residencies in achieving financial sustainability and designing financial models that enable growth and scale.

In service to this goal, NCTR is focused on developing best in class tools and resources, providing individualized consulting and technical assistance, and codifying and disseminating best practices in residency financial sustainability. NCTR offers a complete step-by-step guidance document titled *Design for Impact* (National Center for Teacher Residencies and Public Impact, 2018) a financial sustainability tool that guides programs in budgeting, forecasting, diagnosing, and addressing financial challenges; and offers one-on-one support to residency programs to improve sustainability. Through these efforts, NCTR has developed a clear definition of residency sustainability, identified key levers to achieving sustainability, and captured lessons learned and best practices. As NCTR enter its second decade of building, supporting, and scaling teacher residencies, NCTR is better positioned than ever to support new residencies in launching with sustainable, scalable financial models, and in supporting existing residencies in shifting their current models to be more financially sustainable.

DEFINITION OF FINANCIAL SUSTAINABILITY

NCTR defines financial sustainability as having financial capacity, the resources needed to seize opportunities while maintaining current operations, combined with resistance to financial shocks, the ability to be resilient in the face of occasional, and short-term funding challenges. Financial sustainability is achieved by two ways: (1) minimizing costs; and (2) maximizing revenue. While this may seem simple, in practice it is complex. On the one hand, it is critical that programs develop an efficient but effective cost model that produces strong outcomes, as data on program quality and impact is crucial to garnering continued financial investments from residency partners and funders. However, focusing only on program quality without an eye toward sustainability is problematic as even the strongest program will only have limited impact if it is not affordable or scalable.

MAXIMIZING REVENUE

Having diverse revenue streams is critical to achieving sustainability. In addition to generous contributions from philanthropy, residency programs across the country have experienced success in accessing revenue from the following federal and other grant sources:

- Robert Noyce Teacher Scholarship Program
- Education Innovation and Research Grants
- Teacher and School Leader Incentive Fund (formerly TIF)
- AmeriCorps State and National Awards
- Teacher Quality Partnership Grants
- Teacher Education Assistance for College and Higher Education (TEACH) Grant
- Teacher Cancellation for Perkins Loans
- Teacher Loan Forgiveness for Federal Stafford Loans
- National Education Association's Great Public Schools (GPS) Fund

While grants and philanthropic funding may make launching a new residency program possible, funding from the public-school system is core to long-term residency sustainability. Private funds and one-time grants will never exceed the amount of public funds that already exist with school districts, who often invest in programs and initiatives that are not achieving measurable results for teachers and students. There are various sources of public funding within school districts: Title I (federal funds for economically and educationally disadvantaged students and schools), Title II (federal funds for professional development), funds for tuition reimbursement for teachers, teacher recruitment, new teacher induction and mentoring, professional development, and in some cases discretionary funds districts can leverage as needed to work toward measurable goals for improvement. Rather than identifying new funding to support a residency, districts can reallocate funds from these sources to support residency growth and sustainability.

In more sustainable models, districts compensate residency programs for providing services that lower district costs—such as recruiting, training, onboarding, and retaining teachers in the district's hardest-to-staff schools—and adding value by accelerating student achievement. Losing a single teacher can cost a district up to $20,000 (Learning Policy Institute, 2017), helping to keep highly effective teachers in the classroom, particularly in hard-to-staff schools, represents a cost-savings to the district. In some districts, the district pays the residency program a fixed fee for every residency graduate it hires. In Kansas City, for example, the district pays the Kansas

City Teacher Residency $12,500 per resident hired as a fee for service. This strategy to maximize revenue can be negotiated with the partner district during the design process. Alternatively, a promising practice emerging in the field of nonprofit finance is "Pay for Success," wherein a district would compensate a residency only if they met certain agreed outcomes, such as residents recruited for hard-to-staff positions such as STEM, English Language Learner, or Special Education. For new residency programs, these negotiations should happen with partners as soon as possible, because it is always more difficult to request investment from a district after the fact, rather than to set up the expectation of investment from the beginning.

Working with the district to diversify and expand revenue streams is founded upon a basic premise the residency provides a value to the district. Put simply, residencies are worthy of public funding. Residencies create a steady pipeline of effective teachers that meet district needs, diverging from current teacher preparation pathways. Moreover, the residency model itself provides a value to districts, placing two teachers in a classroom together and offering leadership opportunities to expert teachers. Residencies, then, need to be able to demonstrate their effectiveness and value to districts, and this evaluation plan is best developed during the planning stages (and evolved over time) to be able to approach the district with clear goals and (eventually) results. Ultimately, residencies offer a cost savings to districts in the long term, and residencies can utilize these savings in a value proposition when approaching the district.

In addition to having a diverse portfolio of revenue sources, the type of revenue is another factor to sustainability. Residencies that have recurring (repeatedly available from year to year) and variable (increasing based on the number of residents prepared) revenue sources are better insulated against short-term economic shocks and are better positioned to grow and scale. Per resident, per mentor, or per graduate funding sources are those that will grow as the program grows—in stark contrast to fixed, one-time grants that will deplete, ultimately sunset, and leave a residency program facing a steep fiscal cliff.

MINIMIZING COSTS

In addition to maximizing revenue, residencies must also seek to minimize costs in ways that don't negatively impact programmatic quality or outcomes. Residency programs have three major cost centers: resident costs, mentor costs, and program costs.

Resident stipends are typically the largest line item on any program's budget, yet they are a critical tool for recruiting residents. Research indicates that financial incentives effectively attract candidates of color into the profession

(Hansen, Quintero, & Li Feng, 2018) and setting competitive stipends can be especially crucial when recruiting teachers for hard-to-staff positions, such as STEM, English Language Learner, and Special Education positions. Stipend amounts vary dramatically across the country based on geographic location, cost of living, and competition from other teacher-preparation providers. In an ideal model, districts or schools would contribute part or all of the resident stipend. Not only do residency programs provide a human capital pipeline directly aligned to district needs, train teachers in and for district schools, they also lower student to teacher ratios in residency training sites providing valuable additional manpower in schools to support student learning and achievement. Rather than finding new dollars, districts and schools can reallocate existing, per-pupil funds. For example, the Nashville Teacher Residency works with multiple charter school partners, all of whom pay residents the salary equivalent of a teaching assistant or paraprofessional (around $25,000). In addition to completing their residency training at the school, residents provide direct service to students. For school partners, they are able to provide better support to students while also building their teacher pipeline, and many hire residents to teach at their schools post-residency. For the residency program, this greatly increases sustainability as a major variable per-resident cost is moved off of their books and covered in full by their school partners.

Having residents contribute to the cost of their preparation experience is another cost-saving strategy. Often residency programs are successful in negotiating discounted rates of tuition with university partners or other preparation providers, and those seeking to teach in high-need schools and subject areas typically have a variety of grant, scholarship, and loan forgiveness options that can further offset this cost. In order to prevent tuition costs from becoming a barrier to entry for highly skilled and diverse candidates, some residencies offer deferred tuition, where residents pay back part or all of their tuition in installments while completing a three to five year service commitment post-residency once they are earning a full teacher salary. This can serve to significantly drive down the cost per resident without negatively impacting recruitment. For example, the New York City Department of Education (NYCDOE) covers the entirety of resident tuition during the residency year, approximately $18,000 for residents in training. When graduates begin teaching and collecting a salary, they pay back half of that amount over the course of four years to the Department of Education via automatic paycheck deductions. For a New York City teacher paid biweekly on a ten-month schedule this amounts to a little under $100 in tuition payments per paycheck and creates a valuable deferred revenue stream for the NYCDOE that better positions them to sustain their investments in the residency for the long haul.

Mentor costs represent a much smaller portion of a residency program's overall budget. These costs typically include mentor stipends, funding for mentor professional development, and in some cases funding for substitute teachers to allow for release time for mentors to participate in PD and/or have dedicated time to work with residents during the school day. Residency mentoring is a powerful way to support, reward, and extend the reach of a district's most highly effective teachers and many districts may already set aside funding to support teacher leadership or career ladder roles that can be accessed by the residency program. Title II funds could also be tapped to fund mentor professional development. The case for districts to invest in mentors is a strong one, as one principal emphasized, "As a veteran principal, it is extremely valuable to have two qualified teachers in the classroom together. It is beneficial for the resident to begin the year learning how to put together a classroom, build community see and work with the teacher working in small groups. It is also beneficial in that the district teacher has the opportunity to learn from the resident. It is a win-win for all!" Data indicates that mentors deepen and improve their own instructional practice through participation in the program. Across the NCTR Network, 94 percent of principals agree that residency mentors grew into more effective practitioners through participation in the residency.

In addition to resident and mentor costs, some residency programs continue to offer induction coaching, professional development, and alumni engagement services post-residency. While these represent additional costs for the program, in some cases they are critical to achieving desired outcomes such as teacher effectiveness and retention. Residency partners should strive for efficiency and coordination in post-residency support, so as not to duplicate efforts and drive up costs. For example, if the district already offers robust new teacher induction, the residency program may not need to provide this additional service. If this is not something the district has the capacity to offer; however, the residency program may choose to provide this service in order to ensure a return on investment in the form of strong results for program graduates.

Finally, in order to effectively recruit, prepare, and support residents, mentors, and graduates, residencies have necessary staffing and overhead costs. While residency programs should seek efficient staffing models, for example, leveraging existing personnel from partner institutions before hiring new employees, it is also critical that the program have the right talent, capacity, and infrastructure to achieve the desired outcomes. Further, investing in program evaluation to measure and communicate results is important to getting continued investment in the program.

LESSONS LEARNED

1. Residency Programs Must Better Understand Their Business Models: In order to improve residency sustainability, residency leaders must deeply

understand their programs' business models, and leverage this understanding to better negotiate and support risk-sharing among partners, especially school and district partners who are the long-term beneficiaries. Further, program leaders need to look out more than a single budget cycle into the future both to proactively diagnose and address financial challenges, and to see how planned growth and scale impact cost per resident. Residency sustainability is correlated with residency size and decisions to build residencies cannot responsibly ignore the question of demand from their partner(s) and its effect on the program's expected steady-state size.

NCTR's financial modeling tool, mentioned in the introduction as part of the *Design for Impact* suite of tools, not only provides a diagnostic assessment of financial health but can also be used to help show partners how their dollars can be used to ensure the long-term sustainability of the program (National Center for Teacher Residencies & Public Impact, 2018). Programs can explore various strategies to move toward financial sustainability, understanding how they intend to grow and how they can leverage myriad partners. NCTR residencies are currently using this tool to negotiate and collaborate with partners and funders. Knowing the program's business model, and the long-term financial plan for the residency, allow the program to use concrete numbers and evidence to make the case for cost-sharing among residency partners.

2. Measure, Demonstrate, and Communicate Residency Success: Residency programs provide great value to partner districts and schools. A quality evaluation plan should be designed to measure, promote, and communicate this value. Residencies should ground their evaluation efforts in a programmatic theory of change that articulates short-, mid-, and long-term outcomes. NCTR residencies also create theories of change and program evaluations during development, intending to collect data to measure impact. Programs should know exactly what data they need to collect and when. Programs should also think of how districts, IHEs, and other partners can help them to collect these data. To demonstrate their value, programs can plan to collect a multitude of data. Outcomes should focus on:
    - Increasing Teacher Retention: Programs should collect data showing how long residency graduates remain in the district. When residency graduates are working in a hard-to-staff school or a hard-to-staff subject, data should be disaggregated by those categories. Retaining effective teachers is a powerful demonstration of impact, especially as those new educators persist in positions the district has historically struggled to fill.
    - Improving Teacher Quality: Programs must demonstrate that the residency produces high-performing teachers the district may not otherwise attract or hire. Program evaluation must include multiple measures of

teacher performance, such as student achievement, teacher observation, stakeholder perceptions, and other measures of impact.
- Other Key Benefits: Data should be gathered on other key outcomes the program provides for which you may not be able to attach a monetary value, such as increasing the diversity of the district's teaching staff, demonstrating that a program provides a consistent, reliable pipeline of effective educators that the district otherwise would not be able to acquire on its own.

Program evaluation is critical to getting investments in the residency from partners and funders. In some cases, such as a "Pay for Success" model, evaluation might be a driver for the financial model from the outset. For example, the residency program and district might agree on measurable outcomes for program success, philanthropy or a grant might serve as a temporary funding source, and if independent researchers/ evaluators find that the program has achieved the desired outcomes the residency would then start receiving payment from the district. Program evaluation can also be used as a tool to renegotiate existing financial arrangements, as a program demonstrates proof of concept and thus requests greater or longer-term financial investments from partners or funders. In either case, the financial model can best be understood, negotiated, and revised within the context of the benefits the program provides.

3. Residency Programs Are Worthy of Earned Revenue: If residency programs are indeed providing value to districts, and have data to support this, they are worthy of earned revenue. Despite this, residency programs have typically struggled to get financial support on the basis of the value they provide. The origin of this might lie in many residencies being seed funded by philanthropy or grants, contributing to a mindset amongst residency leaders that they are providing a public service more than a value-creating service worthy of earned revenue.

CASE STUDIES

A number of teacher residencies are financially sustainable while achieving impact goals and ensuring the effectiveness of graduates. Each of these residencies have pursued unique strategies to work toward sustainability, based upon their local context and needs. Here, two residencies, at different stages in their life cycles, purposefully selected distinct—yet sometimes similar—pathways to achieve financial sustainability. Kern Urban Teacher Residency and Dallas Teacher Residency, thus, represent two innovative yet practical models from which other residencies can learn. This section explores each of these residencies in depth, how they cultivated partnerships and shared costs with stakeholders, and key lessons common to both pathways.

Case Study #1

Kern Urban Teacher Residency first partnered with NCTR and graduated its first cohort of residents in the 2016–2017 school year as part of the Next Generation Educator Initiative (NGEI). NGEI, generously supported by the S.D. Bechtel Jr. Foundation, provided grant funding for three years for California State University (CSU)—Bakersfield, to develop a residency program. Currently Kern Urban Teacher Residency has fifty total graduates and sixteen residents in 2018–2019. One hundred percent of graduates have been hired by the school district, 100 percent teach in Title I schools, and 100 percent are certified in EL.

Prior to developing the residency, CSU Bakersfield provided approximately 85 percent of the Bakersfield City School District (BCSD) workforce, so the partnership was already well established when they began collaborating as part of the NGEI grant, and the funding allowed this partnership to deepen by building a residency. At the outset, leadership from both BCSD and CSU Bakersfield agreed upon key investments to ensure both partners had shared financial commitments and were invested in the residency as pipeline for the district.

In its first year, 2016, residents received no stipend. Both the district and university considered what they needed to do to attract and retain highly effective candidates. The next year, the district started paying a resident stipend of $800 per month, with the opportunity to earn substitute money. This figure increased this past year to $1,100 per month, and the district is looking to increase the resident stipend in 2019–2020 to $1,800 per month, again with the opportunity to earn substitute money. BCSD also invests beyond stipends and sub-costs, by purchasing supplies like chromebooks for each resident, Danielson training, and funding for residents and mentors to attend state or national conferences. In addition, the residency has worked to elevate the mentor role so it's a formal rung on the district's career ladder. Overall, the district invested almost $500,000 in the residency this past year and are projecting of a $1 million investment in the upcoming year to increase the resident stipend. The university, too, has worked to make the residency appealing to top candidates and offers a scholarship of $16,000 to offset the cost of tuition, with help from a one-time Bechtel grant.

So, how did Bakersfield City School District and CSU Bakersfield evolve their partnership and mutually invest to build a financially sustainable residency? Kern Urban Teacher Residency saw this grant as an opportunity to develop a sustainable pipeline of effective teachers for their district and meet the needs of students. They recognized the need to invest in top candidates and attract talent into Bakersfield City Schools. Kern approached the grant as a three-year sustainability plan, using the initial funding to get the residency off the ground and evolving their financial model over time. Ultimately, it came down to the numbers. Each year, BCSD loses up to 10 percent of its teacher workforce, representing 120–150 positions, and approximately 200 of its 2,700 teachers are on emergency credential, with no commitment to return the following year. As part of this sustainability plan, BCSD invested in fifty teachers who could guarantee a return on investment and meet the needs of students. So, instead of spending a $50,000 salary plus benefits to recruit each teacher who may leave the district, BCSD instead reallocated available funds totaling that same amount toward the residency and in particular resident stipends. Thus, the residency is viewed as a way to decrease costs for teacher recruitment and longer-term teacher attrition. The district is also seeking to utilize Title II Local Control and Accountability funds (LEAP) in the future to pay for mentor stipends and professional development.

Ultimately, Kern Urban Teacher Residency shows the importance of continually revisiting the program's financial model and partnership. It's also critical to ensure that all partners are invested and committed, particularly as fixed revenues, such as one-time grants, end. Furthermore, if districts are to invest in a residency program, the university needs to offer the district something customized for their needs. Kern Urban is able to produce a consistent pipeline of teachers who will stay in the district and who are certified in the shortage areas needed. Seeing universities reallocate resources to better serve districts is part of having a strong and mutually beneficial partnership and upends the current role of most teacher-preparation providers.

Case Study #2: Dallas Teacher Residency

Dallas Teacher Residency (DTR) first launched in 2014 after receiving funding from local philanthropic dollars, which was later supplemented by state and national grants. Initially, DTR was laser-focused on serving Dallas Independent School District (ISD), and the district did not contribute any funding toward resident or mentor stipends. However, DTR today has thirty-five residents serving both Dallas ISD and neighboring Richardson ISD. One hundred percent of current graduates teach in Title I schools, 86 percent are hired by the school district, and DTR boasts a 96 percent three-year retention rate.

As DTR grew and saw the need for excellent teachers in neighboring schools outside Dallas, the program recognized the importance of diversifying revenue streams and broadening its view on potential district partners. DTR sought to negotiate a new financial model that would allow them to grow and scale. DTR diligently tracked outcome metrics, capturing their track record of success, and approached their expansion school district to show DTR's value and how they were offering a cost-savings to their district. Today, Richardson ISD pays 100 percent of the $20,000 resident stipend.

DTR was able to leverage multiple partners, including Texas A&M Commerce and Texas Wesleyan University, its IHE partners, to achieve financial sustainability and ensure they could scale. DTR approached all partners in the negotiations as real authentic partners who could contribute to a mutually beneficial relationship. DTR recognized the unique value proposition each of the partners brought to table, which helped to facilitate the negotiations. When expanding to Richardson ISD, negotiating with the district to cover the resident stipend in full was a priority and practice DTR wants to replicate with future expansion districts. Up front, DTR worked with its partners to identify clear metrics that would meet everyone's needs, so that they could evaluate the success of the partnership. DTR listened carefully to Richardson ISD's needs and worked with the district to identify the best structure for the district to contribute. Specifically, DTR invoices the district $20,000 per resident and then DTR acts as the actual employer, paying residents as contract workers. Residents then access health insurance and other benefits through the university. By structuring it this way, the district is able to contribute without having to fund benefits or manage all of the potential HR issues associated with hiring residents as employees.

In 2018, after its partnership with Richardson had been established, Dallas ISD set aside $9 million for residency programs. DTR secured a vendor contract with Dallas IDS, and Dallas ISD agreed to pay the $25,000 salary for twenty residents per year, including benefits. This five-year contract benefits the district by creating a consistent teacher pipeline with a partner that has ensured the quality of its graduates. DTR was also able to negotiate with the district, understanding that they were recruiting and selecting high-quality candidates that saved the district resources, and Dallas ISD directly pays DTR $5,000 for each resident they prepare. Furthermore, in 2019, DTR began working with a new university partner, Texas Wesleyan University, which agreed to reduce tuition for the resident by 25%, helping make the residency more affordable for teacher candidates, in addition to paying DTR $2,500 per resident to offset the costs of recruitment. Ultimately, this is a model DTR would like to bring to other expansion districts in the state of Texas.

As these case studies demonstrate, new and existing residency programs can leverage partnerships in various ways to be able to share costs and achieve financial sustainability. In addition, these exemplars show how to move away from fixed revenues, particularly large one-time grants, and develop relationships and partnerships to be able to better attract residents and ultimately serve their communities. Both residencies also utilized data and program evaluations to demonstrate their value to potential partners. In addition, these two programs also relied upon negotiating—and renegotiating—with partners to collaborate on financially sustainable models, indicating that this process is far from static and partnerships should be revisited over the lifetime of a program. Thus, residencies can explore multiple ways to engage partners, cultivate new partnerships, and share costs among partners—for both the benefit of the residency and the schools and community served by that residency.

CONCLUSION

As shown throughout this chapter, residencies operate best if they are initially built with financial sustainability in mind. Only by maximizing and diversifying revenue sources and minimizing costs can the residency ensure quality and be able to grow. Existing residencies have developed myriad paths to achieve financial sustainability, from seeking out diverse revenue sources, collaborating with district and IHE partners, cost-sharing with districts, utilizing a variety of state and federal funds, and demonstrating their value to funders. The work of financial sustainability is never "done" or "accomplished," however, and while it's best to develop a robust financial model with partners from the start, these partnerships need to be tended to, negotiated and renegotiated, and will evolve over time. New partnerships, as in the case of Dallas Teacher Residencies, might be needed in order to scale and better serve students. Data, too, becomes incredibly critical to long-term sustainability, and residencies are best positioned if they develop or co-develop evaluation plans when first negotiating the partnership. All partners can agree upon outcomes and collaborate to work toward those results.

Although this chapter provided an overview of financial sustainability, key levers to sustainability, and lessons learned, NCTR offers a complete step-by-step instructional guide called *Design for Impact* available to network partners. *Design for Impact*'s technical assistance for NCTR partners includes:

- A webinar and accompanying PowerPoint deck that defines financial sustainability and identifies high-potential strategies to improve a residency program's long-term financial health.
- A financial modeling tool that:
    - guides programs as they collect and categorize current financial data,
    - models how multiple strategies could impact a program's financial sustainability, and
    - guides programs as they develop a detailed five-year forecast.
    - *Design for Impact* guidance document provides additional information and action items for residency programs interested in moving forward with the sustainability options highlighted in the technical assistance.

The guidance document leads residencies through multiple strategies, additional examples, helpful tips, and step-by-step guides to achieve financial sustainability. A Financial Modeling Tool (National Center for Teacher Residencies and Public Impact, 2018) accompanies this guide, allowing residencies to diagnose their current financial health, test out multiple strategies to improve financial health, and forecast financial models five years into the future. The Financial Modeling Tool also outlines a comprehensive list of revenue and cost sources, allowing residencies to examine all possibilities to maximize revenues and reduce costs. Additionally, the Financial Modeling Tool helps make the concepts explored here more concrete, which can be utilized when negotiating with partners. This suite of tools, along with NCTR's financial sustainability consulting, is currently being utilized by several residency programs across the country and will help provide us benchmarking data we can use to better understand residency financial models and how to achieve financial sustainability. For more information, go to nctresidencies.org. As NCTR begins our next chapter, we are excited about the opportunity to help grow and enhance our partner programs, in order to advance the residency movement and have an even greater impact on the students and communities we serve. We hope this book has been useful to you as you either begin your journey toward building a residency or developing and enhancing an already existing program. As NCTR has recognized after a decade of engaging and collaborating with partners in this work, financial sustainability is critical to the long-term success of the residency movement, and if we are to truly change teacher preparation writ large, we need to ensure residencies can grow, expand, and meet the needs of their communities. We look forward to what this next chapter brings not only the residencies we support but also the movement toward clinically oriented teacher preparation.

BIBLIOGRAPHY

Allensworth, Elaine, Stephen Ponisciak, and Christopher Mazzeo. "The Schools Teachers Leave: Teacher Mobility in Chicago Public Schools." *University of Chicago Consortium on Chicago School Research.* June 2009. https://consortium.uchicago.edu/sites/default/files/2018-10/CCSR_Teacher_Mobility.pdf.

"Design for Impact: Designing a Residency Program for Long-Term Financial Sustainability." *National Center for Teacher Residencies and Public Impact.* 2018. https://nctresidencies.org/wp-content/uploads/2018/06/Financial-Sustainability-Report-Guidance_Final.pdf.

Guha, Roneeta, Maria E. Hyler, and Linda Darling-Hammond. "The Teacher Residency: An Innovative Model for Preparing Teachers." *Learning Policy Institute.*

September 2016. https://learningpolicyinstitute.org/sites/default/files/product-files/Teacher_Residency_Innovative_Model_Preparing_Teachers_REPORT.pdf.

Hansen, Michael, Diane Quintero, and Li Feng. "Can Money Attract more Minorities into the Teaching Profession?" *The Brookings Institute*. March 20, 2018. https://www.brookings.edu/blog/brown-center-chalkboard/2018/03/20/can-money-attract-more-minorities-into-the-teaching-profession/.

LiBetti, Ashley and Justin Trinidad. "Trading Coursework for Classroom: Realizing the Potential of Teacher Residencies." *Bellwether Education Partners*. July 2018. https://bellwethereducation.org/sites/default/files/TeacherResidencies_Bellwether.pdf.

"What's the Cost of Teacher Turnover?" *Learning Policy Institute*. September 13, 2017. https://learningpolicyinstitute.org/product/the-cost-of-teacher-turnover.

Index

Albuquerque Teacher Residency Partnership, 1–18
alternative certification, 217, 249. *See also* alternative teaching license
alternative teaching license, 26
Alumni, 7, 8, 9, 24, 26, 28, 68, 79, 228
Americorps, 28, 83, 225
application, x, xvii, 10, 25–29, 36–38, 41, 72, 167, 169, 190, 211–12

Boettcher Teacher Residency Program (Colorado), 21–30
Boston Teacher Residency Partnership, 131–52

Carnegie Foundation for the Advancement of Teaching, 161
charter management organizations (CMOs), xv, xvi, 4, 224, 241
child study, 139, 142
clinical experience, xi, xvi, xvii–xx, 3, 5, 58, 84, 89, 102, 115, 117, 120, 123, 127, 158, 188, 189, 211, 242
Coalition to Increase Teachers of Color and Native American Teachers, 207
Colorado State University, 24, 243
Common Core State Standards, 69

continuous improvement, 10, 11, 28, 31, 121–22, 153, 157, 159, 161–62, 169, 177–79, 181–82, 184, 208–9, 243
Costa's Three Levels of Questioning, 172
co-teaching, 15, 32, 35, 67–68, 125–26, 174–75, 207, 211, 213, 215–16
culturally and linguistically diverse students, 65, 66, 69
culturally responsive pedagogy, 67
curriculum coordinator, 39, 45, 57, 60
curriculum maps, 70

Dallas Independent School District (DISD), 232
Dallas Teacher Residency, 10, 232, 234
Danielson, 72, 79, 104–12, 154–55, 162, 164, 167, 177–79, 195, 231
Danielson Framework for Teaching, 162, 195
Darling-Hammond, Linda, 62, 134, 152, 200, 204, 223
Dearborn Stem Academy (DSA), 136
Defense of Learning Project, 160, 162, 167–71, 174
Denver Teacher Residency, xxii
Design for Impact, xxvi, 224, 229, 234–33
do-as-I-do model, 190

Dudley Street Neighborhood Charter School, 131–52

East Harlem Teaching Residency, 83–112
edTPA (Education Teacher Performance Assessment), 72, 76, 86, 170
educational assistants, 4, 7
Education Innovation and Research Grants, 225
endorsement, 35, 64
equity, 27, 32, 65, 68, 69, 85, 86, 88, 90–91, 93, 158, 179, 181, 184, 191, 197, 207–8, 213, 220, 222

financial aid, 5
financial modeling tool, xxvi, 229, 234–35
financial sustainability, 223–24, 229–30, 233–35
Ford Foundation, 22
Fort Lewis College, 24
Freire, Paolo, 152, 203

gateway process, 72, 162
Great Public Schools (GPS) Fund, 225
Grow Your Own, 25–26

Heritage University, xix
high-need schools, xvii, xxii, xxvii, 1, 3, 16, 221, 227
huddling, 72, 74
human resources, xxviii, xxix, 9, 11, 63, 77, 181, 208, 219, 220
Hunter College, xi, xxi, xxvii, xxix, 81, 83–92, 102, 157, 185, 242, 245–46

induction, xi, xii, xvii, 2, 7–9, 18, 63–64, 68–69, 77–80, 86, 135, 158, 163, 168, 178, 188–204, 205, 207, 218, 219, 225, 228, 246
inquiry, 31, 75, 99, 138, 153, 154, 157–62, 167, 169–72, 174, 176, 181–82, 184–84, 188, 241, 246
Institute for Healthcare Improvement (IHI), 121, 161

Jedi Project, 160, 174

Kansas City Teacher Residency, 223–36
Kern Teacher Residency Program, Bakersfield, California, 115–29

learning cycle, viii, 68, 70, 81, 93–98, 100, 103, 191
Learning Policy Institute, xxviii–xxix, 225, 236
learning theory, 67, 69–70

MACP Prepared to Teach Grant, 12
masters in teaching, 64–65
maximizing revenue, 224–26
Memorandum of understanding, 14, 18
Memphis Teacher Residency, xxi–xxii
mentor development, 118, 122, 176, 219
Mentoring Matters, 65
mentor teachers, x–xii, 4, 31, 32–59, 64–65, 69, 71, 74, 86, 123–26, 166, 187, 188, 190, 202, 207, 209, 213–16, 220–21
Metro State University, 24
Minnesota Department of Education, 208, 221

Nashville Teacher Residency, 227
National Center for Teacher Residencies (NCTR), viii–xxix, 1, 4–9, 11, 17, 23, 58, 63, 78, 91–92, 187, 192, 206, 208–9, 223, 224, 228–29, 231, 234–39, 241, 243, 247
National Commission on Excellence in Education, 22
National Council on Teacher Quality, xxi, xxviii
National Education Association, 225
National Network for Education Renewal, xv
Nation at Risk, 22
New Mexico Public Education Department, 3
New Mexico Voices for Children, 1
New Mexico Workforce Connection Department, 6

Index 239

New Site Development Program, 206
New Teacher Center, 31, 46, 49, 51, 53, 192, 246
New Visions for Public Schools, New York City, xi, xxi, xxviii, xxix, 153–86, 245, 249
New York City Department of Education (NYCDOE), xxi, 84, 160, 227, 245
Next Generation Educator Initiative (NGEI), 231
Next Generation Science Standards, 69
No Child Left Behind Act, xvi

parallel learning, 153, 157, 159, 166
paraprofessionals, 26, 77, 211
Pay for Success Model, 226, 230
Peer assistance and review (PAR), 219
Per pupil spending, 21
Plan-Do-Study-Act (PDSA), 121, 122, 125, 129, 161–60
Planning, Rehearsal, Enactment, and Reflection, 68
PRAXIS exam, 26
professional development, xi, xiv, xv, xvii, xxviii, 4, 6, 10, 24, 43, 46, 48, 56–57, 64–65, 68–70, 72, 74–75, 77, 85–86, 89–90, 102–4, 123–28, 134, 138–40, 154, 158, 160–61, 163–64, 166–68, 171, 173, 176–77, 191–92, 195, 198, 201–2, 204, 208–9, 214–15, 219, 226, 228, 232
progress monitoring, 126–27, 162
Public Education and Business Coalition (PEBC), x, 21–30, 246

Queens College at the City University of New York (CUNY), 157, 249

recruitment, vii, x, xiii, xvi–xvii, xxiii, 7, 10 14, 24–29, 31–59, 63–63, 77–78, 125, 135, 158, 159, 168, 181, 200–202, 205, 225, 227, 232, 233, 243
reflective practice, 29, 36, 42, 84, 158

Residency Development Program, xxvii
residency foundations, xxvi
residency outcomes, 254
residency pathway, xxii
Residency Year Curriculum, x, 61–83
Richmond Public Schools, 32
Richmond Teacher Residency, xvii, 31–32, 35, 36, 46, 248
rural, xiv, 21–23, 25–26, 28–29, 34

Saint Paul Public Schools (SPPS), 205–22
Saint Paul Urban Teacher Residency Program, 205–22
San Francisco Unified School District, xxii, 248
Science, Technology, Engineering & Math (STEM), 22
Seattle Public Schools (SPS), 61–82
Seattle Teacher Residency (STR), 61–82
special education, xxi, 15, 64–65, 67–69, 71, 76–77, 80, 134, 141, 158, 174, 206–8, 216, 219–20, 226–27, 242, 247
stakeholders, vii, xvii, xxii, xxiv, 33, 69, 70, 79, 92, 123, 128, 153, 156–57, 162–63, 166–67, 178, 180–82, 184, 205, 209, 211–12, 230
Stanley Teacher Prep, 23
State of Washington Teacher Preparation, 71
stipends, xv, xvii, 4–6, 58, 226–25, 231–32
substitute teaching, 119–20
suburban, xviii, 35

teacher leadership, 32, 38, 45, 57, 65, 214, 228, 248
teacher retention, xxi, 33, 60, 64, 77, 80, 157, 219, 230
teachers of color, 23, 62, 80, 181, 191, 205, 207, 222
teaching academy, 132, 133, 136–39, 141, 143, 144, 145, 148, 150, 247

TeachingWorks, xi, 91–100, 103–4, 245
Texas A&M Commerce, 232
Texas Wesleyan University, 233
Title I schools, 2, 225, 231, 232
Title II, 225, 228, 232
Troops to Teachers, 28
Twin Cities Teacher Collaborative (TC2), 206, 208

University of Chicago Urban Teacher Education Program (UChicago UTEP), 187–204, 246
University of Colorado, 24
University of Denver, 24
University of Michigan, 91, 135, 192
University of New Mexico (UNM), x, 1–18, 244, 246
University of Northern Colorado, 24
University of St. Thomas, 205, 222, 247
University of Washington, 61–81, 242
U. S. Department of Education, xxvii, xxix, 32, 90, 206

Virginia Commonwealth University (VCU), x, 31–60, 248, 249

Western State Colorado University, 24

About the Editors and Contributors

Dr. Cheryl Torrez is a professor in the Department of Teacher Education, Educational Leadership and Policy at the University of New Mexico. She received her Ph.D. in Education from the University of Virginia and her M.A. in Education (Curriculum and Instruction) from California State University, Sacramento. She was an elementary teacher in California for over a decade and served as a Distinguished Teacher in Residence at CSUS. Her research interests include school/university/community partnerships, clinical preparation of teachers, teacher inquiry, and social studies education.

Dr. Marjori Krebs is a professor in the Department of Teacher Education, Educational Leadership and Policy at the University of New Mexico. She received her Ed.D. in Leadership Studies from Bowling Green State University and her M.A. in Educational Theory and Practice from the Ohio State University. Her research interests include project-based and service learning, experiential learning in university and PK-12 settings. She is currently serving as the chair of the Albuquerque Teacher Residency Program design team.

* * *

The National Center for Teacher Residencies (NCTR) is a not-for-profit organization that serves a growing national network of high-performing teacher residency programs. Founded in 2007, NCTR is the only organization in the nation dedicated to developing, launching, and supporting the impact of teacher residency programs. NCTR partners with school districts, charter management organizations, institutions of higher education, not-for-profits, and states to develop and support teacher residency programs as quality pipelines of effective and diverse new teachers. NCTR is headquartered in Chicago with virtual staff located across the country.

Sarah Baird Glover, M.A., is the associate executive director of Education for the Public Education & Business Coalition located in Denver.

Dr. Marisa Bier is currently the program director of the Seattle Teacher Residency. Prior to taking on the role of leading the design and launch of the Seattle Teacher Residency in 2012, Marisa was coordinator of the Secondary Teacher Education Program at the University of Washington. She was responsible for all aspects of the program, particularly ensuring cohesiveness between program curriculum and school practicum experiences, building partnerships with schools in which teacher candidates were placed, and facilitating the work of university coaches who supported teacher candidates in the field.

Marisa brings more than twenty-five years of experience in education to the Alliance, beginning her career as a special education teacher of students with learning disabilities, ADHD, and autism, ages Pre-K through 12th grade. While serving in a leadership role as a site coordinator of her school's university partnership, Marisa developed an interest in teacher education and the role practitioners play in supporting new teacher development. She came to Seattle to pursue her doctorate in Education at the University of Washington, which she received in 2009. There, her studies focused on teacher learning across a continuum from novice to veteran, with a particular interest in learning as it is negotiated within communities of practice.

Publications include:

Zeichner, K. and Bier, M. L. (2015). Opportunities and pitfalls in the turn toward clinical experience in US teacher education. In Hollins, E. (ed.), *Rethinking Field Experiences in Pre-Service Teacher Preparation: Meeting New Challenges for Accountability*. London: Routledge.

Bier, M. L., Kazemi, E., Campbell, S. S., Horn, I., Kelley, M. P., Hintz, A., Saxena, A., Stevens, R., & Peck, C. (2012). Design for simultaneous renewal in university-public school partnerships: Hitting "the sweet spot." *Teacher Education Quarterly*, *39*(3), 127–141.

Dr. Sherryl Browne Graves is the senior associate dean of Education at Hunter College and teaches courses in psychological foundations of education including courses in child development, educational psychology, educational research, cognition and educational technology, and multicultural issues in learning and instruction. Professor Graves' research interests focus on children's understanding of racial and ethnic portrayals in mass media, the effects of diversity in the educational process, and the use of technology in teaching and learning. She has served as a consultant and advisory board members to numerous media organizations including Sesame Workshop, WGBH and KCET Public Television Stations, Discovery Kids and the Public Broadcasting Service. Additionally she has served as a PI on an NSF MSP grant, co-PI on a New York Community Trust early literacy grant and senior advisor on a Foundation for Child Development PreK for All grant. Currently, she is co-PI on a grant from the Robin Hood Foundation to prepare preservice and in-service, K-5 teachers in computational thinking. Dr. Graves is trained in psychology with a doctorate from Harvard University in Clinical Psychology and Public Practice and a bachelor's degree in Psychology from Swarthmore College.

Ashley Clark is the former recruitment, development and partnership director for the Public Education & Business Coalition (PEBC). She focused on identifying recent graduates and career changers interested in entering the education profession. Ashley's work led her to develop strategic partnerships with local and national organizations to develop direct recruitment pipelines and resources that will support preservice and in-service Colorado educators. She continues to work in nonprofit development and teacher recruitment at the Academy for Urban School Leadership's Chicago Teacher Residency. Ashley hails from the Northwest suburbs of Chicago. She received her bachelor of arts in English from Hampton University, master of arts in English from Loyola University of Chicago and is currently enrolled in a master of science in Organizational Leadership program at Colorado State University-Global Campus.

Christine Brennan Davis, M.A., has thirteen years of experience in the education sector. As program director, Christine leads on the design and implementation of NCTR programming and continuous improvement and directly consults partner programs. Prior to joining NCTR in 2010, Christine worked as an instructional coach in Chicago Public Schools and was a high school and middle school English Language Arts teacher in Salem, Massachusetts, and Brooklyn, New York. Christine is a former New York City Teaching Fellow. She has expertise in residency and clinically oriented teacher preparation, district and university partnerships, teacher development, and performance management. She has a bachelor of arts in English from Colby College and a master of arts in Teaching from Brooklyn College. Christine is based in New York City.

Mr. Harry "Doc" Ervin began his tenure as superintendent of the Bakersfield City School District in July 2016. He has led the district's efforts in building curricular, instructional and operational systems and structures that provide system-wide sustainability to support teaching and learning. His personal motto is that he makes every decision in the best interest of children. He has more than twenty-five years of experience in education, having served as a classroom teacher, school principal, and assistant superintendent and superintendent at various school districts across the state.

Dr. Viola E. Florez holds the title of emeritus dean and professor in the College of Education at the University of New Mexico. She has held various executive leadership positions at the University of New Mexico and has served as New Mexico cabinet secretary for Higher Education. Her national presence with educational renewal policy efforts has contributed to building strong university-school partnerships to prepare educators, especially the preparation of novice teachers. She has published extensively addressing teacher development, school-university partnerships, leadership, and educational policy.

Danaya Lamker Franke, M.Ed., is the Saint Paul Public Schools supervisor for SUTR, an educator, and University of St. Thomas adjunct faculty for SUTR.

Lynne Godfrey, M.Ed., is an educational math consultant who works with schools and districts to design and facilitate professional learning with coaches, teachers, and administrators to grow ambitious, equitable learning communities in their schools. As an educator, Lynne served as a classroom teacher Grades 2–8 in Cambridge and Boston, district math coach for Cambridge Public Schools, upper school coordinator and math coach at Young Achievers Science and Math Pilot School and the director of instruction, curriculum and adult development for mathematics at the Dudley Street Neighborhood Charter School and Boston Teacher Residency. It was her work with Bob Moses and the Algebra Project for over thirty years, both locally and nationally, that has influenced and sustains her ongoing commitment to access and equity for all adults and all children in mathematics, where ambitious teaching and learning are a civil right.

Publications include:

Godfrey, L. & O'Connor, M. C. (1995). The vertical hand span: Nonstandard units, expressions and symbols in the classroom. *Journal of Mathematical Behavior, 14*(3), 327–345.

O'Connor, M. C., Godfrey, L. & Moses, R. P. (1998). The missing data point: Negotiating purposes in classroom mathematics and science. In J. G. Greeno and S. V. Goldman (eds.), *Thinking practices in mathematics and science learning*. Hillsdale, NJ: Lawrence Erlbaum.

Holly Gonzales currently serves as the educational coordinator for the Kern Urban Teacher Residency and is a teacher education faculty member at California State University Bakersfield. Holly is a first generation college graduate and CSU Bakersfield alumnus. She earned her bachelor's degree in Liberal Studies and a multiple-subject teaching credential in 2008, and earned her master's in education in 2009. Holly served the students in the Bakersfield City School district for seven years, as an elementary classroom teacher and academic coach. She strives to share her love and passion for serving students in Kern County by modeling a positive growth mindset.

Susan Gonzowitz, M.A., is a senior manager at East Harlem Tutorial Program (EHTP) and the founding managing director of the East Harlem Teaching Residency (EHTR). EHTR is a unique teacher-training program that develops anti-racist educators who will work to transform how young people experience the world. Susan has presented on her work at the American Association of College for Teachers, American Educational Research Association, National Center for Teaching Residencies, New York, Association of Colleges for Teacher Education, and TeachingWorks convenings and conferences. Before designing and launching the residency, Susan worked for three years as the director of the Elementary Program at EHTP and was instrumental in the creation of EHTP's racial equity statement. She has been an adjunct lecturer at Hunter College School of Education for the past five years, teaching both literacy and diversity courses. Prior to beginning her career at EHTP, Susan was employed with the New York City Department of Education, where she was an instructional coach and an elementary school teacher. She received her master's degree in literacy and an advanced certification in school supervision and administration at Hunter College and her undergraduate degree from Skidmore College. She is also licensed in New York State 1–6 elementary education, birth–6 literacy education, and school-building leadership and school district leadership.

Marisa Harford, M.S., is the director of Teacher Residencies at New Visions for Public Schools. For the past ten years, she has worked with the teacher certification team, which prepares highly qualified novice teachers through residency programs, builds capacity in mentoring and support of new teacher development, and crafts sustainable systems and tools for residencies through partnerships with universities and the NYC DOE. Her previous experience includes seven years of secondary-level teaching and instructional coaching at Bronx middle and high schools. She holds a B.A. in English from Yale University, an M.S. in secondary English education from Lehman College, and an advanced certificate in teacher, school and building leadership development from Hunter College.

Publications include:

Harford M., Leopold R., Williams W. T., Chatham E. (2018). Teacher Inquiry as a Vehicle for Developing Pedagogical Content Knowledge in Pre-Service Teachers. In Uzzo S., Graves S., Shay E., Harford M., Thompson R (eds.), *Pedagogical Content Knowledge in STEM. Advances in STEM Education.* Springer.

Rebecca Hendrickson is an independent education consultant who trains and supports teachers working in Chicago Public Schools. She has been an induction coach for UChicago UTEP, the Residency for Residencies Program Director for NCTR, and the associate director of Graduate Training for Academy for Urban School Leadership. Rebecca began her career as a classroom teacher in the New York City public schools.

Dr. Bill Kennedy is the co-director of the University of Chicago's Urban Teacher Education Program, one of the first teacher residencies in the United States. Prior to working at UChicago UTEP, Dr. Kennedy was an induction coach with the Chicago New Teacher Center and was a classroom teacher in New York City public schools.

Dr. Marjori Krebs is a professor in the Department of Teacher Education, Educational Leadership, and Policy at the University of New Mexico. She currently works with teacher candidates at both the graduate and undergraduate levels, along with graduate students earning masters' and doctoral degrees. Her research focuses on teacher preparation and project-based service learning. She is also a children's book author centered on getting children interested in higher education by connecting them with various schools and their mascots.

Jessamyn Lockhart, M.A., is the associate executive director of Preparation for the Public Education and Business Coalition located in Denver.

Marcie Osinsky, M.Ed., has been a leader in the Boston Teacher Residency for the past seventeen years, first, as the founding curriculum director, and now serving as director of the residency for the elementary program. Prior to that work, she was an elementary classroom teacher in the Cambridge Public Schools and the Boston Public Schools. She began her work as a teacher educator at Wheelock College in partnership with the Young Achievers Science and Math School in Boston, where she led the development of a yearlong internship model at the school. Currently, she works at the Dudley Street Neighborhood Charter School engaged with faculty staff and community members in the development and implementation of the teaching academy model. She is deeply committed to the development of new teachers, and continues to grow her practice in teaching teachers to teach with rigor and high engagement for all students.

Publications include:

Osinsky, M. (2008). *Learning to Teach Elementary Mathematics*. In Friedrich, L., Tateishi, C., Malarkey, T., Radin, E., Simons, E. R., & Williams, M. (eds.). (2005). Working Toward Equity: Writings and Resources from the Teacher Research Collaborative, 115–124. Berkley, CA: National Writing Project.

Osinsky, M. (1994). There's More to Heroes Than He-Man. In *Rethinking Our Classrooms: Teaching for Equity and Justice*, volume 1: 84–85. Milwaukee, WI: Rethinking Schools.

Shelley Neilsen Gatti, Ph.D., is an associate professor in special education at the University of St. Thomas. Since 2016, she has worked closely with St Thomas's residency programs in collaboration with Saint Paul Public Schools and Minneapolis Public Schools. Dr. Neilsen Gatti's areas of interest include teacher preparation and evaluation, school-wide PBIS, and assessment and intervention for students with challenging behavior.

Carrianne Scheib, M.P.P., joined National Center for Teacher Residencies in 2017 as director of Data and Impact. In this role, she supports NCTR and partner residencies to systematically use data to measure, demonstrate, and enhance their impact. Prior to joining NCTR, Carrie supported School Improvement Grant (SIG) schools, which rank among the lowest 5 percent of performing schools in the state, to implement the transformation model for school improvement. She also supported districts in multiple states to develop and implement teacher evaluation systems that incorporated measures of student growth. Additionally, Carrie previously served as senior manager of School Performance for Chicago Public Schools, in which she managed over forty school sites. She began her career teaching middle school mathematics in the Mississippi Delta, teaching in one of the ten poorest counties in the nation, as a Teach for America corps member. Carrie received her bachelor of arts and letters from the University of Notre Dame and her master of public policy from the Goldman School of Public Policy at University of California—Berkeley.

Dr. Lilly Siu is the elementary language and literacy coach for Dudley Street Neighborhood Charter School (DSNCS) and the language and literacy instructor for the Boston Plan for Excellence (BPE). She holds a master of arts (M.A.) in Elementary Education from Teachers College, Columbia University, and a doctorate of education (Ed.D.) from Harvard University. For the past thirty years, she has served schools in multiple roles, including educational researcher, curriculum developer, mentor teacher, classroom teacher, and instructional coach. Her work focuses on the social and emotional development of children and student engagement. A native of San Francisco, California, and a graduate of its public schools, Dr. Siu has taught in both the San Francisco Unified School District and the American School in London, and has trained teachers at New College of California, San Francisco State University, and Harvard University.

She is a recipient of the STAR Award from the San Francisco Unified School District and an Incoming Scholarship from Harvard University.

Publications include:

Siu, L. (2011). Finding My Good Side: A Case Study of Student Engagement in a Waldorf-Inspired Community School. Doctoral thesis. Harvard University: Cambridge, MA.

Siu, L. (1993). Attempting to Teach Self Esteem. In Shulman, J. & Mesa-Bains, A. (eds.), *Diversity in the Classroom*. San Francisco, CA: West Ed Publications.

Tamara Sober, Ph.D., is an assistant professor in the Virginia Commonwealth University's School of Education and teaches in the Center for Teacher Leadership's Richmond Teacher Residency program. Dr. Sober has over twenty years of experience in teacher advocacy and teacher leadership at the local, state, and national level. Her scholarship includes social justice education, critical economics for the social studies classroom, and teacher agency. Her passion: recruiting, teaching, supporting, and advocating for teachers!

Publications include:

Sober, T. L. (2017). Teaching about economics and moneyed interests in 21st century democracy. In C. Wright-Maley & T. Davis (eds.), *Teaching for Democracy in an Age of Economic Disparity*, 93–112. New York: Routledge.
Sober-Giecek, T. & Schnapp, S. (2007). *Teaching Economics as If People Mattered.* Boston, MA: United for a Fair Economy.
Senechal, J., Sober, T., Hope, S., Johnson, T., Burkhalter, F., Castelow, T., & Robinson, R. (2016). *Understanding Teacher Morale: A Report of the Metropolitan Educational Research Consortium.* Richmond, VA: Virginia Commonwealth University School of Education.

Amy Steele, M.Ed., is the Saint Paul Public Schools supervisor for teacher development and evaluation, an educator, and University of St. Thomas adjunct faculty for SUTR.

Rachelle Verdier, M.A., is the deputy director for the Urban Teacher Residency at New Visions for Public Schools. For the past eight years, she has worked with the teacher certification team to use her skills in mentoring and professional learning to produce over 220 new teachers for high-needs schools in New York City. In partnership with Queens College and the NYC DOE, she leads the Urban Teacher Residency, an alternative certification program that integrates residents' graduate coursework with hands-on experiences in public schools. Rachelle has over twelve years of experience as a NYC middle school teacher in the sciences and technology, including six years as a staff developer. Rachelle holds a B.A. in environmental science from Boston University and an M.A. in secondary science education from Brooklyn College.

Brandon Ware currently serves as the coordinator of Curriculum for the Bakersfield City School District (BCSD). After a nomadic youth, Brandon and his family planted roots in Bakersfield, California. Emphasizing the importance of education, his mother pushed him to become the family's first college graduate. In 2008, he earned his degree in Liberal Studies with a multiple-subject teaching credential. After teaching for numerous years, he served as academic coach and district-level instructional specialist. Later, he went on to earn his master of arts in Education Administrative Services in 2015. He is a proud product of BCSD and advocate for creating a quality-learning experiences for all students.

www.ingramcontent.com/pod-product-compliance
Lightning Source LLC
Chambersburg PA
CBHW020112010526
44115CB00008B/804